Asynchronous Transfer Mode (ATM)

SECOND EDITION

Technical Overview

Harry J.R. Dutton and Peter Lenhard

PRENTICE HALL PTR, UPPER SADDLE RIVER, NEW JERSEY 07458

Second Edition (October 1995)

For information about redbooks:
http://www.redbooks.ibm.com/redbooks

Send comments to:
redbooks@vnet.ibm.com

Published by

Prentice Hall PTR
Prentice-Hall, Inc.
A Simon & Schuster Company
Upper Saddle River, NJ 07458

The publisher offers discounts on this book when ordered in bulk quantities. For more information, contact

Corporate Sales Department,
Prentice Hall PTR
One Lake Street
Upper Saddle River, NJ 07458
Phone: 800-382-3419; FAX: 201-236-714
E-mail (Internet): corpsales@prenhall.com

For book and bookstore information

http://www.prenhall.com

Printed in the United States of America

10   9   8   7   6   5   4

ISBN   0-13-52044-5

Prentice-Hall International (UK) Limited, *London*
Prentice-Hall of Australia Pty. Limited, *Sydney*
Prentice-Hall Canada Inc., *Toronto*
Prentice-Hall Hispanoamericana, S.A., *Mexico*
Prentice-Hall of India Private Limited, *New Delhi*
Prentice-Hall of Japan, Inc., *Tokyo*
Simon & Schuster Asia Pte. Ltd., *Singapore*
Editora Prentice-Hall do Brasil, Ltda., *Rio de Janeiro*

Contents

iii

Figures

Tables

Preface

This publication is a systems engineering technical paper, *not* a product manual. Its purpose is to assist the reader in understanding the wider issues relating to technology rather than to products. It should be regarded by the reader in the same way as a paper published in a professional journal or read at a technical conference.

Detailed information about IBM products is given here incidental to objectives of the book, and while every effort has been made to ensure accuracy, such information should not be considered authoritative. Authoritative information about IBM products is contained in the official manuals for the product concerned.

Audience

This publication is primarily intended for people who have an interest in the fields of data communications or voice networking. Such people will often be:

Technical planners in user organizations who wish to broaden their understanding of high-speed communications and the direction product development in the industry is taking.

IBM systems engineers evaluating the potential of different systems approaches may find the information helpful in understanding the emerging high-speed technologies.

The information is presented at a "technical conceptual" level and technical detail is only introduced when essential to communicate a particular concept.

Structure

The book is organized as follows:

Chapter 1, "Introduction"

This chapter presents a broad outline of the topics dealt with in detail later in the book.

Chapter 2, "ATM Basic Principles"

This chapter presents the basic principles of an ATM network. It describes in detail the cell format and the routing in an ATM network using label swapping.

Chapter 3, "ATM Adaptation Layer (AAL)"

This chapter describes the ATM Adaptation Layer (AAL) that allows the various traffic types using the ATM network to adapt to the internal network characteristics. The five different AAL types are described in detail.

Chapter 4, "Signaling"

This chapter describes the signaling used to dynamically set up and clear ATM connections.

Chapter 5, "Private Network-to-Network (Node-to-Node) Interface - PNNI"

The PNNI is a very important part of the evolving ATM standards. In addition, it is the first time that there has been any attempt to standardize the internals of a network to this extent. Because of its level of innovation and its general importance, PNNI has been treated in somewhat more depth than other material in this book.

Chapter 6, "ATM Physical Interfaces"

This chapter describes the physical link types used to transmit ATM cells between nodes.

Chapter 7, "Switching ATM Cells"

This chapter describes in detail the different principles for high-speed switching of cells and the performance characteristics of the different solutions. The switch-on-a-chip is described that will be used in various IBM products.

Chapter 8, "Traffic Characteristics"

This chapter gives an overview of the different traffic types that may be transmitted over an ATM network. It describes the characteristics of data, voice, and video traffic and the demands of these traffic types on bandwidth, timing, and delay.

Chapter 9, "Traffic Management"

This chapter discusses some of the principles of traffic management in high-speed networks. In addition it discusses the developing ATM Forum traffic management specifications.

Chapter 10, "Network Management"

This chapter gives an overview of the emerging ATM network management standard.

Chapter 11, "LAN Emulation"

This chapter gives an overview of possible solutions to transport LAN traffic through an ATM network.

Appendix A, "Standards"

This chapter gives an overview of the standards developed by the different standardization bodies involved in ATM.

Appendix B, "SDH and Sonet"

This chapter describes the principles of SDH (Synchronous Digital Hierarchy) and Sonet adopted by the ITU-TC as a recommendation for the international operation of carrier optical networks worldwide.

Appendix C, "Synchronization"

This chapter describes the principles of bandwidth reservation and timer synchronization for real-time traffic in an ATM network.

Special Notices

This publication is intended to help both customers and IBM systems engineers to understand the principles of high-speed communications. The information in this publication is not intended as the specification of any programming interface provided by any IBM product. See the publications section of the applicable IBM Programming Announcement for the specific product for more information about which publications are considered to be product documentation.

References in this publication to IBM products, programs or services do not imply that IBM intends to make these available in all countries in which IBM operates. Any reference to an IBM product, program, or service is not intended to state or imply that only IBM's product, program, or service may be used. Any functionally equivalent program that does not infringe any of IBM's intellectual property rights may be used instead of the IBM product, program or service.

Information in this book was developed in conjunction with use of the equipment specified, and is limited in application to those specific hardware and software products and levels.

IBM may have patents or pending patent applications covering subject matter in this document. The furnishing of this document does not give you any license to these patents. You can send license inquiries, in writing, to the IBM Director of Licensing, IBM Corporation, 500 Columbus Avenue, Thornwood, NY 10954 USA.

The information contained in this document has not been submitted to any formal IBM test and is distributed AS IS. The use of this information or the implementation of any of these techniques is a customer responsibility and depends on the customer's ability to evaluate and integrate them into the customer's operational environment. While each item may have been reviewed by IBM for accuracy in a specific situation, there is no guarantee that the same or similar results will be obtained elsewhere. Customers attempting to adapt these techniques to their own environments do so at their own risk.

The following document contains examples of data and reports used in daily business operations. To illustrate them as completely as possible, the examples contain the names of individuals, companies, brands, and products. All of these names are fictitious and any similarity to the names and addresses used by an actual business enterprise is entirely coincidental.

The following terms are trademarks of the International Business Machines Corporation in the United States and/or other countries:

APPN   IBM
Nways

The following terms are trademarks of other companies:

C-bus is a trademark of Corollary, Inc.

PC Direct is a trademark of Ziff Communications Company and is used by IBM Corporation under license.

UNIX is a registered trademark in the United States and other countries licensed exclusively through X/Open Company Limited.

Windows is a trademark of Microsoft Corporation.

IPX is a trademark of Novell, Inc.

Other trademarks are trademarks of their respective companies.

Acknowledgments

This publication is the result of a residency conducted at the International Technical Support Organization, Raleigh Center.

The author of this document is:

Harry J.R. Dutton
IBM Australia

The project leader was:

Peter Lenhard
IBM International Technical Support Organization, Raleigh Center

Thanks go to the following people for assistance in obtaining information, comments, and review:

Marc Boisseau   IBM Advanced Telecommunications Systems,
                           La Gaude, France

Henri Sourbes	IBM Advanced Telecommunications Systems, La Gaude, France
Alain Blanc	IBM Advanced Telecommunications Systems, La Gaude, France
Jean Claude Beaucousin	
	IBM Advanced Telecommunications Systems, La Gaude, France
Neville Golding	IBM Network Systems, Research Triangle Park, North Carolina, U.S.A.
Bill Ellington	IBM Network Systems, Research Triangle Park, North Carolina, U.S.A.
Raif O. Onvural	IBM Network Systems, Research Triangle Park, North Carolina, U.S.A.
Hal J. Sandick	IBM Network Systems, Research Triangle Park, North Carolina, U.S.A.

Special thanks go to the technical editors:

| **Gail Wojton** | IBM International Technical Support Organization Raleigh, North Carolina, U.S.A. |
| **Shawn Walsh** | IBM International Technical Support Organization Raleigh, North Carolina, U.S.A. |

ITSO Redbooks on the World Wide Web (WWW)

Internet users may find information about redbooks on the ITSO World Wide Web home page. To access the ITSO Web pages, point your Web browser to the following URL:

```
http://www.redbooks.ibm.com/redbooks
```

IBM employees may access LIST3820s of redbooks as well. Point your web browser to the IBM Redbooks Home Page at the following URL:

```
http://w3.itsc.pok.ibm.com/redbooks/redbooks.html
```

Send comments via E-mail to: redbooks@vnet.ibm.com

Chapter 1. Introduction

Asynchronous Transfer Mode (ATM) is a new communications technology which is fundamentally and radically different from previous technologies. Its commercial availability marks the beginning of what promises to be a genuine revolution in both the data communications (read computer) and telecommunications (read telephone) industries.

Around 1988 the telecommunications (carrier) industry began to develop a concept called **Broadband Integrated Services Digital Network or B-ISDN**. This was conceived as a *carrier service* to provide high-speed communications to end users in an integrated way. The *technology* selected to deliver the B-ISDN service is called **Asynchronous Transfer Mode or ATM**.

Today, ATM has expanded to cover much that is not strictly B-ISDN. B-ISDN is a carrier interface and carrier network service. ATM is a technology that may be used in many environments unrelated to carrier services. Holding long and convoluted discussions about the fine distinctions between ATM and B-ISDN is pointless in the context of understanding the technology. For most practical purposes, the terms ATM and B-ISDN are interchangeable. Hence in this book we will use the term ATM almost exclusively.

In 1992 industry forecasters were saying that ATM would begin an experimental phase in 1993, have early commercial products in perhaps 1997 and that the year 2000 would be the year of mass usage. The first commercial products actually became available in 1994 and mass acceptance is beginning. (Even though many of the standards are not scheduled for completion until the end of 1996!)

In the past two years an unprecedented consensus has formed throughout the communications industry that ATM will be the universal networking standard. This consensus has caused the vast bulk of development in the industry to be shifted towards ATM development. Within the last year or so, some 50 organizations have either foreshadowed or announced ATM products.

The almost universal acceptance (among suppliers and developers) of ATM comes from the fact that *ATM is a compromise*:

- ATM will handle all the different kinds of communication traffic (voice, data, image, video, high-quality sound, multimedia, etc.) in an integrated way.

- ATM can be used in both the LAN and the WAN network environments and hence promises a seamless interworking between the two (something we have never had before).

Thus it is effective in a much wider range of communications environments than any previous technology. There are a number of other factors:

- ATM is a new technology designed to operate in the current technological environment (as distinct from older networking systems that are now obsolete).

- ATM is a very cost-effective alternative for building a LAN system. Users can be connected to an ATM LAN system using adapters supporting the transmission speeds according to their individual bandwidth requirements.

But **ATM is a compromise**.

- ATM does not handle voice as efficiently (or as cost effectively) as does an isochronous network.

- ATM does not handle video as easily as isochronous transfer does (although it is probably a lot more efficient).

- ATM certainly does not handle data as effectively or efficiently as a "packet transfer mode" or frame relay system.

- ATM is likely to be problematic in any high error rate environment (such as some slower copper wire connections).

Nevertheless, ATM will handle all types of traffic perfectly adequately and in an integrated way. This means that, instead of having a proliferation of many specialized kinds of equipment for different functions, we can have a single type of equipment and network which will do everything. The wide range of application for ATM means that there will be very large demand for ATM products. It is widely believed that the resulting reduction in costs will more than compensate for marginal inefficiencies in handling any single type of traffic.

A number of factors led to the development of ATM:

1. The advent of very high-speed communication links (especially in the use of fiber optical connections) meant that the technological environment changed utterly. While existing networking architectures will continue to work in the new environment, their performance does not improve (they do not go any faster) when link speeds get faster. Thus a new data network architecture was needed.

2. The very real user demand for data communications services and for ever faster services caused the carriers to look for an integrated way of supplying these services. Running separate and disparate networks is very expensive.

3. Silicon chip technology improved to the point where we can now build very fast (hardware-based) switching systems and these provide an opportunity to perform some applications significantly more efficiently (such as LAN systems).

4. The general belief that integrated packet (or cell) based switching systems will be significantly lower in cost than time-division multiplexing (TDM) systems.

5. The development (again due to improvements in silicon chip technology) of much faster and lower-cost computer hardware made many new applications possible that were not economically feasible before. Multimedia applications, such as personal videoconferencing, are such applications.

1.1 Rationale for ATM Development

One of the driving forces behind ATM development was the need for a new technology that could take advantage of the changes in the technological environment. The current communications technology delivers a very different environment from that of the 1970s when most existing communications protocols were developed.

1.1.1 High-Speed Technology

The evolving high-speed environment may be characterized as follows:

- Very high-speed communications links (10 000 times faster than what was available in the 1970s).

- Extremely low error rates. Traditional copper communications facilities deliver an error rate of about 1 in 10^6 bits transmitted. With optical fiber the rate is a million times better (1 in 10^{12}).

- The cost of digging up roads has not become any less. Thus, it still costs about the same to install a given communications link, but that link is many orders of magnitude faster. Thus, the cost of sending x bits per second is significantly lower now.

- Propagation delay of electricity in a wire (or light in a fiber) is still the same - about 5 μsec per kilometer.

This changed environment means that existing communications protocols are no longer efficient:

- Existing switching node designs, especially when requiring switching decisions in software, just will not handle the data rates possible on current types of connection. New switch designs are needed.

- Error recovery by re-transmission at each stage of a connection is no longer an efficient thing to do. It takes too long and it requires too much logic to process in the available time.

- Existing flow and congestion controls take a very significant amount of processing in a switching node and cannot operate at the required throughput speeds. In any case, they are needed to optimize the usage of bandwidth. Although the cost of raw bandwidth is reducing, bandwidth is not, and will never be, available for free.

Existing networking systems (such as SNA and TCP/IP) *do* function in the new environment. The point is, they just do not go much faster or give much higher throughput. A new communications network architecture is needed. This architecture is based on ATM.

- The system must be capable of switching data at the full speed of attached links.

- Flow and congestion controls *within* the network must be replaced with controls on entry of data to the network.

- Error recoveries must be done from end to end across the network (from end user to end user). The network does not have time to concern itself with error recovery.

- It is not a necessary consequence of high speed, but the opportunity should be taken to have a single integrated network that handles many different types of traffic.

1.1.2 Principles of High-Speed Networks

If the user requirements for an integration of data, voice, video, and image are to be satisfied by ATM networks then clearly they need to be a lot different from traditional packet data networks (such as X.25 networks). Network nodes will need to handle the full data throughput capacity of the new high-speed links (twenty million packets per second - plus) and "higher-layer" network architectures will need to accommodate the unique characteristics of voice and video traffic.

The requirements may be summarized as follows:

Very High Node Throughput

> Nodes must be able to route (switch) data at the peak combined rate of all links connected to them. In corporate networks, this might mean a maximum of perhaps 20 links at 155 Mbps, but this seems a little high for the decade of the 1990s. More likely would be a switch with less than 20 links where perhaps four of them are 155 Mbps and the rest might be at the "T-3" rate of 45 Mbps.

> But corporate private networks are one thing. Public telecommunication networks are something else. The proposal with ATM (B-ISDN) is that packet (cell) switching should become the basis of a multi-function network, which will replace the world's telephone network. To do this, a mainline trunk exchange (probably a cluster of switching nodes) would need to handle perhaps 100 links of 620 Mbps today and perhaps the same 100 links would be running at 2.4 Gbps by the time the system was built.

> Using 53-byte cells, a 2.4 Gbps link can carry just less than six million cells per second *in each direction*.

> The principle is clear. We are going to need the ability to process cells at rates of well above one hundred million per second for Broadband ISDN to become a reality.

Minimal Network Transit Time

This is a critical requirement for voice and has been discussed in "The Effect of End-to-End Network Delay on Voice Traffic" on page 8-12.

Minimal Variation in Network Transit Time

When any traffic with a constant bit rate at origin and destination travels through a network, the variations in network delay mean that a buffer somewhat larger than the largest foreseeable variation in transit time is needed. This buffer introduces a delay and for practical purposes can be considered a net addition to network transit time. This is also discussed in "The Effect of End-to-End Network Delay on Voice Traffic" on page 8-12.

To meet the above requirements networks will need to have the following characteristics:

Totally Hardware-Controlled Switching

There is no way that current software-based packet switched architectures can come to even one one hundredth of the required throughput - even assuming much faster processors.

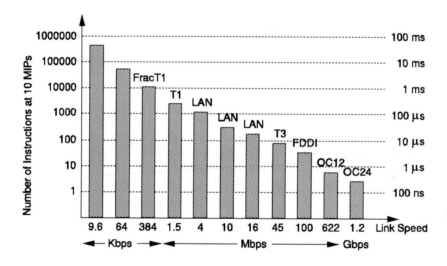

Figure 1-1. *Available Node Processing Time for 53-Byte ATM Cell*

Figure 1-1 shows the amount of time that a processor has per 53-byte ATM cell received on links of different speeds. (Note that the scales on both axes of the graph are logarithmic.) On the left of the figure a scale shows the number of instructions that a 10 MIPs processor would have per cell to make a switching decision before the next cell arrives. Of course, this applies only to one direction of data transfer and to a dedicated link.

Typical packet switches take an average of between 1000 and 3000 instructions to receive a packet, transfer it to an output link, and then start transmitting it towards its destination.

However, there are several hardware switching designs that will meet the required speeds at (predicted) reasonable cost. See Chapter 7, "Switching ATM Cells" on page 7-1.

Suitable Network Architecture

The network architecture must make it possible for the data switching component in a node to decide the destination to which an incoming packet should be routed *at full operating speed*.

The network architecture must provide mechanisms for the stable operation and management of the network, but the data switching element must not need to get involved in extraneous protocols.

Link Error Recovery

Recovery from transient link errors by retransmission (for voice traffic), as is usual for data traffic, can seriously conflict with the requirement for uniform delivery rates. For voice, a delayed packet is worse than a packet in error. However, by the nature of packetization, it is necessary that packets contain a header which carries routing information (identification) so the intermediate switch can route it to the appropriate destination. An error in this information will cause a packet to be routed to the wrong destination *and* a packet to be lost from the correct circuit.

But these very high-speed networks are planned to operate solely over digital (preferably fiber-optical) circuits. Error rates on these circuits are around ten thousand times better than they were for traditional analog data links.

For the data portion of the packet or cell, error checking and recovery can be applied on an end-to-end basis, especially if the error rates experienced on links are very low.

The header portion is not so fortunate. An error in the header can cause a packet to be misrouted to the wrong destination. The network must at least check the headers. (In ATM there is an elegant mechanism that checks the Header Error Check field to obtain cell synchronization. This is described in 6.1.1, "Transmission Convergence Sublayer Functions" on page 6-4.)

Packet Length

Short (less than 64 bytes), fixed-length packets or cells are an attractive option because:

1. Their fixed-length nature gives a uniform transmission time (per cell) characteristic to the queueing within a node for an outbound link. This leads to a more uniform transit-time characteristic for the whole network.

2. The shorter the cell the shorter the time needed to assemble it and hence the shorter the delay characteristic for voice.

3. Short, fixed-length cells are easy to transfer over a fixed-width processor bus, and buffering in link queues is a lot easier and requires less processor logic.

One elegant solution to both the network delay and error recovery problems would be to use very short packets (perhaps 32 bytes) of fixed length. If this is done then Error Correcting Codes (ECC) can be used as a recovery from transient link errors. Two bytes of ECC are required for every 8 bytes of data. A 32-byte packet would then have a routing header (2 or 4 bytes) included within it and 1 or 4 ECC 2-byte groups appended to it (1 if it is thought necessary only to check the header, 2 if the data is to be error recovered also). Therefore, a packet would be either 34 or 40 bytes. (This represents an overhead on the transmission channel in the full ECC case of 20%.) It happens that the use of ECC in this way for a voice packet is considered wasteful and unnecessary. The loss of a packet or two (provided it is relatively infrequent) or the corruption of a few bits of data is not considered to be significant.

The international standard for cell size is now 48 bytes (for ATM). In ATM, the header is checked for validity, but the data within the cell is not (or, rather, that checking and error recovery on the data within a frame (group of cells) is left to the end-to-end protocol called the adaptation layer).

However, there is another side. Video transmission is fine with packet sizes of over a thousand bytes. Data transmission can be achieved with low overhead if the packet size adopted is large enough to carry the largest natural data block as produced by the user's application.

The longer the packet the fewer packets per second must be switched for a given data throughput.

This subject is discussed in more detail in 1.3, "Cell Switching" on page 1-16.

Flow Control

Control of congestion is a critical matter in any packet switching environment. Traditional techniques of flow control are not possible at very high packet rates because they require significant amounts of programmed logic to operate on every packet.

In a high-speed switch, input rate regulation and capacity reservation are the appropriate techniques. These can be agreed by the control processors when a connection is started and enforced at the entry points of the network.

This subject is discussed further in 9.3, "Flow and Rate Controls" on page 9-16.

Congestion Control

Congestion occurs when a node builds up too much data for its internal buffers to process. This can happen even in data networks with very detailed explicit flow controls.

One way to handle congestion is to avoid it. Good flow controls can help in avoiding congestion. Another sure way of handling congestion is to make sure that the maximum demand that can ever be placed on the network can be met at all times. This means running links and nodes at average utilizations of around 10% or 20% at the peak! But this foregoes the benefits of sharing the network.

If the network is to process variable-rate data (say voice) from many thousands of users simultaneously, and if no single user can make a peak demand sufficient to be noticed, then the statistics of the situation work for us. As you add up many variable sources (that are unrelated to one another) the total becomes very stable.

Congestion becomes a problem when there are a number of sources that can individually place a significant demand on the network (such as in variable-rate video). In this case a small number of users (as few as 10 perhaps) might be able to each make peak demands simultaneously and bring the whole network to a standstill. The trick here is to avoid the situation where any single user can make a significant demand on the network.

But some types of traffic change radically over time. Data traffic peaks at different times in a business day. Batch data peaks during the night.

When congestion occurs, packets must be discarded. For some data types (voice, video) coding can be such that low priority packets can be discarded with the net effect of a "graceful degradation" of the service. If these packets are marked as discardable in some way (this is a feature of ATM), then the system can alleviate congestion by discarding these.

If congestion becomes very serious, then the network will need to discard packets not marked as discardable. The network should have a way of prioritizing traffic by service class so that an intelligent packet discard strategy may be adopted.

This packet discard strategy must be performed by the (hardware) data switching element. The discard strategy must be very simple.

Sequential Delivery

If packets applying to one conversation are allowed to take different routes through the network (for load balancing, for example) then they must be resequenced before delivery to the receiver. However, this means that each would have to carry a sequence number (more overhead) and the technique would result in "bursty" uneven delivery. To overcome this, delivery would then need to be buffered sufficiently to even out the bursts. This would add cost, but more importantly it would add to the transit delay and thus degrade the quality.

In a high-speed network this means that each connection must be limited to a fixed path through the network.

Priorities

There is no consensus yet on whether transmission priorities are relevant in a high-speed network. A transmission priority may be given to a packet and that priority enables it to "jump the queue" ahead of lower-priority packets when being queued for transmission within a node.

Within a tightly controlled traditional packet networking system such as SNA, the system of priorities has worked well. It gives better response time to higher-priority traffic and also enables the use of much higher resource (link and node) loadings than would be possible without them.

But at such high speed, with relatively small cells (at the speeds we are considering even a 4KB block is small - in time), many people suggest that the cost of implementing priorities may be greater than it is worth. Most studies of high-speed node technology suggest that the total switching (processing, queueing and transmission) in the kind of node under discussion will be well less than one millisecond.

Other kinds of priority are, however, considered essential. In a large network there needs to be some control and prioritization of the selection of routes through a network depending on the required service characteristics for a particular class of service.

In addition it seems generally agreed that a service class type of priority should be used to decide which packets to discard at times of network congestion.

End-to-End Protocols and "Adaptation"

The characteristics of a high-speed network developed thus far are such that it gives very high throughput of very short packets, but in the case of congestion or of link errors packets are discarded.

To provide a stable service, the network needs to have processing at the entry and exit points of the network. This processing will, for example, break long frames of data up into cells and reassemble at the other end. In addition, for data traffic it should implement a Frame Check Sequence (FCS) calculation to identify frames containing errors. It may also have a retransmission protocol to recover from data errors and lost packets etc. (Or it may just signal to the user that there has been a problem and allow the user to do recovery.)

Each type of network traffic requires different adaptation layer processing.

1.2 ATM Concept

The key concepts of ATM are as follows:

Cells

All information (voice, image, video, data, etc.) is transported through the network in very short (48 data bytes plus a 5-byte header) blocks called "cells".

Routing

Information flow is along paths (called "virtual channels") set up as a series of pointers through the network. The cell header contains an identifier that links the cell to the correct path for it to take towards its destination.

Cells on a particular virtual channel always follow the same path through the network and are delivered to the destination in the same order in which they were received.

Hardware-Based Switching

ATM is designed so that simple hardware-based logic elements may be employed at each node to perform the switching. On a link of 1 Gbps, a new cell arrives and a cell is transmitted every .43 μsec. There is not a lot of time to decide what to do with an arriving packet.

Adaptation

At the edges of the network, user data frames are broken up into cells. Continuous data streams, such as voice and video, are assembled into cells. At the destination side of the network, the user data frames are reconstructed from the received cells and returned to the end user in the form (data frames, etc.) that they were delivered to the network. This adaptation function is considered part of the network but is a higher-layer function from the transport of cells.

Error Control

The ATM cell switching network only checks cell headers for errors and simply discards errored cells.

The adaptation function is external to the switching network and depends somewhat on the type of traffic, but for data traffic it usually checks for errors in data frames received, and if one is found, then it discards the whole frame.

At no time does the ATM network attempt to recover from errors by the retransmission of information. This function is up to the end-user devices and depends on the type of traffic being carried.

Flow Controls

In its original conception, an ATM network had no internal flow controls of any kind. The required processing logic was deemed to be too complex to be accommodated at the speeds involved. Instead, ATM was envisaged to use a set of input rate controls that limit the rate of traffic delivered to the network.

Since its original conception, ATM has changed somewhat. Flow and congestion controls are back on the agenda but in a very different form from those that exist in traditional networks.

Congestion Control

There is only one thing an ATM network can do when a link or node becomes congested. Cells are discarded until the problem has been relieved. Some (lower-priority) cells can be marked such that they are the first to be discarded in the case of congestion.

Connection endpoints are *not notified* when cells are discarded. It is up to the adaptation function or higher-layer protocols to detect and recover from the loss of cells (if necessary and possible).

1.2.1 ATM in the Wide Area Network

In the wide area network environment ATM offers a number of significant benefits:

Integration of Services

The number of specialized services offered by carriers around the world has proliferated in the last few years. This is seen as a direct response to the proliferating needs of users. One of the benefits of ATM is the ability to satisfy most user requirements with a single service and to reduce proliferation of new kinds of networks.

Lower Equipment and Network Cost

It is widely believed that ATM switching equipment will cost significantly less than time-division multiplexing (TDM) equipment to do the same job.

Appropriate Technology to the High-Speed Environment

ATM offers a technology that can deliver service at the very high speeds now becoming available and being demanded by users.

There are two quite distinct environments here:

1. The carrier environment, where ATM is provided as a service to the end user.

2. The private network environment, where a large organization purchases lines from a carrier (or installs them itself) and builds a private ATM network.

The major problem with the wide area environment is government regulation. In most countries, governments regulate the detailed technical characteristics of anything and everything that connects to a public communications network. This is often called "homologation". Part of the homologation process requires protocol testing - the detailed and exhaustive checking of the communication protocol as it is performed by the device being tested.

In years gone by, homologation was an essential task (malfunctioning or badly designed end-user equipment could not only disrupt the network's operation but in some cases actually cause damage to network equipment). Those days have gone forever. Today's communication switches (telephone exchanges, ATM switches etc.) are computers. They have quite sufficient logical ability to rigorously ensure that attaching equipment cannot disrupt or damage the network. But governments (on the advice of the people who do the testing) continue to insist that testing is needed.

Protocol testing is an extremely expensive and very slow task. The requirement for protocol testing has very significantly retarded the growth of (regular) ISDN systems around the world. ATM in the WAN environment will develop only very slowly if this situation continues.

1.2.2 ATM in the LAN Environment

Many people believe that it will be the LAN environment in which ATM gets its first significant usage. There are good reasons:

Users Need a Higher-Capacity LAN System

Existing shared-media LANs were designed and developed in an environment where communications bandwidth (bits per second) was almost free. Compared to the internal speeds (and the possible I/O rates) of early personal computers, the LAN was very nearly infinite.

Most wide area network architectures were developed with the overriding objective of saving the cost of bandwidth. This was done by spending money on devices (in hardware cycles, memory, and software complexity) to optimize (minimize) the cost of bandwidth. When people came to build LANs, the use of existing WAN networking systems seemed inappropriate. Why spend money to optimize a free resource? Thus LAN network protocols save cost by using extra bandwidth. This is *not* inefficient; this is a valid and reasonable adjustment to a changed cost environment (even though that it did not take account of the future need to interconnect LANs over the wide area).

As personal computers and workstations have increased in capability, there has been an attendant rise in the demand for LAN capacity. In the short term, this can be solved by re-structuring large LANs into smaller ones, bridging, routing, and the like, but the improvement in workstation capability and the increase in bandwidth demand does not look likely to slow down, especially when going into multimedia applications. A faster (higher-throughput) LAN system is needed.

ATM Cost/Performance in the LAN Environment

Looking at Figure 1-2 and Figure 1-3 on page 1-14 the performance advantage of a switched system over a shared-medium system is easily seen. In Figure 1-2, let us assume that we have 50 devices connected to a 10 Mbps Ethernet LAN. This is a shared-medium system. Only one station may transmit data at any one time. This means that the total *potential*[1] network throughput is 10 Mbps.

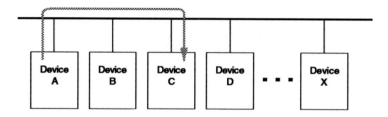

Figure   1-2. *Connection to Shared Medium*

In Figure 1-3 on page 1-14, we have the same devices connected through a switch (let us assume a link speed of 10 Mbps). Each device is capable of sending at full media speed.[2] The total *potential* network throughput here is not 10 Mbps but 50×10 Mbps - or 500 Mbps.

The difference is in the cost. The adapter cards for 100 terminals connected to an FDDI LAN (only 100 Mbps total throughput) will cost about $1,000 each or

---

[1] In reality, of course, quite a lot less.

[2] In this situation, too, throughput is limited by statistical considerations.

a total of $100,000. 10 Mbps adapter cards (if they existed) could cost perhaps $200 each[3] for a total of $20,000.

Of course, with ATM you need a switch, but with FDDI you need a hub. It is expected that ATM switches will cost only marginally more than FDDI hubs. Both systems need a network management workstation.

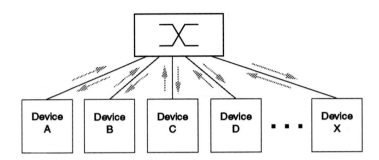

Figure ***1-3.*** *Connection to a Switch*

In the example above, the ATM system has a maximum potential throughput of 10×100 Mbps = 1 Gbps. The FDDI LAN still has a maximum throughput according to the media speed (100 Mbps). The "net" is that an ATM system will deliver much greater throughput than a shared-medium LAN system for a significantly lower cost.

This cost equation also applies to *switched* LANs. The above discussion could apply almost equally to switched Ethernet as to ATM, at least on a cost basis. However, ATM systems have significant advantages over switched LAN systems:

1. Switched LAN systems don't scale up very well at all. It is difficult to build large networks just using switched LANs. You tend to need routers to inter-connect segments of the network. This adds significantly to the cost and cripples the throughput.

2. Switched LAN systems need to use bridges to connect across the wide area. LANs do not have a very good interconnection with the WAN. Another job for a router.

3. Switched LANs don't handle isochronous traffic (video, voice, multimedia) very well at all. Indeed, they do the job very badly.

---

[3] The cost is about the same as an Ethernet adapter **plus** some hardware to convert data frames into cells and back again.

Security

On a shared-medium LAN all of the data traffic passes through every work-station. While some types of LANs have a higher level of security than others, it is true that data security in the LAN environment leaves a lot to be desired.

In ATM, a single end-user station only receives data intended for that station. Thus, users cannot "listen in" to what is going on in the rest of the network.

Asymmetric Bandwidth

In a LAN environment some users will require much higher data throughput than others. Servers, in particular, need much higher throughput than any of their clients. In a shared-medium system, all these devices must have adapters that run at the same speed (the speed of the LAN).

In ATM, individual stations can have connections at speeds appropriate to their capability. A speed of 25 Mbps is faster than any current (ISA bus) PC. Many workstations can easily handle a throughput of 50 Mbps and specialized servers are being built to handle total rates of a few hundred Mbps. This ultimately saves cost, both in the workstations themselves and in the network switching equipment.

ATM Supports Isochronous (Timing-Dependent) Traffic

Perhaps the most discussed near-term application is for multimedia of one form or another on workstations. This usually requires video and sound as well as traditional data. The video and sound components require a system that can deliver data at a timed rate (or can adjust to one). A number of proposed LAN architectures to do this are being explored (isochronous Ethernet, FDDI-II) but ATM offers the potential to allow these applications in an integrated way.

Reduced Need for Routers and Bridges

In an ATM environment there is still a need for routers and bridges but in some network configurations the need is significantly less, for example, where a number of different LAN protocols are used by groups of devices on a set of linked LANs. In an ATM system a number of separate virtual LANs can be set up (one for each protocol) and the need for a router is removed. The bridging function between dispersed locations is performed by ATM without the need for bridges as such. Bridges are only needed to connect between ATM-attached workstations and workstations attached to existing LANs.

1.2.2.1 LAN Emulation over ATM

In order for ATM to be used as a seamless extension of an existing LAN system, the concept of emulating a traditional LAN over an ATM system is being developed. This would enable:

- Use of existing LAN software systems over ATM

- The seamless integration of existing LANs with new ATM services

- The use of ATM to intelligently bridge between existing LANs

The protocols are such that the benefits of ATM can still be obtained but that ATM can be a smooth and logical growth of an existing LAN networking system.

IBM is providing LAN emulation products for use on ATM networks.

1.2.2.2 Multiprotocol over ATM (MPOA) - The Future

While LAN emulation will satisfy most of the immediate requirements for ATM in the campus environment in the short term, it has a number of limitations. These limitations cause the need for intermediate routers and bridges when the network gets large (more than a thousand or so workstations).

A longer term approach is to look at the functions performed by a multiprotocol router and see if these can be performed in an ATM network in a more intelligent way. It turns out that this is indeed the case. Logically, a router breaks down into a directory server function and a forwarding function. These functions don't need to be in the same box - they could be distributed.

But it is possible to go a lot further than this. The router forwarding function might go into *every* end user device leaving only the directory server function out there in the network. You might even build the directory server into your ATM switch (physically but, of course, not logically).

These issues are currently under (sometimes heated) discussion in the ATM Forum. In the three- to five-year term it seems likely that this principle will be applied in real products.

1.3 Cell Switching

The concept of cell switching can be thought of as either a high-performance form of packet switching or as a form of statistical multiplexing performed on fixed-length blocks of data.

A cell is really not too different from a packet. A block of user data is broken up into packets or cells for transmission through the network. But there are significant differences between cell-based networks and packet networks.

1. A cell is fixed in length. In packet networks the packet size is a fixed maximum (for a given connection) but individual packets may always be shorter than the maximum. In a cell-based network, cells are a fixed length, no more and no less.

2. Cells tend to be a lot shorter than packets. This is really a compromise over requirements. In the early days of X.25 many of the designers wanted a packet size of 32 bytes so that voice could be handled properly. However, the shorter the packet size the more network overhead there is in sending a given quantity of data over a wide area network. To efficiently handle data, packets should be longer (in X.25 the default packet size supported by all networks is 128 bytes).

3. Cell-based networks do *not* use link-level error recoveries. In some networks there is an error checking mechanism that allows the network to throw away cells in error. In others, such as in ATM (described below) only the header field is checked for errors and it is left to a "higher-layer" protocol to provide a checking mechanism for the data portion of the cell if needed by the application.

Packets

The term "packet" has many different meanings and shades of meaning depending on the context in which it is used. In recent years the term has become linked to the CCITT recommendation X.25 which specifies a data network interface. In this context a packet is a fixed maximum length (default 128 bytes) and is preceded by a packet level header which determines its routing within the network.

In the late 1960s the term "packet" came into being to denote a network in which the switching nodes stored the messages being processed in main storage instead of on magnetic disk. In the early days, a "message switch" stored received data on disk before sending it on towards its destination.

In a generic sense "packet" is often used to mean any short block of data which is part of a larger logical block.

In ATM the word packet is *defined* to be a unit of data that is switched at the network layer (layer 3) of the ISO model.

Figure 1-4 on page 1-18 shows a sequence of cells from different connections being transmitted on a link. This should be contrasted with the TDM (Time Division Multiplexing) technique where capacity is allocated on a time slot basis regardless of whether there is data to send for that connection. Cell-based networks are envisaged as ones that use extremely fast and efficient hardware-based switching nodes to give very high throughput, that is, millions of cells per second. These networks are designed to operate over very low error rate, very high-speed digital (preferably optical) links.

The reasons for using this architecture are:

- If we use very short fixed-length cells then it simplifies (and therefore speeds up) the switching hardware needed in nodal switches.

- The smaller the cells can be made, the shorter the transit delay through a network consisting of multiple nodes. This principle is described in 1.3.1, "Transit Delay" on page 1-19.

- The statistical principle of large numbers means that a very uniform network transit delay with low variance can be anticipated with the cell approach.

- Intermediate queues within switching nodes contain only cells of the same length. This reduces the variation in network transit delays due to irregular-length data blocks (which take irregular lengths of time to transmit) in the queues.

- When an error occurs on a link (whether it is an access link or a link within the network itself) then there is less data to retransmit. This could be the case but with ATM if a cell is lost for any reason (such as link error or discard due to congestion) the whole frame of which it is part must be retransmitted. In a well designed network using optical links (low error rates) this should not bother us too much.

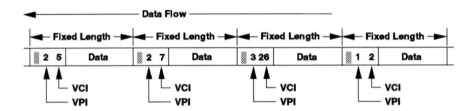

Figure 1-4. Cell Multiplexing on a Link. Cells belonging to different logical connections (identified by the VPI and VCI) are transmitted one after the other on the link. This is not a new concept in the data switching world, but it is quite different from the fixed multiplexing techniques used in the TDM approach.

The reasons that cell switching has not been popular in the past are:

- High error rate analog links potentially cause too high an error rate to allow end-to-end recovery. In most cases, link-level error recovery is needed.

- Processing time (load due to processing instructions), both in the network nodes themselves and in the attaching equipment, is greatly increased. As described elsewhere in this document, most software-driven data switching equipment takes about the same amount of processor time to switch a block regardless of the length of that block. (This is not exactly true due to the effects of I/O interference but that is usually small.) For example, if a 1 KB block is broken up into eight 128-byte packets, then the load on the network switching nodes is multiplied by eight.

  The use of hardware logic for routing in cell-based switches minimizes this effect. However, even in a system where hardware-based routing is used there is significant overhead in the end-user equipment needed for breaking the user data block up into cells and in doing adaptation layer processing.

- The additional bandwidth taken up by headers. The network routing header is necessary, but it takes link capacity to transmit and is an overhead. In the example above, where a single block is broken into 8 smaller packets, then we have multiplied the overhead by 8. This is why packet and cell networks are designed to use very short headers. The need for very short headers is perhaps the primary reason for using connection-oriented protocols.

   In the days when a 2400 bps link was considered "fast" this was a significant overhead. In 1995 the cost of link capacity (or bandwidth) is reducing daily and this overhead is no longer considered significant.

- Hardware technology had not progressed to the point where total hardware switching was economically feasible (it has been technically possible for some years).

- In the older technology end-to-end error recovery processing added a very significant cost to the attaching equipment. (Significantly more storage and instruction cycles required.) This is needed with cell networks today, but hardware cost has become much less and this is no longer a problem.

- If the network is designed to do its congestion control by discarding data, and if error recovery is done by the retransmission of whole blocks, then there is a very nasty "multiplier effect" which can severely impact network performance. This is discussed in 9.2.2, "Congestion in ATM Networks" on page 9-6.

The cell technique is intended to provide the efficiencies inherent in packet switching without the drawbacks that this technique has had in the past. Because cells are small and uniform in size, it is thought that a uniform transit delay can be provided through quite a large network and that this can be short enough for high-quality voice operation.

1.3.1 Transit Delay

When data is to transit a network consisting of a number of switches then the shorter the packet (or cell) size the shorter the network transit delay will be.

Assume User A, in Figure 1-5 on page 1-20 has a block of 1024 bytes to send through a 3-node network to User B. Assume also that the link speeds are the same, the nodes are infinitely fast, there is zero propagation delay, and that there is no other traffic.

- User A sends to Node 1 and takes (for our discussion purposes) 4 units of time.

- Node 1 sends to Node 2 also taking 4 units of time.

- Node 2 sends to Node 3.

- And so on until the message arrives at User B.

The total time taken has been 4 times 4 units = 16 units of time.

Now, if the 1024-byte block is broken up into four, 256-byte packets then the following scenario will occur:

- User A sends the first packet to Node 1, taking 1 unit of time.

- Node 1 sends this packet to Node 2, but while this is happening User A is sending packet 2 to Node 1.

- While User A is sending the third packet, Node 1 is sending a packet to Node 2 and Node 2 is sending a packet to Node 3.

- This happens through the network until the last packet arrives at User B.

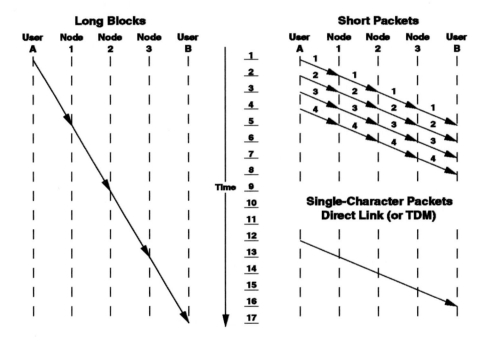

Figure 1-5. *Effect of Packetization on Transit Time through a 3-Node Network*

It is obvious from the diagram that sending the message as small packets has reduced the network transit time to 7 units compared with the 16 units needed without packetization. This is due to the effect of overlapping the sending of parts of the message through the network.

The section of the figure headed "Direct Link" refers to what happens in the limit as we keep reducing the packet size. When we finally get to a packet size of one character, we have a network throughput equivalent to a direct link or TDM operation of the nodes. Transit time in this case is 4 time units.

Chapter 2. ATM Basic Principles

The conceptual structure of an ATM network is shown in Figure 2-1.

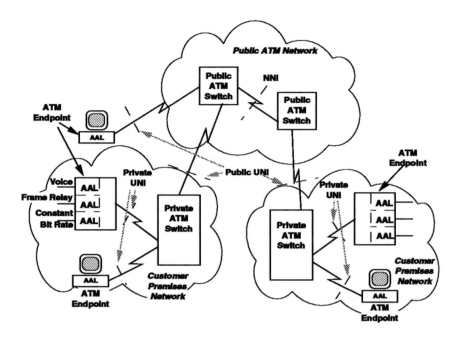

Figure   2-1. *ATM Network Structure Overview*

ATM Networks

In Figure 2-1, there are three quite separate ATM networks, two private and one public.

Private ATM networks are sometimes called "customer premises networks" and indeed they will very often be confined to a local area such as a building or a campus. However, a private ATM network can be distributed over a wide area by the use of carrier (non-ATM) links between ATM nodes. Such links could be copper-wire leased lines, "dark" fibers,[1] or Sonet/SDH[2] TDM connections.

---

[1] A dark fiber is a fiber connection provided by a carrier that is not restricted, just like a copper-wire "leased line". It is dark because there is no light in the fiber until the user puts it there.

[2] See Appendix B, "SDH and Sonet" on page B-1.

2-1

ATM Switches

Four "ATM switches" are shown in the figure. These perform the backbone data transport within the ATM network. They are usually classified as either "Private ATM Switches" or "Public ATM Switches". The difference between private and public ATM equipment could be trivial in some cases but will often be quite major. Public and private switches will differ in the kinds of trunks (links) supported, in accounting and control procedures, and in the addressing modes supported. There is also the obvious question of size. Public network equipment will usually need much higher throughput than will private equipment.

Public ATM switches are sometimes referred to as network nodes (NNs). This is incorrect, as the term network node is not defined in ATM standards - even though there is a network node interface (NNI).

Private ATM switches and networks are sometimes called customer premises nodes (CPNs) or customer premises networks. Again, this terminology, while useful, is not defined in the ATM standards.

ATM Endpoint

The ATM endpoint is a piece of end-user equipment that interfaces to an ATM network in a native way. An endpoint sends and receives ATM cells on link connections defined by ATM standards. An endpoint (and only an endpoint) contains an ATM Adaptation Layer (AAL) function.[3]

An ATM endpoint connects to the ATM network over the User Network Interface (UNI).

User Network Interface (UNI)

The UNI is specified exactly by the applicable standards. It is structured according to the reference model for ISDN, as illustrated in Figure 2-11 on page 2-23.

There are two somewhat different UNIs, called "public" and "private". The public UNI is for connection of end-user equipment to a public ATM network. The private UNI is for use within a single organization's premises or for a private network using lines leased from the PTT.

---

[3] However, it must be noted that ATM switches will often contain ATM endpoint functions as well as switch functions.

The major differences between the two are:

1. Link types allowed

   Some of the link types allowed at the private UNI use protocols that only work over very short distances (such as 100 meters). These would be obviously inapplicable to a public network interface.

2. Addressing formats

   Public ATM networks will use E.164 addresses (similar to telephone while private networks will probably use addressing techniques derived from LANs or from OSI.

3. Which organization specifies them

   The public UNI is defined and controlled by the ITU-T. The private UNI is defined by the ATM Forum.

Network Node Interface (NNI)

As shown in Figure 2-1 on page 2-1, this is the trunk connection between two network nodes (NNs). As the standard has evolved, three distinct "flavors" of the NNI have emerged:

1. The **NNI-ISSI** will be used to connect ATM switches within a local area and belonging to the same telephone company. In the US, this equates to nodes which are in the same LATA (Local Access Transport Area).

2. The **NNI-ICI** is the "intercarrier" interface and will typically be used to interconnect ATM networks operated by different telephone companies. This could be the interface between the local carrier and the longline carrier (in the US) or an international connection.

3. The **Private NNI** allows connection of different ATM switches in a private network environment.

The differences between these interfaces is mainly one of emphasis. For example, the addressing formats used are likely to be different and you might not need accounting at a private NNI, whereas you certainly do need it at the NNI-ICI.

Links

There may be one or many physical link connections between the nodes. These are shown as shaded areas in Figure 2-2 on page 2-5. The multiplexing of virtual paths and virtual channels over a physical link connection is shown in Figure 2-3 on page 2-7.

Links between nodes may be carried as "clear channels" such as over a direct point-to-point connection, but may also be carried over a Sonet/SDH connection or over a PDH[4] connection.

Network Internals

In Figure 2-1 on page 2-1 the ATM public network is shown as a cloud. Representation of public networks as a cloud has become traditional since the first public data network standard, X.25. One of the reasons for the cloud representation was that the standard defined only the interface to the end user and the services to be provided by the network. The internals of X.25 networks are not covered by any standard. *Things are different in ATM.* The internals of the ATM network are in the process of rigorous standardization and so, while the end user may still see it as a cloud (because its internal detail will be masked from the end user), its internal protocols will be exactly understood.

Cells

As mentioned earlier, the ATM network transports data (including voice and video) as 53-byte "cells". The objective is to provide a very short, constant transit time through the network. Within the network, there are no error recoveries (there is error detection for cell header information). Flow and congestion control is done not by the detailed interactive protocols of traditional data networks, but by controlling the rate at which traffic is admitted to the network (and a strong reliance on the statistical characteristics of the traffic). When network congestion is experienced, there is no alternative - cells must be discarded.

ATM Adaptation Layers (AAL)

End users of an ATM network will be of two kinds:

- Those that interface to the ATM network directly, through either the public UNI or a private UNI

- Those that do not know anything about ATM, and interface using a non-ATM protocol (such as frame relay)

In either case, a significant amount of logic is required *over and above what is provided by ATM* in order to use the network productively.

For all types of users there are common tasks that must be performed in order to connect to the ATM network. In its definition, ATM includes processing for these common tasks. This is called the ATM Adaptation Layer (AAL). The AAL is the real end-user interface to ATM.

---

4 See 6.2.3, "PDH-Based Physical Connections" on page 6-14.

The AAL *never* interfaces to an external link or device. Rather, the AAL provides a programming interface and end users are connected to the ATM network by program functions external to ATM. The AAL only provides some common attachment functions - many protocol layers are usually required above the AAL for useful work to be performed.

Figure 2-1 on page 2-1 is perhaps a little misleading in the positioning of the AAL. End users using voice or frame relay or whatever must attach through an AAL *but a lot more than just the AAL code is needed.* AAL just provides a more convenient, standardized way of accessing the network from a program. The program then interfaces with other external links such as voice or frame relay or higher layers of some other communication protocol.

2.1 Virtual Channels and Virtual Routes

Perhaps the key concepts in ATM are those relating to how data is routed through the network. Figure 2-2 illustrates these concepts.

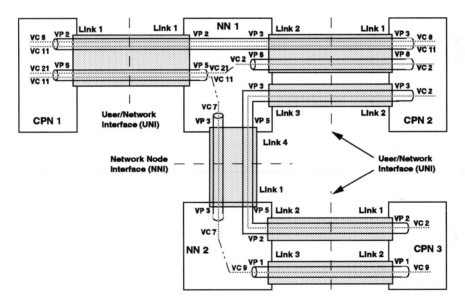

Figure   2-2. *Routing Concept in an ATM Network*

Virtual Path (VP)

As illustrated in Figure 2-2, a virtual path (VP) is a route through the network representing a group of virtual channels (VCs). VPs may exist:

1. Between ATM endpoints (as between CPN 1 and CPN 2 and between CPN 2 and CPN 3)

2. Between ATM switches and ATM endpoints (as between NN 1 and CPN 1, NN 1 and CPN 2, and NN 2 and CPN 3)

3. Between ATM switches (as between NN 1 and NN 2)

A VP may be routed through an ATM switch by reference only to the VP number, or it may terminate in an ATM switch. A VP entering an endpoint always terminates in that endpoint.

Virtual Channel (VC)

The concept of a virtual channel is defined in ATM as a unidirectional connection between end users. However, the use of the acronym VC for many other purposes in communications (such as the virtual circuit in X.25) means that its use is often confused.

Virtual Channel Connection (VCC)

A virtual channel connection is the end-to-end connection along which a user sends data. The concept is very close to that of a virtual circuit in X.25. The major difference is that a virtual channel connection carries data in one direction only, whereas a virtual circuit is bidirectional.

While a VCC is defined to be unidirectional, it must be noted that VCCs *always occur in pairs*, one VCC in each direction. Thus, a bidirectional communication channel consists of a pair of VCCs (that have to follow the same physical path through the network).

The concepts of VC and VCC are likewise almost the same. The acronym VC is most often used in a generic context and VCC in much more specific ways.

Virtual Channel Link (VCL)

A virtual channel link is a separately identified data flow within a link or a virtual path. A virtual channel connection (VCC) through the network is a sequence of interconnected (concatenated) VCLs.

The relationship between links, VPs and VCs is summarized in Figure 2-3 on page 2-7.

Links within Nodes

An ATM node may have many links attached. The maximum number of links and their addressing (numbering) within the node is *not* within the scope of the ATM standards.

VPs within Links

Within each link there are a number of VPs. The maximum number is defined by the number of bits allocated to Virtual Path Identifiers (VPIs) within the ATM cell header (8 or 12 bits).

VCs within VPs

Each VP has a number of VCs within it. The maximum number is restricted by the number of bits allocated to Virtual Channel Identifiers (VCIs) within the cell header (16 bits).

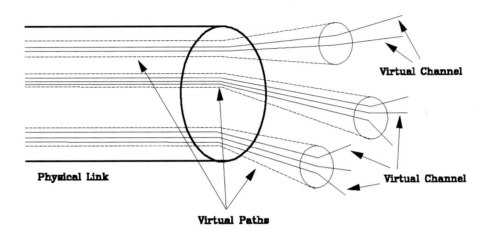

Figure   2-3. Link, Virtual Path and Virtual Channel Relationship

As far as the architecture of ATM is concerned, each link may have all possible VPs and each VP may have all possible VCs within it. (In practice, nodes will limit the maxima to much smaller values for practical considerations, such as table space within a node.)

It is important to note that the scope of the numbering of each entity is just within the entity above it in the hierarchy. For example, all VPs may exist on all links - so VP number 2 may exist on link number 3 and there may be a VP number 2 on link number 7, but they are unrelated to one another. There could be a VC number 17 in *every* VP in a node.

VPs and VCs are only numbers! They identify a virtual (logical) path along which data may flow. They have *no* inherent capacity restrictions in terms of data throughput.[5] That

---

[5] There are deliberate restrictions imposed on the rate of entry of data into the network, but this is not relevant here.

is, dividing the link into VPs and VCs has nothing whatever to do with division of link capacity. You could saturate any link no matter what the speed with data on just one VC - even if the link had all possible VPs and VCs defined!

A good analogy is the US road system, where a single physical road can have many route numbers (sometimes up to 30 or more). The cars traveling on the road may consider themselves to be following any one of the numbered routes. But at any point in time all the cars on the road may consider themselves to be using the same route number.

2.2 Cell Format

The cell formats at the Network Node Interface (NNI) and the User Network Interface (UNI) are illustrated in Figure 2-4 and Figure 2-5 respectively.

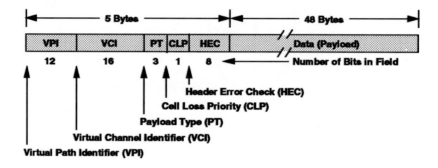

Figure 2-4. ATM Cell Format at Network Node Interface (NNI)

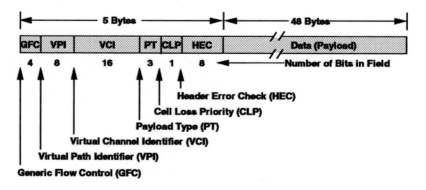

Figure 2-5. ATM Cell Format at User Network Interface (UNI)

Cell Size

An ATM cell is always 48 bytes of data with a 5-byte header; it may *not* be longer or shorter. This cell size was determined by the CCITT (now called the ITU-T) as a compromise between voice and data requirements.

Generic Flow Control (GFC)

At the present time the GFC function has not been standardized. However, from the two cell headers it should be noted that the GFC field does *not* appear in the cell header on the NN interface. Therefore, it is not carried through the network and has only local significance between the ATM endpoint and the ATM switch to which it is attached.

VPI and VCI

The most important fields in the cell header are the Virtual Path Identifier (VPI) and the Virtual Channel Identifier (VCI). Together these identify the connection (called a virtual connection) that this cell belongs to. There is no "destination network address" because this would be too much of an overhead for a 48-byte cell to carry.

The VPI/VCI together are similar in function to the Logical Channel Identifier in X.25 or the DLCI of frame relay in that they do not identify the destination address of the cell explicitly, but rather they identify a connection which leads to the desired destination.

Reserved Values

There are a number of reserved VPI and VCI values that are used for signaling, operation and maintenance, and resource management. The range from VCI=0 to VCI=15 is reserved by the ITU-T. The range from VCI=16 to VCI=31 is reserved by the ATM Forum. This applies to VCIs within all VPs.

Empty Cells

A cell with both VPI and VCI values set to zero indicates that the cell is unassigned (empty). Unassigned cells are used on physical links that have framed structures (generally PDH and SDH). On these links, when there is no data to send the sender must send something; thus, an empty cell is sent. At the receiver, these cells are immediately discarded. On links that are unframed (such as the 100 Mbps optical link derived from FDDI), the gaps between cells are filled with idles and therefore empty cells are never transmitted.

Any given ATM node may implement fewer than the possible maximum VPI and VCI numbers. In fact, most nodes will do this. When a node implements less than the maximum, then it must use an integral number of contiguous bits and these must be the low-order bits of the field. VC and VP values of 0 have reserved usages.

Payload Type (PT)

Three bits are available for payload type (PT) identification, hereafter named bit0, bit1, and bit2 in the sequence of their occurrence in the three-bit field. The first bit, bit0, determines if this cell is for a user data flow (when set 0) or for operations administration and management (OA&M). If the cell carries user data (bit0=0) then bit1=1 means that congestion was experienced somewhere along the cell's route (bit1=0 means no congestion on the route).

Bit2 is used by "higher layers". At the present time it is only specified for AAL-5 where bit2=1 means that this cell is the end of a block of user data (bit2=0 means this cell is the beginning or the middle of a block).

Cell Loss Priority (CLP)

When set to 1, this bit indicates that the cell is of *low* priority. That is, if the system needs to discard cells to relieve congestion, then this cell should be discarded first. It is incorrect, but in some publications this bit is referred to as the DE (Discard Eligibility) bit.

Header Error Check (HEC)

This field allows the *correction* of all single-bit errors in the header part of the cell *or* for the *detection* of most single and multi-bit errors. The "or" in the previous sentence is critical. When the algorithm determines that there is an error, it has no reliable way of determining whether that error is a (correctable) single-bit error or an (uncorrectable) multi-bit error.

What to do in this situation requires further study. If the overwhelming majority of errors are single-bit, then it seems the best thing to do is to correct them and to tolerate the fact that some misrouting will occur on cells that really had multi-bit errors. Or, you could play it safe and discard all cells where the algorithm says there is an error.

In addition to its use for error detection, the HEC field is used for determining cell boundaries on some types of physical links.

When the link is unsynchronized and cell boundaries are unknown (such as during link initialization), the receiver will scan its input data looking for 5-byte groups such that the 5th byte is a valid HEC for the previous 4 bytes. When this condition is detected, the receiver waits for 48 bytes to go past and then tries again if the next 5 bytes received also pass the test as a valid header. This process is repeated a specified number of times. When the check is successful for the defined number of times, the receiver declares that it has obtained valid cell synchronization. The chances of invalid synchronization being gained are very low.

2.3 Network Characteristics

2.3.1 Connection-Oriented Network

An ATM system is a connection-oriented system. There is no way to send data in an ATM network except on a pre-established connection (VCC). The system uses either call-by-call (switched circuit) setup or semi-permanent connections (set up by OA&M procedures).

2.3.2 Connectionless Operation

There is a connectionless mode of operation defined. This operates "over the top" of the ATM network. There are one or many "connectionless servers", which are just connectionless routers within the ATM network. Each user that requires connectionless service has a connection to the connectionless server.

In this mode of operation the first cell (or cells) of a group carries the full network address of the destination within its data (payload) field. Subsequent cells belonging to the same user data block do not carry a full network address, but rather are related to the first cell by having the same VPI/VCI as it had.

In a sense, connectionless operation is external to the ATM network since it operates at a layer above ATM and operates using pre-established ATM connections.

2.3.3 Guaranteed In-Sequence Delivery

Cells delivered to the network by an ATM endpoint over a virtual connection are transferred to the partner ATM endpoint in the same sequence as they were presented to the network. This is very important as it means that the end user (or the adaptation layer function) does not have to resequence cells that arrive out of order. But it also restricts the network to using a single path for any given virtual connection (at any particular point in time).

The payload (data) part of a cell may contain errors. Transmission errors within the data portion of the cell are *not* detected by the network (this is up to either the end-user equipment or the adaptation layer).

2.3.4 Broadcast and Multicast

Broadcast and multicast operation are available in ATM. In reality, there is no true "send it to everyone, I don't care" form of broadcast. A broadcast is a multicast with all users connected.

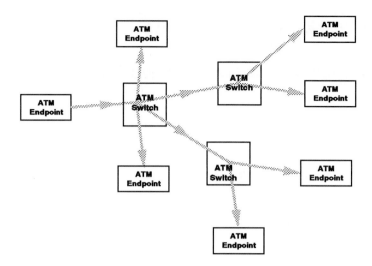

Figure   2-6. *Multicast Tree*

Multicasting takes place over a tree structure, as illustrated in Figure 2-6. Its official name is "point-to-multipoint connection".

- Communication is from the root of the tree to each "leaf".

- Data may be sent from a leaf to the root[6] but there is no leaf-to-leaf communication possible over the same connection.

- For any endpoint to have the ability to send to all other endpoints in the multicast group, there must be a separate multicast tree built on which it may send data.

- Data is copied as late as possible for every outgoing link in the structure. Multiple copies of the same data *never* appear on the same link.

- The VPI/VCI is swapped at each branch point when the data is copied, and thus there is no relationship between the VPI/VCIs used on each stage of the route.

  This is mentioned to contrast the operation with an alternative that was discussed as an option. That is, if a reserved VPI/VCI was used at each endpoint, then the VPI and VCI numbers for a given broadcast tree would be the same at each endpoint. This is not how multicast works in ATM (although it is a common misunderstanding).

---

6 This depends on which "release" or "phase" of ATM we are using. Leaf-to-root communication is not supported in ATM Forum phase 1.

- Multicast trees may be set up and changed by signaling (switched setup) or defined by the network administrator (semi-permanent).

While any-to-all multicast is not yet specified in ATM, it is expected that the function will become available in the future. It is called "multipoint-to-multipoint connection".

2.3.5 Quality of Service (QoS)

Each virtual channel connection has a given quality-of-service characteristic associated with it. This QoS specifies an average bandwidth as well as a maximum peak (instantaneous) allowed bandwidth. In serious overload situations, when the network cannot recover from overload by discarding only cells marked as low priority, the network can select which cells to discard depending on the QoS characteristic on the VC.

The QoS parameters defined by the ITU-T are as follows:

- Cell Transfer Delay (Network Latency)

- Cell Delay Variation (Jitter)

- Cell Transfer Capacity (Speed - average and peak allowed rates)

- Cell Error Ratio

- Cell Loss Ratio

- Cell Misinsertion Rate

A VP also has a QoS associated with it. VCs within a VP may have a lower QoS than the VP, but they cannot have a higher one.

2.3.6 Cell Discard and Loss

Cells may be lost or discarded by the network. The network does *not* detect the loss of cells and does *not* signal the end user when it has discarded cells from a particular connection.

Some variable-bit-rate encoding schemes for voice and for video are structured in such a way that two kinds of cells are produced:

- Essential cells which contain basic information to enable the continued function of the service

- Optional cells which contain information that improves the quality of the service (voice or picture quality)

If the end-user equipment marks a cell as low priority, that cell will be discarded first if cells need to be discarded due to network congestion.

If discarding marked cells is insufficient to relieve the network congestion, then the network may optionally use the QoS to decide which cells to discard next. How (and if at all) the QoS is used to select cells to be discarded is not defined in the standards.

In this case, a lower quality of service may be specified which would allow the network to discard cells belonging to these virtual connections in situations of extreme congestion.

In cell-based networks where congestion is handled by cell discard, and recovery is accomplished by retransmission of full blocks rather than individual cells, there is a potential problem in congestion situations. See 9.2.2, "Congestion in ATM Networks" on page 9-6.

2.3.7 Congestion Control

There is no flow control in an ATM network of the kind that is standard in traditional packet switching networks (such as SNA). That is, windowed link protocols and procedures such as "pacing" cannot be efficiently performed in the high-speed environment.

In ATM, when a connection is requested, the parameters of that connection (service class, requested average throughput rate, and requested peak throughput rate) are examined and the connection is allowed only if the network has sufficient capacity to support the new connection.

This is a lot easier said than done. Any system that allocates capacity in excess of real capacity on the basis of statistical parameters allows the possibility (however remote) that by chance a situation will arise when demands on the network exceed the network resources. In this case, the network will discard cells. The first to be discarded will be arriving cells marked as lower priority in the CLP bit (cells already queued in buffers will not be discarded). After that, discarding will take place by service class or randomly depending on the node's implementation.

2.3.8 Input Rate Policing

At the entry point to the network, the ATM switch monitors the rate of data arrival for a VP or a VC according to the negotiated QoS parameters for that connection. It will take action to prevent an ATM endpoint from exceeding its allowed limits.

The ATM endpoint is expected to operate a "leaky bucket" rate control scheme (see 9.3.2.6, "Leaky Bucket Rate Control" on page 9-26) to prevent it from making demands on the network in excess of its allowed capacity.

Depending on the network (and the user's subscription parameters) the network may either:

- Discard cells received in excess of the allowed maxima.

- Mark excess cells with the CLP (cell loss priority) bit to tell the network that this cell is of low priority and may be discarded if required.

Since there is no real control of flow within the network this function is very important.

Another function that is performed at the entry point to the network is collecting traffic information for billing. There is no standard as yet, but it seems certain that many public networks will have a charging formula taking into account the average and maximum allowed cell rate as well as the actual traffic sent. In fact, it is quite possible that some administrations will charge only for the maximum allowed capacity and connect time (the network must provide for the capacity if the user has a circuit even if that capacity is not used). This kind of system is used in other industries. In some countries electricity is billed for according to peak usage rate regardless of the total amount of electricity used.

2.3.9 End-to-End Data Integrity

There is no end-to-end data integrity provided by the ATM network itself. This is the responsibility of the end-user equipment. The "adaptation layer" function (implemented in the ATM endpoint) provides an error checking function such that errored data is discarded but it does not provide recovery of lost data. This must be provided by the using system externally to the ATM network.

2.3.9.1 Priorities

In traditional data networks (like SNA), connections often have priorities depending on the type of traffic and its importance. Traffic of high priority will be transmitted on any link before traffic of a lower priority. There are no priorities of this kind defined in the ATM standards. There is no priority field (as distinct from cell loss priority) in the cell header.

To guarantee the requested QoS for a VCC (for example, maximum end-to-end delay and delay variation) ATM switches can (and better do) implement a buffer management and transmission scheduling algorithm that ensures that real-time traffic is scheduled for transmission over a link before, for example, ABR traffic and that a link's buffer queue for real-time traffic holds only a few cells; a real-time cell that does not arrive in time is useless for the receiver anyhow. That means, that during the setup of a VCC, intermediate ATM switches on the connection's physical path have to look at (and remember) the QoS requested for that connection.

2.4 Data Transfer Mode (Routing)

ATM networks route data internally using a process called "logical ID swapping". This is important because the network is constrained to deliver cells on a virtual connection in the same order in which they were presented to the network. (Of course, different virtual connections between the same pair of ATM endpoints may go by different routes.)

In ATM, there are two IDs for each virtual connection: the VPI and the VCI. Some ATM switches may only know about and switch VPs. Other switches will know about and switch both VPs and VCs.

An ATM switch must keep a table of VPI values relating to each physical link that it has attached. If a VP "passes through" the switch, its associated VPI entry contains a pointer to the outbound link where arriving data must be routed together with the VPI on the outbound link. If the VP terminates in the particular ATM switch, then each ATM switch must keep a table of VCIs for each terminating VP. This table contains pointers for the further routing of the data. The VC may be, for example, a signaling channel and terminate in this particular ATM switch. Alternatively, the VC may be logically connected to another VC through this ATM switch in which case the ATM switch must route the data to the appropriate outbound connection (identified by the link, VPI, and VCI).

When the ATM switch routes the cell onward using only the VPI, then the VPI number is changed. (VPIs only have meaning within the context of an individual link.) When the ATM switch routes the cell by using both the VPI and the VCI, then the outgoing cell will have a different VPI and VCI.

2.4.1 Logical ID Swapping (Principle)

Logical ID swapping is an internal network technique for routing data through a network of packet-switching nodes. It is widely used in a number of different data networking systems (X.25, APPN, frame relay) and has been selected as the routing technique (transfer mode) to be used in ATM.

The basic concept in logical ID swapping is that of a connection carried through the network by a series of pointers in successive nodes along the route. Each data packet sent carries an identifier (called a logical channel identifier or LCID)[7] in its header which specifies the particular logical connection to which this packet belongs. There is no global connection identifier (at least not one used for making the routing decision for the individual packets). The LCID is unique only within a particular link and therefore when a virtual circuit (channel in ATM) passes through a switch from one link to another the LCID must be changed (because it is different in each link).

In Figure 2-7 on page 2-17 there is a logical connection between an end-user system connected to Link 1 (LCID 8) on Node A and another end-user system attached to Link 6 (LCID 4) on Node B. In operation the procedure works as follows:

1. The end-user system places data to be sent on a link to the network (in the example, Link 1 on Node A).

---

[7] In ATM this is the VPI and/or the VCI.

2. The user data has a header appended to it which contains a logical channel identifier (in the example, LCID 8).

3. Node A receives the block and looks at the header. It finds that the received block has LCID 8.

4. The node then looks at the connection table for LCID 8 on Link 1 (the node knows which link the data was received on).

5. The node finds that logical channel 8 on link 1 is connected to logical channel B on Link 3.

6. The node then changes the LCID within the data header from 8 to B.

7. The node then queues the data for transmission on Link 3.

8. When Node B receives the data it sees that it belongs to logical channel B. (Notice here that both nodes know the same LCID at each end of the link because it is the same link. The LCID only has meaning in the context of the single link between Node A and Node B.)

9. Node B then repeats the process changing (swapping) the LCID to 4 and sending it out on Link 6.

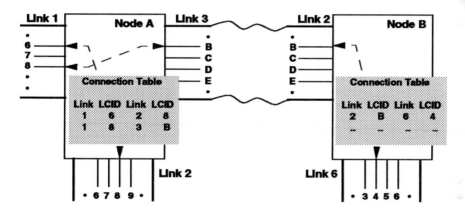

Figure 2-7. *Logical ID Swapping*

2.4.2 Setting Up the Route

In order to set up a route, the routing tables along the path of a virtual connection (within each switch) must be set up correctly. This is initiated in two ways:

1. By OA&M (operation, administration, and maintenance) procedures

This means that the connection is predefined, or rather, set up and changed by a system operator through a management system. In this case the switching function is not usually called a switch but rather a **cross-connect**.

2. By dynamic request from an endpoint

This is called switched call setup and is discussed at length in Chapter 4, "Signaling" on page 4-1.

2.4.3 Logical ID Swapping in ATM

In ATM, two levels of logical ID (the VPI and the VCI) are used and thus logical ID swapping in ATM is a two-stage process. The procedure is shown in Figure 2-8.

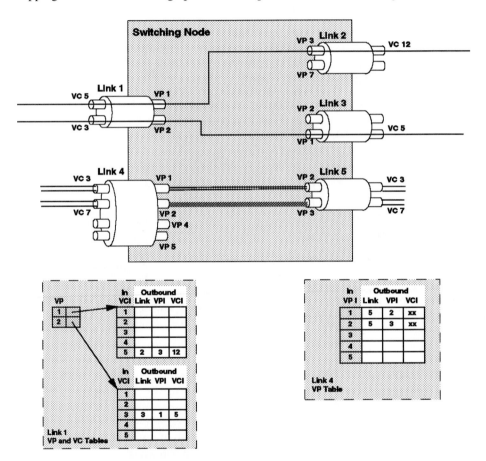

Figure *2-8. Logical ID Swapping in ATM*

- Looking at Link 1 we see that there is a VP with VPI=1, which has a VC with VCI=5 within it.

- A connection exists between Link1/VPI=1/VCI=5 and Link 2/VPI=3/VCI=12.

- We can see that the VP with VPI=1 on Link 1 terminates within this ATM switch.

- Necessary routing tables for Link 1 are shown.

  - There is a VP table with an entry for each VPI on the link.

  - Because each of the two illustrated VPs on Link 1 terminate in this node the table entry for each VP is minimal. It consists only of a pointer to a VC table.

  - There is a VC table for each VP that terminates in this switch.

- When a cell arrives on Link 1 with VPI=1 and VCI=5 the switch first looks to the routing table for Link 1. It locates VPI=1 in the VP table and uses this to find the VC table.

- The switch then looks to the VC table for the entry for VCI=5.

- From the table entry it discovers that the cell is to be routed to Link 2 with VPI=3 and VCI=12.

- It changes the cell header to reflect the new VPI and VCI values and routes the cell to Link 2.

In Figure 2-8 on page 2-18, the case of VPI swapping is shown for Link 4. This case is very simple because the VCI does not change. The VP table shows an outbound link ID and a new VPI but not a VCI. The VPI is used to locate the appropriate table entry and the cell is routed accordingly (and the VPI is updated).

Since the VPI and/or VCI fields in the cell header have been changed, then the HEC field in the cell header must be recalculated before the cell can be transmitted. This is because, when a cell is switched from one link to another the VPI is *always* replaced[8] (regardless of whether the VCI is replaced or not) and the HEC is always recalculated.

It is important to note that there is a separate VP table for every inbound link and a separate VC table for each VP that terminates in this node. The ATM standards do not define *how* an ATM switch structures and manages its VPI/VCI swapping tables. Actual implementations may be completely different from the conceptual view we have taken to describe the logic of the label-swapping process. But however the implementation is done, the routing decision has to be made very fast; there is not much time before the next cell arrives.

---

[8] Although it may be replaced with the same value it had before.

Multicast and broadcast operations (described in 2.3.4, "Broadcast and Multicast" on page 2-11) are achieved by having multiple destination entries in the VP or VC tables. The system copies each cell once for each outgoing link as indicated in the table entry.

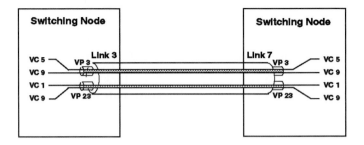

Figure **2-9.** *VPIs and VCIs within a Link.* VPI and VCI numbers are the same at each end of a link (because there is nothing within the link that can change them).

2.5 Some Definitions

The formal definitions of VC and VP related concepts rely on an understanding of ATM label swap routing. These are illustrated in Figure 2-10. Although some of these terms were introduced earlier, they can now be treated with more precision.

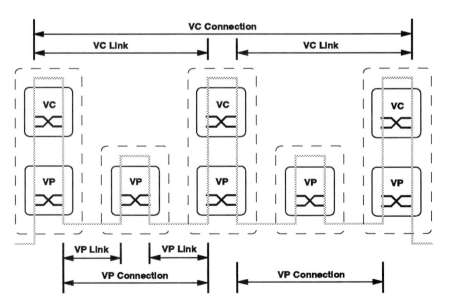

Figure **2-10.** *VP and VC Concepts*

Virtual Channel (VC)

The best definition of a virtual channel is "a logical association between the endpoints of a link that enables the unidirectional transfer of cells over that link".

This is not the definition used by either the ATM Forum or the ITU-T. The ATM Forum defines it as "a communication channel that provides for the sequential unidirectional transport of ATM cells". The ITU-T defines a VC as "a concept used to describe unidirectional transport of ATM cells associated by a common unique identifier value".

Thus, the Forum definition appears to equate to a VCC where the ITU-T definition equates to a VCL.

Virtual Channel Link (VCL)

A VCL exists from the point where a VCI value is assigned to where it is translated or terminated. Since it exists within a VP it may pass through a number of ATM switches (if the VP is switched). It is unidirectional.

Virtual Channel Connection (VCC)

This is a concatenation of VCLs extending from one end user to another through the ATM network. The endpoint is actually a Service Access Point (SAP).

VCCs always exist in pairs (one for each direction).

Virtual Channel Switch (VCS)

This is the VC switching function shown in Figure 2-10 on page 2-20. A VCS connects VCLs together to form VCCs. To do this it terminates VPCs and translates (changes) VCI values.

Virtual Path (VP)

This is a group of virtual channels associated in such a way that the group can be switched through the network without the switching element ever knowing about the separate existence of VCs. Thus, all VCs within a VP travel on the same path through the network. VCs within a VP may have lower QoS characteristics than the VP, but may not have higher ones.

A VP may exist through a short sequence of nodes (for example on a backbone) or it may extend from ATM endpoint to ATM endpoint.

Virtual Path Link (VPL)

A VPL exists between the point where the VPI value is assigned and where it is translated or the VP is terminated. In practice, this means that a VPL exists only within a point-to-point link between ATM switches. When a link arrives in an ATM node the VPI is always translated, so the VPL only extends over the range of a single inter-switch ATM link.

It should be noted that ATM links between switches can run over SDH, for example, and be "networked" (switched) through the SDH network. This operates at the layer below the ATM layer and is unknown to ATM.

Virtual Path Connection (VPC)

This is a concatenation (sequence) of VPLs that extends between virtual path terminations. This is the virtual path. It is unidirectional.

Virtual Path Switch (VPS)

The VPS is the processing function that connects VPLs to form VPCs. This function translates the VPI values and directs cells to the correct output link on a particular ATM switch.

Virtual Path Terminator (VPT)

This processing function terminates the VP and makes the VCs available for separate and independent routing.

Virtual Path Connection Identifier (VPCI)

This is the identifier of the VP connection returned by the network when call setup is performed. It is 16 bits long.

The VPCI is used in the signaling protocols instead of a VPI. The VPI is only unique within a single ATM link. In the case of a simple ATM concentrator device, multiple downstream connections are concentrated onto a single upstream connection. The upstream connection is connected at the UNI. This means that a single signaling channel at the UNI is controlling multiple downstream links. The VPCI has additional bits to allow the link to be uniquely identified.

In the first versions of ATM the VPI and VPCI will be "numerically equivalent".

2.6 The ATM Reference Model

In standards development there are two reference models that apply to ATM. The first is the B-ISDN reference model as illustrated in Figure 2-11 on page 2-23. Interfaces between functions shown in the model are the same ones as in regular "narrowband" ISDN (N-ISDN) but are subscripted with the letter B to indicate broadband.

The model (as shown in Figure 2-11 on page 2-23) is not used very often to describe ATM as the interfaces have been given other (more convenient) names.

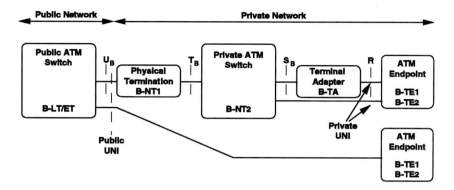

Figure 2-11. *B-ISDN User-Network Interfaces Configuration*

U_B represents the physical wire interface between the public network and a user. In N-ISDN the physical protocols for the U interface were not internationally standardized (but there are country-level standards).

T_B represents a different physical layer interface to the carrier network but cell-level protocols are not affected.

Both U_B and T_B interfaces are called the **Public User-Network Interface** (public UNI).

S_B is the private UNI interface. This is very similar to the public interface, but there are many differences in the types of link protocols allowed, in signaling and in accounting etc.

R is the same interface as the S_B interface except that a simpler interface link layer protocol is used (one without OA&M capability).

The functions of the "boxes" involved are as follows:

B-LT/ET is the Line Termination and/or the Exchange Termination. It represents the public ATM switch.

B-NT1 represents the physical line terminating equipment. In N-ISDN, the NT1 is usually a separate piece of equipment supplied and owned by the carrier. In B-ISDN, B-NT1 is a function that will usually be built into the end-user equipment.

B-NT2 is the private ATM switch function. In narrowband ISDN, NT2 is a PBX.

B-TA is the terminal adapter function. In the standard, this function is provided to allow for the adaptation to ISDN of non-ISDN devices. In this model, the ATM endpoint is still an ATM device but the link protocol between it and the TA is not a standard ATM link protocol.

It would be legitimate to have here a device that interfaced ATM to frame relay (for example). The R interface would then be a frame relay interface.

B-TE is an ATM endpoint or TErminal.

Figure 2-12 shows the way in which ATM is usually represented in the ISO's reference model for Open Systems Interconnection (the OSI model).

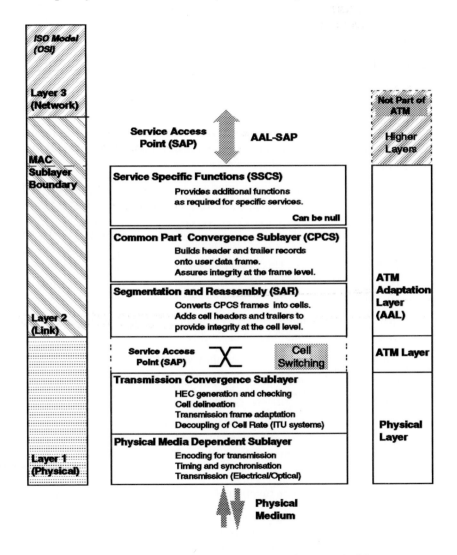

Figure 2-12. ATM Function Placement in the ISO Reference Model

Physical Layer (Layer 1) of the ISO model represents the functions of the core ATM cell-switching network. Of course, the ATM physical layer now becomes only a part of the OSI physical layer.

Link Layer (Layer 2) of the OSI model is not completely covered by ATM. Indeed, the service access point (SAP) interface of the ATM adaptation layer is equivalent to the MAC sublayer of the ISO model's layer 2. To perform a full ISO link layer you need to have some network end-to-end protocol there to perform error recovery by re-transmission.

Some people contend that this is an erroneous way of looking at the subject and that the ATM layer should be regarded as equivalent to layer 3 (networking) of the ISO model and the adaptation layer as the lower part of ISO layer 4. This is an interesting academic point but won't help us build networks.

2.7 Private UNI Versions

There are three "versions" of the ATM Forum private UNI that are of current interest. These are called Versions 3.0, 3.1, and 4.0. As might be expected, 3.1 is more functional than 3.0 and 4.0 will have more function than 3.1.

UNI Versions 3.0 and 3.1 are incompatible. For example, an adapter card at level 3.0 will *not* interface to a switch at level 3.1. At the present time some suppliers offer alternative code options so that products can obey either. In the future it is expected that some switches will be able to dynamically detect the level of adapter to which they are attached and use the appropriate version. When this happens, however, it would still not be possible for an adapter at one level to communicate with an adapter at the other level. There is some suggestion that some switches will actually convert the protocols in the future to allow this latter kind of interaction. However, at the time of writing the authors were unaware of any product that performs this function.

The major differences between UNI 3.0 and 3.1 are as follows:

1. Alignment with the ITU Q.2931 signaling specification.

   UNI 3.0 was based on a subset of the ITU Q.93b signaling specification but contained a number of additional functions (for example, SCR, MBS traffic parms, point-to-multipoint call setup, etc.). UNI 3.1 is based on the ITU Q.2931 specification.

2. UNI 3.1 uses a new version of SSCOP.

   The Service Specific Connection-Oriented Protocol is a data-link protocol used for reliable delivery of signaling packets. This is based on ITU Q.2100, Q.2110 and Q.2130. UNI 3.0 was based on just Q.2100.

UNI version 4.0 doesn't exist. UNI 4.0 is referred to quite often even in ATM Forum documentation. However, the ATM Forum has decided not to release a UNI 4.0. Instead, the individual components that make up the UNI will have their own specifications and will be released as and when they are ready. Thus there will be:

- Signaling 4.0

- Traffic management 4.0

- Management specifications

- Individual physical-layer interface specifications

This is intended to allow specifications to be developed and released with minimum delay.

2.8 End-User Interface

Figure 2-13 on page 2-27 shows the data flow from one end user to another over an ATM network. There are several important things to notice about this structure:

- Each box in the figure represents an ATM endpoint in a separate physical device.

- The *only* way to interface to ATM is through a program of some kind. That is, within the ATM endpoint, the physical layer, ATM layer, and adaptation layer are rigorously defined by the ATM standards. The "primitives" which the user program uses to interface to the AAL (at the AAL service access point - SAP) are also rigorously defined.

  However, the ATM code can interface to *nothing* else. It forms the interface between user code and the ATM network. This means, for example, that if we want to support a voice connection there is a *program* sitting between the ATM AAL-1 (which handles constant-bit-rate voice) and the physical adapter that connects to some source of voice information. ATM does *not* connect to a voice line directly (nor to anything else).

- When a user program sends data, that data is processed first by the adaptation layer, then by the ATM layer, and then the physical layer takes over to send the data to the ATM network. The cells are transported by the network and then received on the other side first by the physical layer, then processed by the ATM layer, and then by the receiving AAL. When all this is complete, the information (data) is passed to the receiving user program.

- The total function performed by the ATM network has been the *non-assured* transport (it might have lost some) of user information from program to program.

- The user program mentioned here is quite obviously **not** end-user code in the normal sense of the term. In order to make the network useful, a very significant amount of processing (protocols) must be performed.

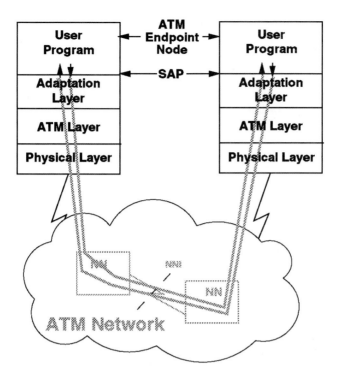

Figure **2-13.** *Data Flow through an ATM Network*

Looked at from a traditional data processing viewpoint, all the ATM network has done is to replace a link connection with another kind of link connection - all the "higher-layer" network functions must still be performed.

Chapter 3. ATM Adaptation Layer (AAL)

In order to make an ATM network practical, it is necessary to adapt the internal network characteristics to those of the various traffic types that will use the network. This is the purpose of the adaptation layer.

An ATM network carries cells from one end of the network to the other. While the cell header has error checking in it (this is necessary because of the possibility of misrouting cells which had bit errors in the header), there is *no* error check on the data part of the cell. In addition, cells can be lost or discarded during transport and in error situations (this depends on the specific network equipment) cells could get out of sequence and/or get duplicated.

3.1 Overview

The function of the adaptation layer is to provide generalized interworking across the ATM network. This function is, however, very basic indeed. In the case of data, the AAL takes frames (blocks) of data delivered to it, breaks them up into cells and adds necessary header information to allow rebuilding of the original block at the receiver. This involves checking for errors. *The AAL does not do any error recovery.* In the case of data, if a frame being received has any errors at all, then it is discarded and not delivered to the receiving end. Error recovery is the responsibility of a "higher-layer protocol".

One way of looking at the adaptation layer is to regard it as a special form of Terminal Adapter (TA) within the ISDN model.

3.1.1 Service Interface

Figure 3-1 on page 3-2 shows the logical structure of an ATM network.

The "service interface" is the interface to higher protocol layers and functions; that is, the service interface is the boundary of ATM. The AAL connects the service interface to the ATM cell-switching network. Note that the service interface is an *internal* interface within a device. It is specified as a series of logical primitives which will be implemented very differently in different products. The service interface definition does not include the means of physical delivery of the service primitives.

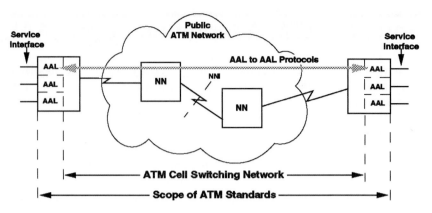

Figure **3-1.** *The ATM Adaptation Layer (AAL)*

3.1.1.1 AAL Service Classes

The ITU-T has defined four different generic classes of network traffic that need to be treated differently by an ATM network. These classes are designated Class A to Class D. Originally, there were four different "AAL types" proposed - one for each traffic class. This changed during the standards definition process as the problem came to be better understood. The four service classes, plus a class X, are summarized in Figure 3-2.

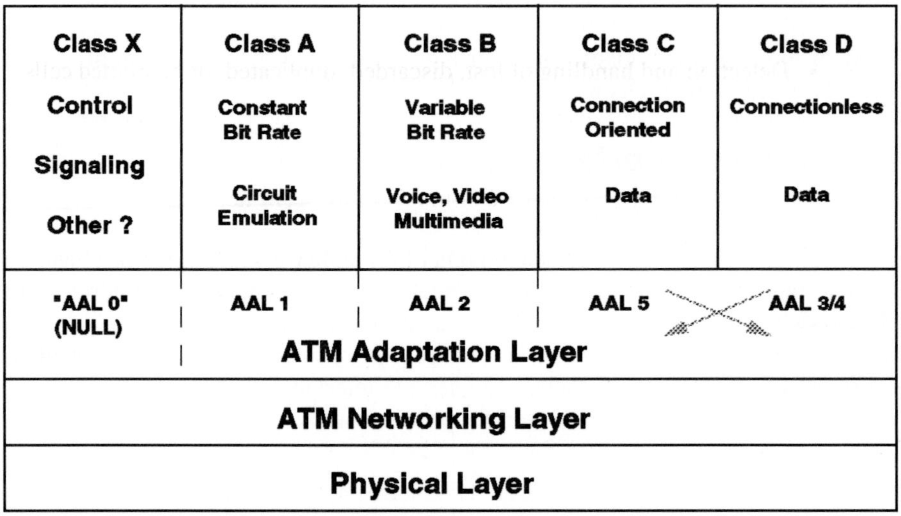

Class X	Class A	Class B	Class C	Class D
Control	Constant Bit Rate	Variable Bit Rate	Connection Oriented	Connectionless
Signaling				
Other ?	Circuit Emulation	Voice, Video Multimedia	Data	Data
"AAL 0" (NULL)	AAL 1	AAL 2	AAL 5	AAL 3/4
		ATM Adaptation Layer		
		ATM Networking Layer		
		Physical Layer		

Figure **3-2.** *Service Classes and AAL Types*

Class X (User Defined)

This is a connection-oriented ATM transport service where the requirements (variable or constant bit rate, traffic type, timing, etc.) are user-defined. The only things that the network is involved with are the required bandwidth and QoS parameters.

Class X connections would be provided by AAL-0.

Class X is not defined in the ITU-T recommendations; it is, however, discussed in ATM Forum material.

Class A (Circuit Emulation)

This service emulates a leased line. It is intended for constant-rate voice and video applications etc.

These applications have the following characteristics:

- There is a constant bit rate at source and destination.
- There is a timing relationship between source and destination.
- There is a connection between end users of the service.

The adaptation layer must perform the following functions in order to support this service:

- Segmentation and reassembly of data frames into cells
- Handling (buffering) of cell delay variations
- Detection and handling of lost, discarded, duplicated, or misrouted cells
- Recovery of the source clock frequency (in a plesiochronous way)
- Detection of bit errors in the user information field

Class B (Variable-Bit-Rate Services)

This is intended for voice and video traffic that is basically isochronous at the level of end-user presentation, but which may be coded as variable-rate information.

These services have a variable flow of information, need some timing relationship between the ends of the connection and are connection oriented.

The services provided by the AAL for class B are:

- Transfer of variable-bit-rate information between end users
- Transfer of timing between source and destination
- Indication of lost or corrupted information not recovered by the AAL itself

The requirements here are quite complex, for example:

1. Many video applications will be primarily one-way and go to multiple destinations (multicast). However, typical one-way video is not too sensitive to network delay (a few seconds is fine).

2. Other video applications (such as videoconferencing) require a complex multicasting or hubbing regime. Videoconferencing requires synchronization of video and voice. It also has quite strict end-to-end delay requirements.

It is the class B traffic that produces nightmares for network engineers. High-bandwidth, and variable loads require complex rate control structures because of their unpredictable nature and because their data rates can often peak at a significant percentage of the network resources being used. In other words, unless your network is designed correctly Class B traffic can disrupt its operation with great ease.

It should not be surprising that AAL type 2 (the AAL which provides service for class B traffic) is as yet undefined.

Class C (Connection-Oriented Data)

This is traditional data traffic as known in an SNA or X.25 network.

These services are connection-oriented and have a variable flow of information.

Two services are provided called "message mode" and "streaming mode". Message mode provides for the transfer of single frames of user information. Streaming mode provides transport for multiple fixed-length frames of user data.

An AAL for class C must provide:

- Segmentation and reassembly of frames into cells

- Detection and signaling of errors in the data

In addition, it could provide other services such as the multiplexing and demultiplexing of multiple end-user connections onto a single ATM network connection. There is strong disagreement as to the need for this last function, however.

Class D (Connectionless Data)

This service has several uses in sending ad-hoc data, but could be used, for example, to carry TCP/IP or LAN interconnection traffic where the protocol in use is inherently connectionless.

These services are connectionless and have a variable flow of information. It is intended to support connectionless networking protocols such as IP and services that transfer data character-by-character (such as an "ASCII TWX" terminal).

Like the other three types of service, class D requires:

- Segmentation and reassembly of frames into cells

- Detection of errors in the data (but not retransmission)

In addition to these basic services, class D specifies:

- Multiplexing and demultiplexing of multiple end-user data flows onto a single cross-network data flow (for single-character transmissions)

- Network layer addressing and routing

It can be seen that the functions provided by the AAL are very basic ones. They are similar to those provided by a LAN at the MAC layer. This is the level of function provided by the AAL (of course, the AAL handles many types of service in addition to data). For data applications, either a logical link layer protocol (such as IEEE 802.2) or a higher-layer protocol that provides end-to-end data integrity will still be needed for successful operation.

3.2 Structure

There are now five different AAL types:

- AAL-0 means no AAL function is being performed. Cells are transferred between the service interface and the ATM network transparently.

- AAL-1 provides function for service class A.

- AAL-2 provides the required functions for variable-rate service class B. As yet there are no defined standards in this area.

- AAL-3/4 provides service for both classes C and D. AALs 3 and 4 were combined during the standards definition process as it was realized that the same process could perform both functions. It is quite complex and regarded by some as over-designed.

- AAL-5 provides functions for both classes C and D, but is significantly simpler (but it is also less functional). Some people think it will be fine for class C traffic, but AAL-3/4 will still be needed for connectionless traffic. Others disagree.

There is also a Signaling AAL (SAAL) defined; this adaptation layer does not provide user-to-user services but is a series of AAL functions that support signaling connections between ATM switches and/or between an ATM endpoint and an ATM switch (network). This is described in 3.8, "Signaling AAL" on page 3-24.

The internal logical structure of AAL-3/4 and AAL-5 is shown in Figure 3-3 on page 3-6. AAL-1 has a much simpler structure, but the principle is the same.

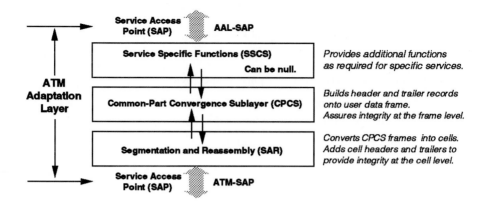

Figure **3-3.** *Structure of Sublayers in AAL-3/4 and AAL-5*

- Data is received in frames (for AAL-3/4 these can be up to 64 KB).

- A service-specific function may be performed here, if needed, to provide a more standard service interface (SAP) for common protocols. One such function has already been defined for frame relay. This layer will, however, often be null.

- **CPCS** stands for Common Part Convergence Sublayer. This operates on whole frames of user data, and the exact function depends on which AAL is being used.

- **SAR** means Segmentation and Reassembly. This is the layer that takes data and builds a stream of 48-byte cells. Again, functions depend on which AAL we are discussing.

- The interfaces between the sublayers shown in the figure are defined as logical primitives - they are not SAPs. This means that there is no intention to allow an external programming interface between the sublayers.

3.2.1 Terminology

As data flows through the AAL it is processed by (up to) three sublayers and changes its form (has different headers appended and is segmented or reassembled) as it is processed by the different sublayers.[1] At different points data is called by different names:

---

[1] The objective of this book is to explain ATM in an understandable way. This means the minimal use of jargon terms and acronyms. Unfortunately, however, at some points it is necessary to use the terminology because we cannot obtain understanding in any other way. This is one of them.

Service Data Unit (SDU)

This is data as it appears at the interface between a particular layer or sublayer and the layer immediately above. Thus, when data is presented to the AAL at its service interface (or service access point - SAP) it is called an AAL-SDU. This also applies in the other direction when data is delivered to a user by the AAL at the AAL-SAP.

Interface Data Unit (IDU)

An SDU may be segmented into multiple data blocks at an interface and these shorter segments are called IDUs.

Protocol Data Unit (PDU)

This is data as it appears at the interface between a particular sublayer and the sublayer immediately below. That is, the PDU is an SDU which has the sublayer's protocol information (headers and trailers etc.) appended.

Figure 3-8 on page 3-16 shows the flow of data through an AAL (for clarity most of the data naming has been left out). This figure needs to be studied in conjunction with Figure 3-3 on page 3-6. The naming works this way:

- A frame of user data is presented to the AAL at the service access point (SAP). At this point the data is called:

  - An AAL-SDU (the service data unit to be processed by the AAL)

  - An SSCS-SDU (the service data unit to be processed by the SSCS sublayer)

  - A CPCS-SDU (if there is no SSCS sublayer and the data unit is to be processed by the CPCS)

  All these names can apply to the same data and we have not started processing it yet.

- When the CPCS sublayer has finished its processing the resultant data unit is called a CPCS-PDU. It is now a Protocol Data Unit because it contains protocol information for the named sublayer.

- Now the data is passed to the Segmentation and Reassembly (SAR) sublayer and its name changes immediately. It is now a SAR-SDU. Although it contains protocol information meaningful to the CPCS, it is just data to the SAR and thus viewed from the SAR the data unit is an SDU.

  So a CPCS-PDU is *exactly* a SAR-SDU - it is all in your point of view.

- When the SAR has finished its processing, the resultant (many) data units are called SAR-PDUs.

- These are then passed to the ATM layer where they are called ATM-SDUs. They then have their ATM headers appended and are renamed ATM-PDUs or cells for short.

It is a very simple concept but the source of endless confusion.

3.3 AAL-0

This is the "null" AAL and corresponds to a process that connects the AAL service interface directly to the ATM networking service. Some people suggest that this might be used for network control and service messaging; however, the network control and service messages are the ones that simply *must not* get lost or corrupted.

Basically this interface allows the equipment designer and/or the end user to ignore standards and do what they like. This is simply not a very good idea.

3.4 AAL-1

AAL-1 is used for class A (constant-bit-rate) traffic. This means that the input and output to the network is in the form of a constant, timed stream of bits. In practice, this may take the form of data in an SDH or PDH frame where the frame rate is constant but data exists in different parts of the frame so that it arrives in the network in short bursts with periods of nothing in between. However, the received data stream is continuous and is locked to a timing reference.

The functions of AAL-1 are:

- Receive the data and package it into cells for transport through the network.

- Transmit the data to the end user on the other side of the network with the same timing that it had when it was received.

There are a number of challenges in doing this:

- Since the data stream is continuous, groups of data bytes must be placed into cells and the continuous data stream reconstructed at the other side of the network.

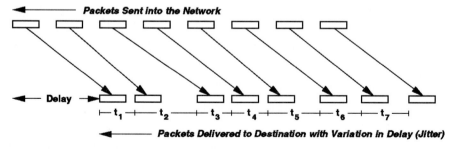

Figure   3-4. *Latency and Jitter*

- As shown in Figure 3-4, when cells are transported through the network they take different times (from one another) to transit the network. This causes "delay jitter". The receiver must retain sufficient buffering such that delay jitter does not result in overrun or underrun of the data stream.

  When doing this, it is generally a requirement that the end-to-end delay be minimized and therefore that buffering in the receiver be minimized.

- If the data being received was timed from our ATM network clock and the data being delivered was also timed from the same clock then we do not have much problem - the data stream will be received and transmitted at the same rate.

  But real life is not like this. It will be necessary to receive data and to transmit it on links that (while having the same nominal data rate) are not controlled by the same network clock. Indeed, this is the normal case. We must receive data using a derived clock (clocking derived from the received data stream) and then re-transmit at the other side of the network using some other clock.

  This would be fine if the clocks were *exactly* the same. But they cannot be the same. Crystal controlled oscillators of the same nominal rate vary from one another by quite large amounts (1 in 10^6) for example.

  In this case, it is necessary to do something to ensure that the timing of both bit streams is the same.

- This must be done in the ATM environment where cells may be lost or corrupted in transit.

3.4.1 Data Transfer

Data transfer operation is very straightforward, but does vary with the specific type of traffic transported. The cell format for AAL-1 is shown in Figure 3-5.

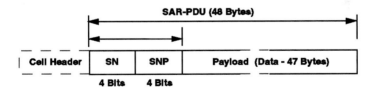

Figure 3-5. Cell Format (SAR) for AAL-1

The cell payload starts with two fields of four bits each:

Sequence Number (SN)

> This field contains a three-bit sequence number (which operates in a cyclic fashion) and a one-bit "CS Indication" (CSI) bit. The CSI bit is used for a number of purposes depending on the type of traffic.

Sequence Number Protection (SNP)

This field provides Cyclic Redundancy Check (CRC) bits to protect against errors in the Sequence Number field.

In operation, data just fills up each cell in turn (up to 47 bytes per cell) and the cell is sent as soon as possible. The data is passed to the AAL across its SAP in blocks, which were assembled from the external continuous data stream by an external process.

At the receiver end the reverse takes place. Cells found to have errors in the SN field are discarded but no error recovery (by retransmission) is attempted.

In order to minimize delays caused by cell assembly and playout, it is possible to send cells which are not full. This is particularly useful in the case of very slow-speed (4800 bps for example) data transfer. However, in ATM you must always send full cells - you cannot send less than 53 bytes. What happens here is that the AAL-1s are set up so that they agree to use fewer bytes than 48 in the cell. This can be specified when the circuit is provisioned (defined) or by sending a message between the AALs at the time of switched circuit establishment.

3.4.2 Clock Recovery

The biggest challenge in AAL-1 is clock recovery.

- If data is delivered to the network (even slightly) faster than it can be processed (transmitted at the other side of the network) then at some time data will have to be thrown away. In the meantime, while data is building up in network buffers, there will be an increase in network latency.

- If data is transmitted out from the network faster than it is received, then at some time the receiver will have nothing to transmit.

This means that you have to do something to ensure that the speed of output is closely matched to the speed of input. The network is asynchronous, but the circuit being transported is *synchronous*.

Note: Traditional data networks do not have this need or function. Synchronization of the output port to the speed of the input port is only needed with Constant Bit Rate (CBR) traffic.

There are two ways of handling this:

Synchronous Residual Time Stamp (SRTS)

SRTS relies on having an exact reference clock available at both ends of the network connection (that is, it must have the same clock at both AAL-1s). This reference clock is related to the network clock but will normally be much slower (it will be a multiple of network clock cycles).

The SRTS method is illustrated in Figure 3-6 on page 3-11.

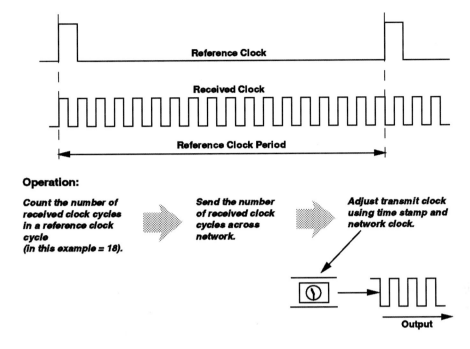

Figure *3-6. Synchronous Residual Time Stamp Clock Recovery*

1. As data is received, the clock cycles are counted to determine how many cycles there are in a reference clock period.

2. This time stamp is then sent across the network.

3. The reference clock, together with the time stamp, is then used to control an oscillator which drives the output link.

4. The SRTS is continually updated so that variations in the input clock rate are accommodated.

If you want to use SRTS, then the network must be strictly synchronized and clock distribution becomes a critical part of network design. SRTS is a particularly good method of operation and results in minimal requirement for buffering in the receiver and therefore minimal end-to-end network delay.

Adaptive Clock (AC)

With the adaptive clock method (as illustrated in Figure 3-7 on page 3-12) you do not need a network-wide reference clock.

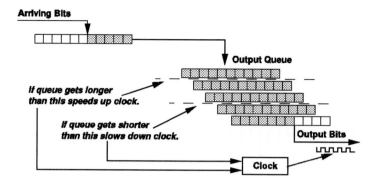

Figure 3-7. *Adaptive Clock Technique*

1. Data is received by the network and built into cells.

2. Cells are sent through the network to the destination AAL-1.

3. At the destination there is a buffer queue.

4. There is a notional level in the buffer queue which the system tries to maintain. That is, we might have the objective of having 200 bytes of data queued waiting for transmission.

5. In concept, all we need to do is speed up the transmit clock whenever the queue gets longer than our desired length (in this case 200 bytes) and slow it down when the queue length gets shorter.

6. Of course, it is not as simple as this. Data is transported in cells, so the queue is refilled in 47-byte increments. There is delay jitter across the network. Even if the data was being fed to the network at *exactly* the rate of data being sent from the network, there would be variations in the length of the output queue.

7. This means we need to use "set points". Instead of having a desired number of bytes in the queue, we have two queue levels: an upper limit and a lower limit (expressed in bytes).

8. When the queue length falls below the lower limit, then the transmit clock is slowed down. When it gets above the upper limit, then the transmit clock is speeded up.

9. The gap between the upper and lower limits depends on the jitter within the network.

This is quite a good method and improves as the speed of the data stream increases. The problem is that in order to have a playout queue you have more data queued than in the SRTS method. This queue represents a network end-to-end delay. For example, voice at 64 Kbps takes almost 6 ms to fill a cell. If we have an average queue length of 4 cells in the playout operation, then that is 24 ms of additional end-to-end delay. As speed increases this becomes less and less of a problem because a small number of cells in the playout queue represents less and less time.

3.4.2.1 Structured Data Transfer (SDT)

Most ATM physical transports use framed physical layer protocols of one kind or another (Sonet/SDH or PDH). Many (or rather most) of these are based on a 125 μsec clock cycle. SDT is the transport for these protocols.

SDT uses an additional header byte in the AAL-1 SAR header. The presence of this header byte is indicated by setting the CSI bit in the SAR header. This additional byte is a pointer (offset from the start of a cell) that indicates where a frame (or other grouping of data) begins. Since the start of a frame may not always be present in a cell, the header byte is not always present either. This pointer is just for synchronization and you do not have to indicate the start of each logical grouping. (Indeed, it is possible to have two logical groups in a single cell - as with T1 transport for example - and there is only one pointer.)

Structured data transfer uses either the SRTS or AC method for clock synchronization.

3.5 AAL-2

AAL-2 processes a stream of data like AAL-1 does with the critical difference that the data stream is variable in rate. Coded (compressed) voice and video are the primary examples here.

AAL-2 is currently absent from the draft standards and so details are not available.

One of the key problems that faces the designers of AAL-2 is how to handle the synchronization of multiple (variable-rate) data streams. This is the most important technical challenge facing the development of multimedia systems.

3.6 AAL-3/4

Derived from the SMDS standard, AAL-3/4 is a high-function, relatively complex AAL. One objective of the design was to retain compatibility with SMDS.

AAL-3/4 provides end-to-end[2] transport for both connection-oriented (Class C) and connectionless (Class D) data. There are many options:

Service Modes

Data transport takes place in either of two modes, message mode or streaming mode.

In *message mode* single blocks of data (called AAL-SDUs) are received from the user at the service interface and delivered to another service interface elsewhere in the network.

In *streaming mode* a (possibly unending) stream of data blocks separated in time from one another is transported across the network.

Delivery Assurance

When data is transported across the ATM network it will sometimes be corrupted or lost during transit. The question is how to handle these conditions.

A cell may be discarded for congestion reasons, or it may be lost if a link error caused a data error in the cell header (this is detected using the HEC). Cells with uncorrectable errors in their headers are unconditionally discarded. However, cells may have correct headers, but errors in the data portion.

There are three things we can do:

1. Deliver only correct SDUs to the destination (omitting any that had missing cells or had errors).

2. Perform end-to-end error recovery and deliver a correct sequence of SDUs with none missing.

3. Do no end-to-end error recovery but pass all data (even errored data) to the destination. In this case the AAL would signal the user that errors had been detected in the data.

AAL 3/4 allows all three alternatives.

- *Assured operation* is the mode which requires re-transmission in the case of error. This mode is allowed in the ITU-T draft standard, but details of its operation have not been defined. When this function is implemented it will be as a part of a Service Specific Convergence Sublayer (SSCS).

- *Non-assured operation* covers the case where the AAL does not attempt any retransmission of data for error recovery. In non-assured operation, the user may decide whether delivery of errored SDUs is desired or not.

---

[2] In this context end-to-end means from one AAL service interface (see Figure 3-1 on page 3-2) to another AAL service interface somewhere else in the network.

In the great majority of uses, the non-assured case where errored data is not presented to the end user will be the mode of choice.

Blocking and Segmenting of Data

In message mode, an option is provided to allow blocking of short SDUs into larger units for transport through the network (of course, these larger units are going to be broken up into cells by the SAR function).

In streaming mode, there are a number of options for segmenting and re-blocking the SDUs during transit.

All of these blocking and segmenting options are simply allowed functions of the SSCS. At the present time no SSCS implements them. However, in streaming mode, in the absence of an SSCS, a single AAL-SDU may be presented to the SAP as multiple AAL-IDUs. If there is no SSCS they will be reassembled into a single CPCS-SDU before processing by the CPCS.

Multiplexing of Connections

A feature is provided to allow multiplexing of several AAL-to-AAL connections onto a single ATM VCC. This is described in 3.6.5, "Multiplexing Connections" on page 3-19.

Multipoint Operation

Point-to-multipoint operation is possible where an AAL-3/4 is simultaneously communicating (with the same information) with multiple destinations.

3.6.1 AAL-3/4 Method of Operation

The overall logic of AAL-3/4 operation is shown in Figure 3-8 on page 3-16.

- A user data frame (of course, including higher-layer protocol headers) is passed to the AAL over the service interface. In this context it is called an **AAL-SDU (AAL Service Data Unit)**.

- Assuming the absence of a service-specific function, the CPCS pads the data out to a multiple of four bytes and appends its header and trailer records.

- The new data unit is called a **CPCS-PDU (CPCS Protocol Data Unit)**.

- The CPCS-PDU is passed to the Segmentation and Reassembly (SAR) sublayer which segments the CPCS-PDU into 44-byte units and pads the last one to an exact 44 bytes.

- The SAR then adds its own header and trailer to the data segment and this is now called a **SAR-PDU**.

- Lastly an ATM header is added and the SAR-PDU becomes an ATM cell.

- The cell is carried through the network and presented to a matching AAL at its destination.

- The reverse process is then undertaken, first by the SAR sublayer and then by the CPCS.

- A reconstituted cell is passed across the service interface to the destination end user.

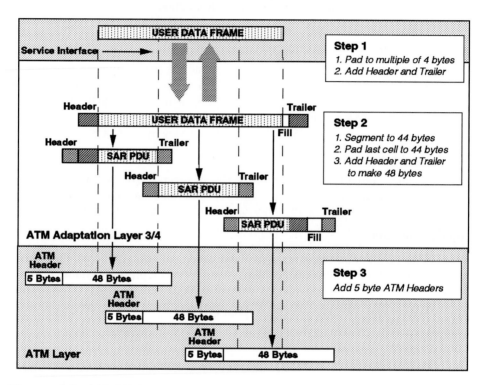

Figure *3-8.* *AAL 3/4 Operation*

3.6.2 Common Part Convergence Sublayer (CPCS)

The CPCS-PDU format is shown in Figure 3-9.

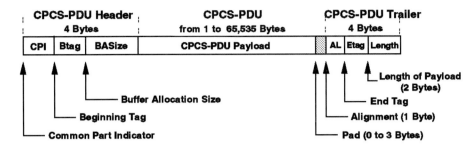

Figure   3-9. *AAL-3/4 CPCS-PDU Header*

The fields have the following meanings:

Common Part Indicator (CPI)

> This field specifies how the other fields of the CPCS-PDU are to be interpreted. For example, it specifies the coding used in the Length and BASize fields.

> The current ITU-T specification (I.363) shows only one possible value - all bits equal to zero. This specifies that both BASize and Length fields are coded as the integer number of bytes. Other possible values are "for further study".

Beginning Tag (Btag)

> When the CPCS builds a header and trailer for a single PDU it places the *same* value into both the header and the trailer. When the next PDU is built the value is incremented. The value wraps around.

> When a CPCS-PDU has been reassembled, the value of Btag in the header must match the value in the trailer. This is one of the criteria used by the CPCS to ensure that the PDU has been reassembled correctly after it has been received.

Buffer Allocation Size Indication (BASize)

> This value is intended to tell the receiver how much buffer space to allocate to the PDU in reassembly buffers. It may be equal to or larger than the PDU size.

Pad Field

> This field is added to the data to ensure that the resulting length is a multiple of 4 bytes. This ensures that the trailer part of the PDU will be on a 32-bit boundary - making the trailer easier and faster to process.

Alignment Field (AL)

>   The real trailer record is 3 bytes long. In order to ensure that these fields can be processed quickly by a 32-bit word processor, the alignment byte is included. It is all zeros.

End Tag (Etag)

>   This is the matching tag to Btag.

Field Length

>   This is the real length (in bytes if the CPI field says all zeros) of the CPCS-PDU payload (user data). This is another check to determine whether the CPCS-PDU has been reassembled correctly.

3.6.3 Segmentation and Reassembly Sublayer (SAR)

The SAR-PDU format is shown in Figure 3-10.

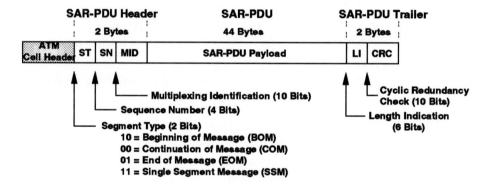

Figure 3-10. SAR-PDU Format for AAL 3/4

The fields have the following meanings:

Segment Type (ST)

>   These two bits indicate where the individual segment belongs in the larger SAR-SDU (when it is built by the CPCS it is called the CPCS-PDU, and when it is received by the SAR it is called the SAR-SDU).

Sequence Number (SN)

>   These four bits are used to number the SAR-PDUs in sequence (modulo 16). This is used to verify the correct sequence of cells when the SAR-SDU is rebuilt.

Multiplexing Identification Field (MID)

> The use of this field is discussed in 3.6.5, "Multiplexing Connections" on page 3-19.

Length Indication (LI)

> This field specifies how much data is in the variable part of the cell. All cells except the last of any SAR-SDU should be full (LI=44). The last cell is typically short and therefore LI may take any value (a multiple of 4 because the SAR-SDU is already padded to make sure this is true) from 4 to 44.

Cyclic Redundancy Check (CRC)

> This polynomial is calculated over the whole SAR-PDU except for the CRC field itself. It is used to detect (but not correct) errors in the SAR-PDU.

3.6.4 Error Detection

It can be seen from the above description that there are many ways in which errors can be detected.

1. The ATM layer provides assurance that cells delivered to any endpoint were sent by the partner user, because the cell header is protected by a CRC. However, cells may have been lost in the network or they may be delivered to the AAL with errors in the data (because the data part of the cell is not covered by a CRC at the ATM layer).

2. At the SAR sublayer:

   - The data content of a received cell is protected by the CRC on that cell.

   - The Sequence Number field is used to detect missing cells or cells arriving out of sequence.

   - The Segment Type bits in conjunction with the MID field ensure that each SAR-SDU is reconstructed such that the first SAR-PDU had a "begin-of-message" indicator in it, the last had an "end-of-message" indicator in it, that all cells form a correct sequence, and all have the same MID value.

3. At the CPCS sublayer, the Btag and Etag fields (which were transported as data but not processed by the SAR) are checked to be the same. An additional check is that the Payload Length field in the CPCS-PDU must match its real length.

This would seem to be enough checking.

3.6.5 Multiplexing Connections

AAL 3/4 has the capability of allowing multiple AAL connections to use the *same* ATM VC simultaneously. This is done in a quite unexpected way.

A conventional way of providing such multiplexing would be to provide an identifier in the CPCS-PDU header to identify the connection to which a particular CPCS-PDU belonged. CPCS-PDUs would then be processed in a single thread by the SAR. The result would be that on a single VC a group of cells belonging to one CPCS-PDU would be sent followed by a group of cells from the next CPCS-PDU. **This is not how multiplexing is done.**

Each AAL connection has a logically separate instance of the AAL (although obviously this will be implemented as multiple tasks executing in the same block of code). Thus SAR-PDUs belonging to *different* CPCS-PDUs can be randomly intermixed on the same ATM VC. When they arrive at the partner AAL the problem is how to assemble them into correct CPCS-PDUs again - to which CPCS-PDU does each cell belong.

That is what the Multiplexing Identification (MID) field is used for. The MID is an arbitrary number that is chosen by the sending SAR to identify a group of cells as belonging to the same CPCS-PDU. When a SAR-PDU is received that has a Beginning of Message (BOM) segment type this is interpreted as being the beginning of a new logical data block (SAR-SDU/CPCS-PDU). The MID value is then saved and used to identify subsequent cells that belong to this particular SAR-SDU.

This facility is there to provide compatibility with SMDS. SMDS (IEEE 802.6 Metropolitan Area Subnetwork) is a type of LAN. That is, SMDS is connectionless.

- Data is sent on the LAN in 53-byte cells.

- It would be too inefficient to put the full LAN addresses (16 bytes) into the header of each cell.

- So when a data block is sent as a stream of cells, only the first contains the real destination address. Subsequent cells contain the MID value to enable the receiver to identify cells that belong to this data block.

- Other traffic using the LAN will insert cells into the middle of a stream from any particular sender so this identification process is necessary.

- It gets more complex because multiple senders may want to transmit to a single destination at the same time. This happens in a conventional LAN (where data is sent in blocks) but each block is a unit itself. In SMDS the receiver has to assemble the parts of a block as they are received and it is possible that parts of *different* blocks may be intermixed. This happens, because different senders may decide to send to the same destination simultaneously.

Thus, the idea of the MID was born. Actually, what they are doing is establishing short term "connections" over a connectionless medium. The first cell of a data block is routed according to its full LAN address (connectionless routing) and establishes the MID identifier (a form of connection identifier) so that subsequent cells in this block can be identified.

3.7 AAL-5

Originally called "SEAL" (Simple and Efficient Adaptation Layer), AAL-5 was designed to operate significantly more efficiently than was AAL-3/4 - of course, it does not have all of the functions of AAL-3/4.

With the exception of connection multiplexing, AAL-5 has the same list of allowed options as described above for AAL-3/4. That is:

- Message mode and streaming mode

- Assured delivery

- Non-assured delivery

- Blocking and segmentation of data

- Multipoint operation

As with AAL-3/4 these allowed options will be implemented as part of service specific sublayers (SSCS) as these are defined.

In normal operation (without an SSCS) a single AAL-SDU will be mapped into a single CPCS-PDU using non-assured mode of operation and discarding any data where errors are detected. This provides the same function (although on a connection-oriented basis) as a LAN provides at the MAC layer. Of course, to provide assured operation, a higher-layer protocol (such as IEEE 802.2) will be needed.

3.7.1 AAL-5 Method of Operation

AAL-5 operation (as illustrated in Figure 3-11 on page 3-22) is extremely simple:

1. An AAL-SDU is received at the AAL-SAP.

2. It may or may not be processed by an SSCS.

3. The data is passed to the CPCS and becomes a CPCS-SDU. The CPCS appends its control information as a single trailer record and inserts pads so that the length of the new CPCS-PDU is a multiple of 48 bytes. The information present in the CPCS trailer is sufficient to provide assurance that the PDU has been reassembled correctly by the SAR after it has been carried through the network.

4. The CPCS-PDU is then passed to the SAR and becomes a SAR-SDU.

5. The SAR segments this into 48-byte SAR-PDUs (but note, there is no header or trailer information added).

6. The SAR passes these 48-byte segments to the ATM layer and indicates the last one in the group as a parameter in the call to the ATM layer.

7. The ATM layer builds an ATM header and includes the End-of-Message (EOM) flag in the last SAR-PDU of the SAR-SDU.

The reverse process happens on reception.

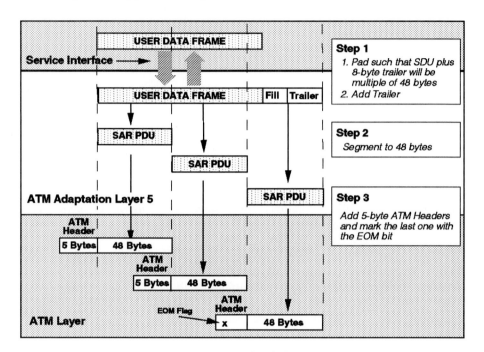

Figure **3-11.** *AAL-5 Operation*

3.7.2 Common Part Convergence Sublayer (CPCS)

The CPCS-PDU format for AAL-5 is shown in Figure 3-12 on page 3-23. The meanings of the fields in the CPCS trailer are as follows:

CPCS-PDU Payload

In the absence of an SSCS this will be just the data passed to the AAL over the service interface (the AAL-SDU). If an SSCS is present it may perform other functions such as blocking or re-blocking or even transmit protocol data messages of its own.

The payload has a maximum length of 65,535 bytes.

Pad

The CPCS pads out the data frame so that the total length, including the CPCS trailer, is a multiple of 48 bytes. This is so that the SAR does not have to do any padding of its own. The pad is inserted at the end of the data, but before the trailer, so that the trailer will be in a predictable position when the CPCS-PDU is reassembled. This also helps with boundary alignment to speed up processing.

CPCS User to User Indication (CPCS-UU)

This is used to pass information from one CPCS to its communicating partner.

Common Part Indicator (CPI)

Right now this is zero and exists for boundary alignment, but other uses are under study.

Data Length

This field is very important because it tells us how much of the received data is CPCS-SDU and how much is pad. It is also a check on the loss (or gain) of cells during transit.

Cyclic Redundancy Check (CRC)

This field provides a validity check on the whole CPCS-PDU except for the CRC itself.

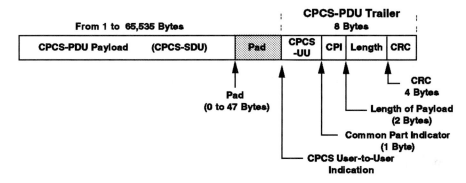

Figure   3-12. AAL-5 CPCS-PDU Header

3.7.3 Segmentation and Reassembly Sublayer (SAR)

The header format for the SAR-PDU is not shown because it does not exist. For AAL-5, there is no SAR header or trailer information present in a SAR-PDU.

All that the SAR sublayer does is to take the SAR-SDU (CPCS-PDU) and break it up into 48-byte units (before it is passed to the SAR it has been padded to a multiple of 48 bytes in length). In the reverse direction it receives a stream of cells and builds them into a SAR-SDU to pass to the CPCS.

The SAR does have one bit of header information. This is the last bit of the Payload Type (PT) field of the cell header. This is discussed in 2.2, "Cell Format" on page 2-8. It indicates that this cell is the last of a logical group (last cell in the SAR-SDU).

As the SAR does not build the cell headers (that is done by the ATM layer), information needed to build the ATM header is passed to the ATM-SAP as parameters rather than data.

3.7.4 Error Detection

AAL-5 relies completely on the CRC and the Data Length fields to detect errors. This will probably deliver the same level of data integrity as AAL-3/4, but it could also result in somewhat more data being lost.

For example, if the last cell in a CPCS-PDU is corrupted or lost, then AAL-5 cannot know that this is the end of the PDU. It will continue to receive SAR-PDUs and attach them to the end of the previous CPCS-PDU. When a SAR-PDU indicating an ending does arrive, *both* concatenated CPCS-PDUs must be discarded. AAL-3/4 would only have discarded the first.

3.8 Signaling AAL

The signaling AAL provides reliable transport for signaling traffic. It is structured as shown in Figure 3-13.

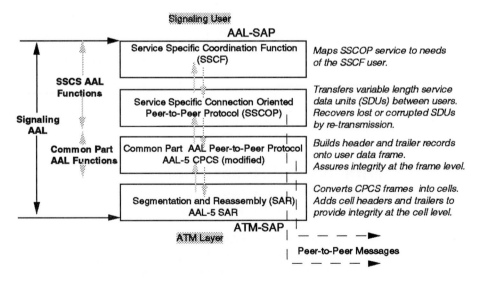

Figure   3-13. Signaling AAL Structure

The signaling AAL has the following characteristics:

- The Common Part AAL peer-to-peer protocol and the SAR function are only trivially different from AAL-5.

- The SSCOP function has an end-to-end protocol, which provides error recovery by retransmission for corrupted or lost data.

- The SSCF is a "glue" layer that connects the SSCOP to the signaling user. There may be a number of different SSCFs depending on the needs of the particular end user.

Chapter 4. Signaling

Signaling is the process used for *dynamic* setup and clearing of ATM connections (VPCs and VCCs) at the UNI.[1] In ATM, connections may be *permanent* in which case they are set up by OA&M processes (system definition or system management) or they may be *switched* in which case they are set up by signaling.

If a connection is permanent, then if the network fails and is re-started the circuit is restored. If a switched connection is lost through a failure, then it is the responsibility of the endpoint to request another connection - the system will not restore a lost switched connection.

The key elements of ATM signaling are:

Out-of-Band Signaling

> Signaling takes place on separate VCs from the VCs used to carry data. This is the same principle as is used in regular Narrowband ISDN (N-ISDN) where the "D" channel is used to initiate calls. It is quite different to the way in which X.25 works. In X.25, the CALL packet is sent on a free virtual channel and when the call is established, this virtual channel then is used for data transfer. In ATM, a request to set up a connection is sent to the network over a special signaling channel. During the setup of the connection the network tells the end user which VPI/VCI will be used for the connection.

Signaling Channels

> Because ATM is very flexible, the standards bodies have left plenty of scope for using multiple signaling channels from each endpoint.
>
> 1. VCI=1 (regardless of VPI value) is reserved for the use of "meta-signaling".
>
> 2. VCI=2 (regardless of VPI value) is reserved for general broadcast signaling.
>
> 3. VCI=5 VPI=0 is used for point-to-point and point-to-multipoint signaling from an ATM endpoint to the local network.
>
> 4. VCI=5 VPI≠ 0 is used for point-to-point signaling with other endpoints and other networks.

---

[1] There are also signaling functions being defined for use at the NNI. These are not yet fully defined and are not described in this book.

4-1

Meta-signaling

Meta-signaling is the process of setting up additional signaling channels from an ATM endpoint. This will be used in the future, but is not used in the first ATM implementations.

Broadcast Signaling

Broadcast signaling will be important in future releases of ATM, but in the first release it is not used.

Point-to-Point Signaling

This is the default.

Scope

When a VC or VP connection is set up by an OA&M procedure (a "permanent" VC/VP connection) within the ATM network, only the parameters of the required connection are considered. ATM endpoints that use permanent VC/VP connections must be configured to match the characteristics of the network. This is a manual procedure and there is *no* automatic checking to make sure that the parameters match.

When a VP or VC connection is set up by signaling however, the call setup message carries sufficient information for complete end-to-end setup of the VC or VP connection. For example, AAL parameters are carried in the Setup request and are passed to the remote end AAL. Some higher-layer information is also passed end-to-end.

ATM Channels

Characteristics of connections that may be set up through signaling:

- Connections may be point-to-point and/or multipoint.
- QoS (including bandwidth) requirements of connections may be symmetric or asymmetric.
- Each connection setup request creates a single connection (either point-to-point or multipoint).

Class B and Class D Services not Supported

Class B (AAL-2) has not yet been defined by the standards in sufficient detail to enable specification of parameters for VC establishment.

Class D (connectionless) is implemented in ATM by having connections to a connectionless server (which may be within the network). Call establishment procedures for this are not needed.

Third-Party Connection Setup

Connection setup by a third party (one not involved in the data transfer) is *not* allowed in ATM Release (Phase) 1.

This means that party A cannot send a request to set up a connection between party B and party C (where the initiating party is not otherwise involved in the call). In time it is expected that this function will be added.

4.1 Addressing

ATM channels are defined as sequences of identifiers which define paths through the network. A path goes from one endpoint to another. At no point in the transfer of data through an ATM network is an address needed.

Addresses are essential for many reasons, not the least being to identify ATM endpoints for the purpose of setting up and clearing virtual connections.

4.1.1.1 Addressing in Interconnected Networks

The kind of problem that has to be solved here is illustrated in Figure 4-1. Three separate interconnected networks are illustrated. How does user 1 in network A place a call to user 1 in network C. This is only possible if the addressing structure has been carefully planned.

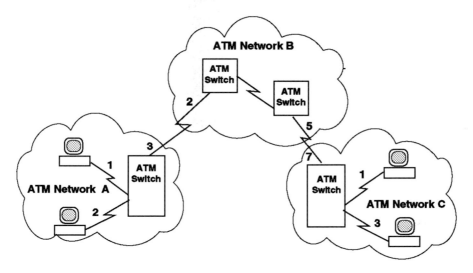

Figure **4-1.** *Addressing in Interconnected Networks*

- If each network is quite separate and each has its own addressing range so that (as in this case) the same address can appear in two networks, then we could qualify the network address with a network identifier and call the addresses C1 and A1. To do this we would have to set up a way of allocating and administering network identifiers.

- If we organized things so the same address could not appear in multiple networks, then each network would have to have a directory including all accessible devices (this is impractical in most cases). Alternatively we could search the network using broadcasts to look for a destination user name (as is done in interconnected LAN networks).

- In X.25 networks we did not have either of the above situations (except in the public network environment). When X.25 users place a call, they specify a destination address in their own network. So, if device 2 in network A in the example tried to call device 1 in network C, then it *must* place address 3 (the connection to the next network) in its destination address field. When the packet arrives at the connection to the next network how do you determine the destination address for the next stage?

   Ways were found to do this in X.25 - all of them are unnatural and inelegant. This was because the people who designed X.25 never foresaw the need to use a public network to interconnect two private networks.

In ATM the situation will be significantly better than we had with X.25 (we did learn something). ATM uses a structured address which allows the network to determine the routing for calls to interconnected networks.

4.1.1.2 ATM Address Formats

The address formats used in ATM are shown in Figure 4-2 on page 4-5. There are three different address formats used here:

ITU-T (E.164) Format

   This format is essentially a telephone number style address. It is specified by the ITU-T and will be used by public (carrier provided) ATM networks.

DCC (Data Country Code) Format

   This format carries LAN addresses as specified by the IEEE 802 recommendations.

ICD Format

   This is the format specified by the International Organization for Standardization (ISO) for Open Systems Interconnection (OSI).

The ATM Forum specifies that equipment must support all three formats in private networks. Networks supporting the ITU-T specification (mainly public ATM networks) only need to support the ITU-T address.

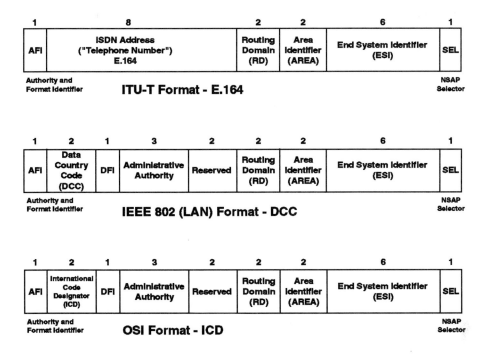

Figure 4-2. *ATM Address Formats*

Some people have objected to the use of 20-byte addresses. Twenty bytes is 160 bits or about 10^{40} possible addresses. This is sufficient address range to uniquely number every cell in every human body on earth! This is said to be wasteful.

The reason the address is so long is because it is structured. Structured addresses greatly simplify the task of locating particular endpoints and, in any case, the addresses are only carried in the setup request and so the overhead is minimal.

4.2 Call and Connection Control Operation

There are three functions provided in ATM signaling for call and connection control. These cover call setup, call clearing and status. The following signaling messages are defined:

1. Call Establishment

   - Setup
   - Call Proceeding
   - Connect
   - Connect Acknowledge

2. Call Clearing

- Release
- Release Complete

3. Status

- Status Enquiry
- Status

4. Point-to-Multipoint Messages

- Add Party
- Add Party Acknowledge
- Add Party Reject
- Drop Party
- Drop Party Acknowledge

4.2.1.1 Signaling Message Format

Every signaling message contains the following parts:

Protocol Discriminator (1 Byte)

> This is used to specify which address format is used. E.164 = 45. ICD (OSI) = 47. DCC (IEEE 802) = 39. No other values are allowed.

Call Reference (4 Bytes)

> This is for the benefit of the calling system. It enables the calling system to easily reference the instance of the call when a reply is received (so that it can have multiple requests outstanding). This is a meaningless 32-bit pattern to ATM, so the endpoint system could place a 32-bit control block address in here.

Message Type (2 Bytes)

> This identifies which type of signaling message this is. Connect, Call Proceeding, Setup, Release, Add Party are some of the message types.

Message Length (2 Bytes)

> This specifies the length of the contents of this signaling message.

Variable-Length Information Elements

> The different information elements are specific for each message type and are included in a message as required.

4.2.1.2 Information Elements

The following information elements may be present in the above signaling messages. For each message type some elements are mandatory and some are optional.

AAL Parameters (4-20 Bytes)

This carries the required AAL characteristics from the sending AAL to the receiver. For example, the CPCS-SDU maximum size can be included here so that the receiving AAL knows the maximum size of a data block that it should ever receive.

ATM User Cell Rate (12-30 Bytes)

This element contains several fields that specify the forward and backward average and peak cell rates requested for this connection.

Broadband Bearer Capability (6-7 Bytes)

This element indicates requested broadband bearer characteristics. It specifies whether the data stream is constant or variable bit rate, requires end-to-end timing or not, and is or is not susceptible to clipping.

Broadband High-Layer Information (4-13 Bytes)

This information is transferred transparently across the ATM network and is used for compatibility checking by the receiving endpoint. This applies to the protocol layers above ATM.

Broadband Repeat Indicator (4-5 Bytes)

A number of elements in the signaling message may be repeated. This element specifies how repeated elements shall be interpreted.

Broadband Low-Layer Information (4-13 Bytes)

This element is also used for compatibility checking, but at a different level to that of the high layer information. For example, if two systems are communicating using ATM as a physical connection for an X.25 network protocol, this element contains things like the default packet size and the default window size.

Called Party Number (Max 25 Bytes)

This is the identification of the destination endpoint with which we wish to set up a connection.

Called Party Subaddress (4-25 Bytes)

This is used in the situation where the destination endpoint is in a private ATM network using OSI NSAP addressing, and where the connection must traverse a public ATM network that only supports E.164 addressing.

Calling Party Number (4-26 Bytes)

The number of the originating party to the call.

Calling Party Subaddress (4-25 Bytes)

Again, this is for the situation where the calling party uses an OSI NSAP address over a public ATM network that only supports E.164.

Cause

This optional element contains codes to identify the cause in exception conditions.

Call State

This reports the current state of a call or global interface.

Connection Identifier (9 Bytes)

This element identifies the VPI and VCI values to be associated with this call. Note that here the VPI is not used. Instead a "Virtual Path Connection Identifier" is used. In Release 1 the VPI and the VPCI are identical. However, this is not necessarily true. When an ATM "concentrator" is present, a single link at the UNI may be split into a number of (lower speed) links. When this happens, a single signaling channel has to support multiple real link connections. The VPCI allows additional bits to select which real link is to carry the VP/VC.

QoS Parameters (6 Bytes)

This indicates the requested QoS class for each direction of a connection.

Broadband Sending Complete (4-5 Bytes)

This may be present (optionally) to indicate the completion of the called party number. It exists only for compatibility with some types of public network. The ATM Forum specifies that this should be ignored by the network when it is received.

Transit Network Selection (4-8 Bytes)

This is to identify a specific transit network when more than one transit network is possible.

Endpoint Reference (4-7 Bytes)

This identifies the individual endpoints of a point-to-multipoint connection.

Endpoint State

This element contains the state of an endpoint in a point-to-multipoint connection.

End-to-End Transit Delay

This element is not supported in Release 1 of ATM.

Restart Indicator

> This element identifies the class of the facility to be restarted.

4.2.1.3 Call Establishment (Setup)

The calling ATM endpoint requests the establishment of a connection with another ATM endpoint by using the procedure shown in Figure 4-3.

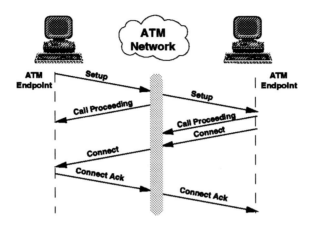

***Figure 4-3.** ATM Switched Circuit Setup Protocol*

A setup request message is sent on the signaling channel (default VPI=0 VCI=5) from the requesting ATM endpoint to the network.

4.2.1.4 Circuit Disconnect (Clearing)

The procedure for clearing (disconnecting) a call is shown in Figure 4-4.

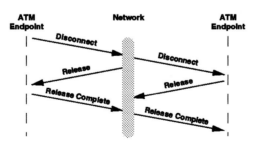

***Figure 4-4.** ATM Switched Circuit Disconnect Protocol*

4.3 Meta-Signaling

The meta-signaling protocol will be used to set up and clear signaling channels in addition to the default signaling channels. This is needed because of the great flexibility of ATM systems - a single signaling channel (like the N-ISDN D-channel) will not be sufficient. Meta-signaling uses the default VPI=0 VCI=1.

Three kinds of signaling channels may be set up:

1. Point-to-point

2. Selective broadcast (multicast)

3. General broadcast

Meta-signaling is very simple and every signaling message is sent in fixed format in a single cell. No AAL protocol is used for meta-signaling.

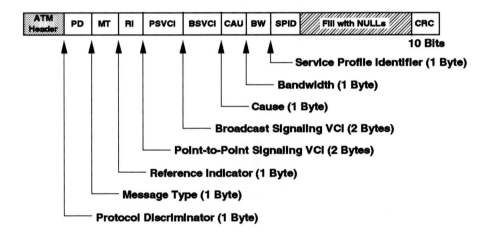

Figure *4-5.* *ATM Meta-Signaling Cell Format*

There are three procedures:

Channel Setup

> This uses a message called "Assign Request" and receives either an "Assigned" response or a "Denied" response.

Channel Clearing

> This is accomplished using a message called "Remove Request" with appropriate responses.

Check Request

This can be used at regular intervals to check if everything is still connected (a heartbeat signal). Its major use is to determine the status of a requested signaling channel.

The problem is that there is no AAL procedure in meta-signaling. The meta-signaling payload is protected by a CRC field, but if a cell is discarded by the system for any reason there is no way for the requester to know what happened. For example, if an ATM endpoint sends an assignment request and never sees a matching response, then either the original request or the response has been lost. The check message is used to determine the status of the system when we are not sure.

Chapter 5. Private Network-to-Network (Node-to-Node) Interface - PNNI

There are several interfaces defined in ATM which have been referred to in other parts of this book. These are:

- User Network Interface (UNI)

- Network Node Interface (NNI)

- Private Network-to-Network Interface (PNNI)

- B_ISDN Inter-Carrier Interface (B-ICI)

- Data Exchange Interface (DXI)

- Switch-to-Switch Interface (SSI)

In this chapter, PNNI is treated in rather more depth than the rest of the material in this book. This is because of PNNI's importance. Further, while PNNI is derived from many existing protocols, it is elegant and innovative in its conception. Study of PNNI gives an insight into the problems to be faced in constructing large networks.

The PNNI is an ATM Forum specification for connecting either ATM nodes (switches) or ATM networks. Thus, "PNNI" stands for either "Public Node-to-Node Interface" or "Private Network-to-Network Interface" depending on the particular context in which PNNI is being used. Thus, the PNNI can be used either as an interface *between* different ATM networks or as an interface between ATM switches *within* a single ATM network.[1] These uses are illustrated in Figure 5-1.

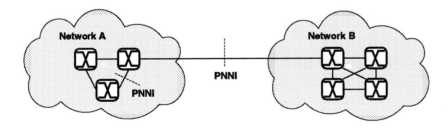

Figure 5-1. PNNI Usage

---

[1] This raises the question of precisely what constitutes a "network". You may, for example, wish to consider two networks connected through PNNI to be a single network. This is open to debate.

5-1

To the extent that PNNI defines a node-to-node (switch-to-switch) interface, it is specifying the internal operations of the network itself. This is quite unusual in networking systems generally. For example, X.25 (a data networking standard superficially similar to ATM) defines only the *interface* of an end user to the network - it does not define the internal operations of the network in any way. In recent years LAN bridge standards, IP, telephone network standards (especially signaling), and some router standards have begun to specify many aspects of internal network interfacing. But PNNI goes much further than most of these. PNNI is one of the first attempts to "standardize" the internal operations of a communications network.

Perhaps the most important aspect of the PNNI is the fact that it is a *private* interface. The concept of a private interface is that the connected switches are controlled (or owned) by the same user organization. Thus, each switch can "trust" the other.

There are many situations where we actively want to *prevent* a device at one side of an interface from doing anything that might compromise the equipment at the other side of the interface. For example, if we connect consumer equipment to a public network through the ATM UNI, we want to prevent the user equipment from doing anything that might disrupt the operation of the public network. This leads to a very important requirement for this kind of connection - the requirement that the interface *isolate* the end user from the internals of the network. This isn't too restrictive when it applies to the connection of end-user equipment to a public network. However, when we are building an interface *between switches* a requirement for complete isolation would result in both a significant reduction in network function and less than optimal network operation. Thus, the design of a switch-to-switch interface needs to balance the need for isolation with the cost in reduced functionality.

In the PNNI, both sides of the interface are "trusted" to some extent even if they were made by different manufacturers. This enables the exchange of detailed information about the topology and operational state of the network and results in a much more functional interface than would be possible otherwise.

5.1.1 Objectives of the PNNI

The objectives of the PNNI can be summarized as follows:

Function

> Provide an interface between ATM switches such that full-function networks of arbitrary size and complexity may be constructed. There should be full support for both switched and permanent VC and VP connections including multipoint support. The network must provide QoS on an end-to-end basis.
>
> The PNNI should also be an interface between ATM subnetworks.

Scalability

The PNNI must be simple enough for use in small networks (and by small switches) and yet must scale up to extremely large size. One statement of the objective suggests that PNNI might be used to construct a "global ATM Internet" (that is, perhaps tens of thousands of switches).

Multi-Vendor

The PNNI should allow networks to be built where both switches and end-user workstation equipment are supplied by different manufacturers.

Proprietary Subnetworks

The PNNI should allow for the construction of subnetworks using proprietary (non-PNNI) internal protocols. These protocols could be extensions of PNNI or something quite different. It is generally accepted that it would be a bad thing if PNNI were to stifle innovation.

This is achieved by defining PNNI as an interface between "switching systems". A "switching system" is defined as a set of one or more switches that act together to appear as a single switch for the purposes of routing. PNNI is therefore the definition of an *interface* between switches or switching systems and other systems with which they are connected.

Open Implementation

PNNI should *not* presuppose any particular method of internal switch operation. This should be kept as open as possible to allow people to develop innovative techniques.

Dynamism

The network topology should, to the maximum degree possible, be self-defining and should involve a *minimum* of user setup or tuning.

Efficiency

It is important that the protocols employed should be as efficient as possible. This is a difficult issue because many design decisions are trade-offs between many goals. For example, optimal route determination implies that the process making the route calculation has access to an accurate network topology that includes information about loadings on resources in the network. To ensure accurate topology information it is necessary to send a large number of topology update messages through the network. The more accurate you need the topology information, the more often these updates must be sent, and the more traffic that is generated.

Usefulness

PNNI phase 1 is intended to be a complete, long-term architecture which may be added to but will not be changed in the foreseeable future.

The PNNI is a very simple and elegant concept which nevertheless offers an extremely powerful function.

5.1.2 Functions

The basic function of the PNNI is to define the structure of an ATM network such that the setup of VC and VP connections from end-to-end through the network can be supported. This means, that when an end user (across the UNI) requests a new connection a route for the connection must be chosen and the connection set up. In order to do this, PNNI has a number of different functions:

Topology and Routing

In order to choose a route through the network, we need to know the topology of the network together with information about its current state. (Current committed loading on links, for example.) The protocol used to distribute topology and link state information in PNNI is called "routing".

Path Selection and Signaling

The process that the network goes through to set up a switched (temporary) connection (VCC or VPC) is called "signaling".

Traffic Management

At a superficial level, PNNI is not concerned with traffic management. The complex traffic management protocols that are used for ABR connections operate across the PNNI and do not directly concern the PNNI itself. At another level, in planning and setting up connections across multiple PNNI interfaces, link state information (allocated bandwidth, etc.) must be taken into account and this is of course a traffic management issue.[2]

Network Management

Good network management is, of course, essential to the operation of any large network. Network management for PNNI is being developed as part of the wider network management specifications and does not form part of the PNNI specification. However, the Management Information Blocks (MIBs) that apply to PNNI are defined within the specification.

---

[2] This applies to CBR, VBR and some ABR connections.

5.1.3 Concepts

Figure 5-2 illustrates a relatively small ATM network.

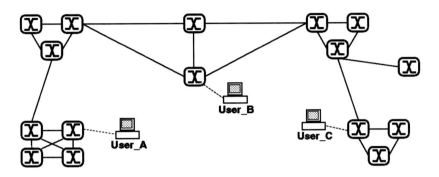

Figure **5-2.** *PNNI Network*

When User_A places a call request to set up a connection with User_C the network must:

1. Locate User_C

   This implies that either the switch to which User_A is connected has a complete network directory, or that it has connection to a switch (or to a server of some kind) which does have this information. In PNNI, every switch carries a topology database and network directory sufficient in scope to do some basic route planning. However, detailed planning is a cooperative process in which many switches along the route participate.

2. Plan a route through the network to User_C that satisfies the QoS requested

   This might have been done in many different ways; for example, it might be calculated hop-by-hop through the network as a setup request is forwarded, or it may be done by reference to a central route server which has a detailed network database.

   In PNNI, every switch maintains a database which reflects a partial view of the network. This "partial view" varies in the amount of detail contained in it. A switch has very detailed topology and state information about switches in its immediate vicinity (its sub-network). However, it carries less and less information depending on how far (in a logical sense) it is from the particular part of the network in question. Because the nodes' network topology databases vary in the amount of detail held, the route calculated varies in the amount of precision with which it is expressed. The route is made more precise as the connection setup request is forwarded and processed by the switches along the chosen route. The switches along the route add detail to the route consistent with their knowledge of the topology.

3. Set up the connection

In PNNI, the originating switch sends a setup message which proceeds hop-by-hop (switch-by-switch) through the network along the preplanned route. As the route itself is contained in the setup message, the protocol used to navigate the setup request along the chosen path is an example of a *source routing* protocol.[3]

5.1.3.1 Cell Header

The ATM 5-byte header used by PNNI is the standard NNI format as shown in Figure 2-4 on page 2-8.

5.1.4 Building the Network Topology (Routing)

In order to plan a route through the network the originating switch must have available to it the following information:

A network directory function to enable the switch to locate the destination endpoint.

A network topology map to enable the switch to calculate possible routes to the destination endpoint.

Up-to-date state information to enable the switch to determine if required QoS characteristics can be met on any particular alternative route under consideration. This is a part of the topology map.

This information does not necessarily have to be stored within the switch itself but must be available to it (for example from a server). If each switch is to maintain its own database, then there must be a protocol for building this database and for keeping the information in it up-to-date.

This could potentially involve creating a very large amount of network traffic. In an extreme case, this might mean sending changed network state information throughout the network *every* time there was a change in the state of one of the network's resources (switch or link between switches).

This may not be too hard in small networks, such as in the example network of Figure 5-2 on page 5-5. However, as the network gets larger the amount of additional network traffic required to keep all switches' databases current gets larger exponentially. In addition, the load on individual switches grows as the number of topology update messages received increases. Experience with other types of networks (for example, router networks) shows that you can reach a point where the bandwidth used for administrative

---

[3] In principle, this is the same protocol as used for session setup in IBM APPN networks (navigating the BIND) and NBBS. A similar process is also used for routing frames through a network of token-ring bridges.

traffic to keep the network operating is *greater* than the bandwidth left over to transmit (productive) user data!

A mechanism is clearly needed to limit the topology update traffic while maintaining the network function. This is not as difficult as it sounds when it is realized that most networks are structured according to geography and that individual switches just do not need to know about the whole network topology.

In PNNI the "routing" protocol is responsible for propagating network state and topology information. This protocol is designed to limit the amount of information needed in each switch while still providing a mechanism for the construction of good routes through the network.

5.1.4.1 Routing Hierarchy

The key to understanding PNNI topology services is the principle that a "switching system" can be either a real physical switch (one box by itself) **or** it can be a "virtual" switching system composed of an interconnected group of switching systems. This definition of a virtual switch is *recursive*; that is, the concept of a switch is used in its own definition. Consequently, a virtual switch can also be a group of groups of switches. To avoid confusion, we call a virtual switch a *Logical Group Node (LGN)*. This concept is illustrated in Figure 5-3 on page 5-8.

The network from our previous example in Figure 5-2 on page 5-5 is now shown in three different views:

1. A high-level view consisting of Nodes X, Y, and Z.

2. A mid-level view consisting of Nodes X.A, X.F, Z.C, Z.D, and Z.E.

   Notice here that node Y is represented at the middle level as well as at the top level. This is just a convenient way of representing it. There is *no* middle level in the hierarchy making up node Y. Y consists of 2 physical switches. This is fine. There is no requirement that the layering structure be uniform throughout the network.

3. A low-level (physical level) view consisting of all 16 ATM switches.

Notice that at each level we have a view of an interconnected network of nodes which is itself a valid view of the total network. As mentioned above, the network is constructed as a hierarchy of Logical Group Nodes (LGNs). In our example, switches X.A.1, X.A.2, and X.A.3 make up LGN X.A. LGNs X.A and X.F make up LGN X.

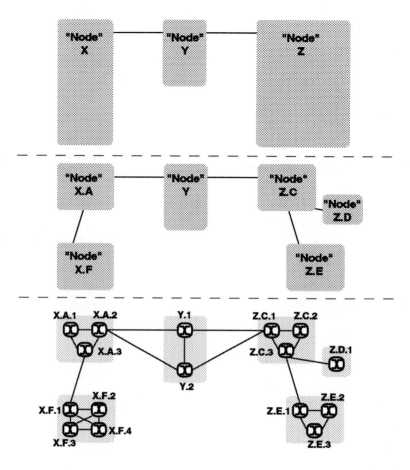

Figure 5-3. *Hierarchical Network Views.* The 16-switch network from previous examples is shown here in three different views. A "high-level" view consisting of 3 nodes, a mid-level view consisting of 6 nodes and a physical view consisting of all 16 nodes.

The key to constructing this hierarchy is in the ATM address. Each physical ATM switch is uniquely identified by its ATM address that has to be defined in the switch.[4] The 20-byte ATM address (according to one of the formats described in 4.1.1.2, "ATM Address Formats" on page 4-4) is taken as a bit string and structured as illustrated in Figure 5-4 on page 5-9.

---

[4] This is the default case. As will be seen later, the hierarchy may be built using user-defined ID information, which is different from the ATM address.

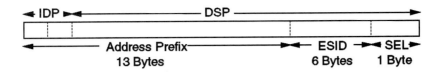

Figure 5-4. Address Structure in PNNI

The ATM address is structured into a 13-byte (104-bit) address prefix followed by a 6-byte end system identifier and a 1-byte selector (subaddress). The idea is that the address prefix alone uniquely identifies a physical switch and all its connected end devices. That means, a certain switch and all ATM devices connected to this switch share the same address prefix that should be different from all address prefixes assigned to other switches and their devices in one (PNNI-connected) network. In real life, this will not always be possible (for example, because a switch may connect via the UNI to an external network). How to deal with that more complicated case is described in 5.1.4.3, "Foreign Addresses" on page 5-11.

The user (system planner) is free to partition the 13-byte address prefix into any number of levels up to 104 (that is, 1 bit per level).[5]

Each logical group node (LGN) is composed of a *peer group* of LGNs or switches. A peer group is a group of *interconnected* nodes with an arbitrary number of high-order ATM address bits in common. At the lowest level, this is just a number of connected switches with some number (defined by the system planner) of high-order address bits that are the same. A peer group can be viewed as a single node at the next higher level. When a peer group is viewed in this way it is called a *logical group node*.

Peer Group Definition

A peer group (PG) is a group of interconnected switching systems or LGNs which have the same peer group ID. That is, they have some arbitrary (but defined in the context of each particular network) number of high-order bits of their address prefixes in common.

A logical group node is defined recursively. At the lowest level, an LGN is composed of a group of interconnected switching systems. At higher levels an LGN is composed of a group of interconnected LGNs.

---

5 While it is possible to conceive of a PNNI network of 104 levels it is extremely unlikely that any network will have more than a very few levels (perhaps 3 to 5 even in a large network). Because the computing load of maintaining a large number of levels is considerable and also because of complexity, it is felt that early product implementations may have limitations in that range.

> **Logical Group Node (LGN) Definition**
>
> A logical group node is an abstract representation of a peer group as a single logical node for the purpose of representing that PG in a higher level of the PNNI hierarchy.

In order to form a PG, a group of nodes must have a group of high-order (leftmost) address bits in common (that is, the same). This is illustrated in Figure 5-5.

> **Logical Node (LN) Definition**
>
> A logical node is any node that obeys the PNNI protocols at its external interfaces. An LN could be a single switch but will often be a group of switches connected together by non-PNNI (proprietary) protocols.

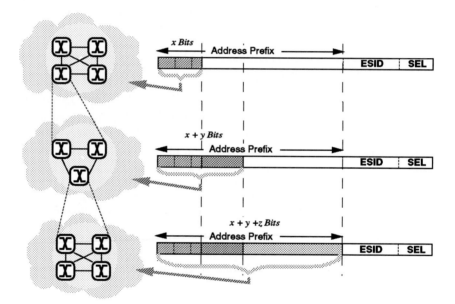

***Figure* 5-5.** *Addressing Hierarchy*

- At the highest level illustrated, the LGNs that make up the high-order LGN have their x high-order bits the same.

- At the next level, the 3 LGNs illustrated have their x+y high-order bits the same.

- At the lowest level illustrated, the LGNs (now they are real, physical switches) have their x+y+z high-order bits the same.

The concept is further illustrated in Figure 5-3 on page 5-8. The switches in the lowest level have been labeled with their hierarchical addresses.[6] Switch X.F.4 is a part of LGN F which itself is a part of LGN X.

You can have up to 104 levels in the hierarchy and the number of bits used for any level is arbitrary within the restriction that the total number of bits used must be equal to or less than 104. ATM addresses have a structure which is ignored by this process but which would limit the practical number of levels to significantly less than this theoretical 104.

It should be noted that small networks might consist of a single LGN (be a single peer-group). There is no requirement for a hierarchical structure unless it is necessary for network operation.

5.1.4.2 Peer Group IDs

The bit string that identifies a peer group is known as a "Peer Group ID" (PGID). This ID may be created in default from either the ATM address or the node ID. However, it may also be explicitly specified as a bit string unrelated to either the ATM address or the node ID.

5.1.4.3 Foreign Addresses

In order for a switch to be part of a PNNI network it must have an address prefix which conforms to the hierarchical structure discussed above. However, a particular switch may also have an address which does not conform to the rules. In addition, a switch may have attached to it end systems whose ATM addresses do not have the same prefix as the switch itself.

In order to allow for this situation there is the ability of a switch to have associated with it a *foreign address*. Because they are not systematic or predictable, foreign addresses must be distributed to *every* switch in the network - otherwise you couldn't find them to set up a call.

5.1.4.4 Peer Groups and Level Indicators

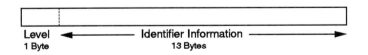

Figure 5-6. *Peer Group Identifier*

---

6 Note that the format and the periods (.) used to separate segments of the address in the picture are just a convenience for the purpose of writing down the addresses. The periods do NOT appear in the real address.

Peer groups exist in many hierarchical levels. As discussed above, these levels are indicated by an arbitrary number of high-order bits (0 to 104) in the address prefix. In PNNI, a peer group identifier (PGI) consists of the 13-byte identifier (Address Prefix field) preceded by a one-byte binary number. This number is called the level indicator and identifies the number of bits that are significant within the Identifier field for the peer group addresses by this PGI. The lower the level indicator number the higher the "level" of the peer group. Level numbers are a good, quick way of finding the position of a particular peer group within the hierarchy.

5.1.4.5 Peer Groups and Logical Group Nodes

The concepts of "peer group" (PG) and "logical group node" (LGN) are just two different ways of looking at the same thing. The definitions are almost the same. A group of interconnected switches that have an agreed number of their address prefix bits the same is called a peer group. When we look at a peer group as a complex (virtual) node within a higher-level peer group, then we call it a logical group node (LGN). Viewed as a single (complex) node it is called an LGN. Viewed as an interconnected group of switches and LGNs it is a peer group.

5.1.4.6 Links between LGNs

At the lowest level, individual switches are interconnected by real, physical ATM links.[7] At higher levels, however, LGNs are interconnected by logical links which may or may not map to a single physical link. In Figure 5-3 on page 5-8, the links Y.1-Z.C.1 and Y.2-Z.C.1 are seen as separate links at the lowest level but as a single *aggregated link* at the higher levels.

5.1.4.7 Link State Routing

At the lowest level in the hierarchy, when a switching system becomes operational it exchanges "Hello" packets with neighboring nodes.[8] These Hello packets contain a number of things, but the most important part is the PGID of the sending node. When a node receives a Hello packet from its neighbor, it compares the peer group ID received from its neighbor with its own PGID to determine whether this adjacent node is part of its peer group or not.

If the neighboring node is part of the same peer group, then the link and node information are stored as part of the peer group topology. The node builds a *PNNI Topology State Packet* (PTSP) message that lists all its adjacent links and their characteristics (such as the ATM address of the node to which the link is attached). This PTSP message then is *flooded* (broadcast) to all adjacent members of this peer group. Flooding is performed

---

[7] Later in 5.1.4.18, "Links between Switches" on page 5-22 we will see that at the lowest layer you can have VP connections instead of physical links here.

[8] This happens after the physical-layer initialization protocols are complete.

by each node sending a PTSP message to its link-connected peers, which then send the PTSP message to all their link-connected peers except the one from which the message was received. Of course, every node receiving a PTSP message has to check if it was already received before and will ignore duplicates.[9] This enables each node in the peer group to maintain an identical copy of the peer group's topology database.

The detailed PTSP information about resources in a particular peer group is never propagated to nodes outside the peer group. Of course, PTSP information may affect the characteristics of the PG when viewed as an LGN. LGN structure (the summarized topology of the PG) *is* propagated throughout the higher-level PG.

5.1.4.8 Topology Aggregation

Within each PG, nodes (or switches) exchange topology and link state information with each other so that each has a detailed topology and link state map of its own peer group. In Figure 5-3 on page 5-8, switches X.F.1, X.F.2, X.F.3 and X.F.4 all understand the detailed topology of logical group node X.F.

At higher levels, however, all of the detailed information is not necessary and is, in fact, quite undesirable. Information about a peer group is aggregated to form a logical image of the peer group as a single LGN. The most important aspect of this aggregation is what to do about links to other LGNs. Where there are multiple parallel links between two LGNs (perhaps terminating in different real switches) there is a question as to whether these should be aggregated to form a single logical link or whether they should be kept separate. In addition, it is sometimes desirable that some part of the internal topology of the PG be represented outside.

Consider Figure 5-7 on page 5-14. In a typical real switch, there is effectively infinite capacity within the switch to route data from any input link to any output link dependent only on the loading of the links concerned. LGNs are different from real switches because they can (and will often) have an internal routing capacity significantly less than a real switch would have. The LGN in the figure (hopefully not a typical structure) has good capacity between C and D but much less between D and A, B and C, or A and B. It is desirable that key aspects of this structure should be known in the higher-level PG so that good routes can be planned.

By default, in PNNI, each LGN is seen as a single switch of infinite internal capacity. However, in cases like the one in the figure a more detailed abstraction of the LGN is used.

---

[9] The process of flooding (broadcasting) topology information to all members of a peer group (with all the logic necessary to ensure integrity of the peer group's topology database) is very similar to the process in APPN.

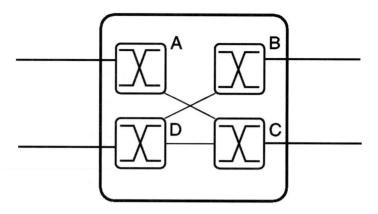

Figure 5-7. *Possible Internal Structure of LGN.* This illustrates the problem of aggregating peer group topology into the form of an LGN.

5.1.4.9 Peer Group Leader (PGL)

But the LGN is more than just a theoretical abstraction. There must be some real processing performed to do the aggregation, store the data, and represent this peer group within the higher-level peer group. This is done by the *peer group leader.* Topology aggregation may also be performed by logical nodes - that is, nodes that are composed of groups of switches that do not use the PNNI protocol internally.

Peer group leader (PGL) can be any node in a peer group, and the node acting as a PGL is selected based on a priority system. The PGL has *no* special privileges within the group. Its function is to form an image of the peer group as if it were a single node (that is, build the image of the LGN) and participate in the topology exchange protocols within the higher-level peer group on behalf of its peers. This means that the PGL *is* a single node (the LGN) in the higher-level peer group. In this way, it passes (summarized) information "up" the hierarchy.

The PGL also passes topology information *down* the hierarchy to its peers within the group. This information is a summarized network topology of the total network obtained from the LGN. This enables each switch on the lowest level to know enough about the overall network to construct a route. Without this, a switch would not have enough information to build routes outside its own (lowest-level) peer group.

It is important to notice that the PGL performs only one function - that of a "gateway" for passing topology information about the PG up the hierarchy and topology information about the network down the hierarchy. Each switch in the network keeps a detailed view of network topology and uses this to construct routes through the network (set up VCs). The PGL takes no part in setting up VCs or in planning routes on behalf of other nodes.

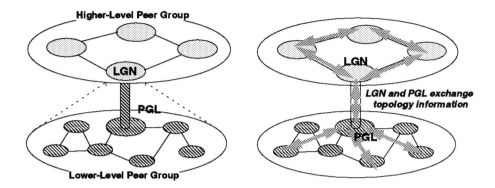

Figure 5-8. *Peer Group Leader and Logical Group Node.* The left-hand figure shows the duality of PGL and LGN. The right-hand figure shows the flow of information.

5.1.4.10 A Switch's View of the Global Topology

Topology aggregation results in each switch "seeing" a restricted (but adequate) view of the total network's topology[10]. Figure 5-9 on page 5-16 shows the network as viewed by switches X.F.1, X.F.2, X.F.3, and X.F.4. Each of these switches sees an exact topology only for its own peer group and a summarized topology for the remainder of the network. In addition, broadcast (flooded) Link State Update (LSU) messages received by these switches only relate to the LGNs that they can "see". This is a very significant reduction in network traffic compared to a network without hierarchical structure.

Reduction of topology update traffic is the whole reason for the PNNI hierarchy. The hierarchy enables us to:

1. Very significantly limit the amount of data needed within each node's topology database.

2. Very significantly limit the network broadcast traffic needed to keep the databases up to data.

---

[10] This is sometimes referred to as a "fish eye view".

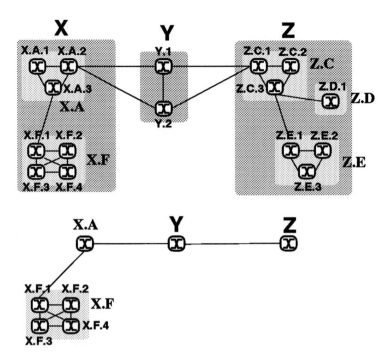

Figure 5-9. A Switch's View of the Global Topology

5.1.4.11 Uplinks

An uplink is the logical connection between a higher-level node and a lower-level node. Within a peer group, each LGN must know about connections to other LGNs (peer groups) on the same or higher levels. However, an LGN within a PG *cannot* know about individual nodes (LGNs) within other peer groups because that would imply understanding network topology within other PGs. For example, in Figure 5-9 the link X.F.1 to X.A.3 is considered an "uplink" at each end. This is because X.A.3 does not "see" switch X.F.1 as a peer. Rather, X.A.3 only sees node X.F as a higher-level LGN. The same is true in the other direction; switch X.F.1 sees the LGN X.A and not the switch X.A.3 as the termination of its external link.

When a node discovers that one of its links connects to a different PG from its own, it recognizes that for this link it must become a *border node*. At this stage the link is known as an "outside" link. A border node does not initially know the real network address of any external node (external to its PG) to which it is directly link-connected - this is discovered via the Hello protocol. But other nodes within the PG need to know about the external connection as a connection to a higher-level LGN.

When the node discovers that it is a border node on some link it extends the Hello protocol to include information about higher-level LGNs. This enables border nodes to discover the *lowest, common, higher-level PG of which both connected PGs are members.*

In Figure 5-10 on page 5-18, node X.1.2 has a link connection to Node X.2.1, but they are in different PGs. From the Hello protocol, node X.1.2 will discover that its PG X.1 is a peer of PG X.2 in PG X. Thus, the link between X.1.2 and X.2.1 is viewed by X.1.2 as a link to the higher-level node (LGN) X.2. This is a *logical* entity called an *uplink* because it is a logical connection from a lower level to a higher one.

Once the node discovers a common PGID via the Hello protocol, it can build a PTSE to describe the uplink and flood this information to all other members of its peer group.

5.1.4.12 Peer Groups of LGNs - Horizontal Links

As discussed above, peer groups may consist of LGNs. In fact, all peer groups above the lowest level do consist of LGNs by definition.

When forming a peer group of LGNs there must be a connection (or a path) on which to exchange the summarized topology information between peers. At the lowest level, this is not a problem since peers are directly connected (either by a physical link or a VP connection), and a special VC (VCI=18) is reserved for the Hello protocol between peers. This is called the "Routing Control Channel" (RCC) and is a permanent VC connection since it is always present and does not need to be set up.

At higher levels however, the logical links which exist between LGNs do not necessarily map to a direct physical connection. For example, in Figure 5-10 on page 5-18 the logical link between LGN X.1 and LGN X.2 would map to the physical link between X.1.1 and X.2.1, but neither of these physical nodes is a peer group leader! The connection between LGNs is accomplished by setting up a *switched VC* connection between them. This is done even though the network has not been fully set up yet. The PGLs within each adjacent PG know the topology of their own PGs and (by definition) PGs at lower levels will have been already set up. This is sufficient for an LGN to request (and get) a switched VC connection set up to the other PGL(s).

Once a VC connection is set up between the PGLs of LGNs at the same level, then the Hello protocol is used in the same way as at the lowest level to set up the PG and to exchange topology within the PG.

The Hello protocol runs continuously at each level. That is, Hellos are sent at intervals on a timed basis to ensure that an accurate picture of the network state is maintained.

5.1.4.13 Building the Hierarchy

Figure 5-10 shows a sample network represented in the style used in ATM Forum documentation. The network is built dynamically by a recursive generation of LGNs level by level from the bottom up.

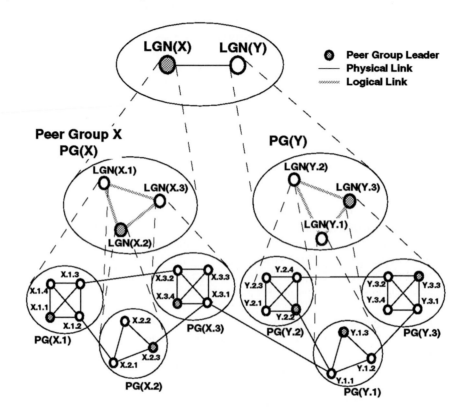

Figure   5-10. *Network Hierarchy Example*

In summary, the operation proceeds as follows:

1. Initialize physical links (and VP connections) between switches.

2. Exchange Hello protocol messages between physical peers.

3. Complete the lowest-level PGs (using the flooding protocol between peers).

4. Identify uplinks (as far as possible).

5. Build horizontal links.

6. Exchange Hello messages at the next-higher-level PGs.

7. Complete this level's PGs (perform topology flooding between LGNs).

8. If this is the highest level then we are done.

9. Go to step 4.

It can be seen that at each level the structure of a PGL is the same with two exceptions:

1. At the highest level there need not be a PGL (because the function is not needed).

2. At the lowest level each node is a real switch or logical node.

5.1.4.14 PNNI Communication between Switches

It is important to notice that all PNNI communication is done through "routing" rather than through ATM switched connections. That is to say, *all* PNNI administrative traffic such as Link State Update (LSU) messages, call setup messages, etc. are *routed* (not switched) through the network. User data however, is *always* switched.

Every switch (and LGN) is connected to all adjacent switches through an ATM VC connection. This uses a reserved VC (VPI=0, VCI=18 on a physical link or VCI=18 on a VP connection). These VC connections allow distribution of information among the control points of a peer group. PNNI messages travel through the network hop-by-hop from one node control point to the next. This allows for processing to be done at each switch along the path.

Connection of higher-level LGNs are made peer-to-peer from LGN to LGN and make use of switched VCCs, which are switched through unrelated nodes at lower levels. Thus, routing takes place between peers when we are performing the flooding protocol within a PG, and in this environment intermediate VC connections may well be switched through the network. When setting up a new call the setup message is always routed from node to node at the lowest level.

End users communicate with one another through VCCs which travel through the switching elements of each node and are *never* routed.

5.1.4.15 Address Summarization and Reachability

In the default case of PNNI, the ATM address of each node is used to construct the hierarchy (of PGs, LGNs, etc.). Each switch must be configured with an address that obeys rules such that the hierarchy may be constructed. In practice, this may be too restrictive - network designers may wish to use a *different* address for the purpose of reachability (or indeed multiple addresses) from the address used for constructing the hierarchy.

When a switch receives an incoming call request it must be able to decide where in the network is the desired destination of the call. This means that information about reachability must be available to every switch. In an extreme case, every switch might have a different address from every other switch with no systematic relationship at all between them. If this was done, then every switch in the network would need to have a directory with an entry for every other switch in the network. This directory would need to be kept up to date continuously as changes occurred. Practical experience with router networks shows that this can lead to a very large amount of network traffic. In addition, it could require a very large amount of storage and processing in each switch in a large network.

So, addresses may be summarized. When two addresses are summarized the x high-order bits of the address must be the same. LGNs summarize the addresses of lower-level switches/LGNs in order to propagate only summarized information.

5.1.4.16 Advertising Topology

The major purpose of PNNI routing is to enable each node to have sufficient topology information to process a call setup request. The information required is not the same in each node of the network (unless the whole network is a single PG). The information needed falls into three general classes:

1. Network structure

   Each node must have a view of the total network. As seen above, this is a partial view and is detailed within a particular node only for the PG of which this node is a member.

2. Link state information

   Information about the current loadings of links (and current capacity commitments) is needed by the node in order to be able to plan routes. Many parameters are possible here. The mandatory ones are:

   - Maximum Cell Transfer Delay (MCTD)
   - Maximum Cell Delay Variation (MCDV)
   - Maximum Cell Loss Ratio (MCLR)
   - Administrative Weight
   - Available Cell Rate (ACR)

3. Reachability information.

   When a node receives a call request it must be able to decide where the destination node is within the network. It may be that the hierarchical network address structure is sufficient to make the decision. However, it is possible for a node to have an address (or addresses) associated with it that is *not* part of the PNNI hierarchical structure. This might happen for example when a PNNI node is connected to an "external" (non-PNNI) network. Thus, these "foreign" addresses must be propagated to every node in the PNNI network. However there is a mechanism available to limit the scope of this propagation.

The information must be propagated initially when the network is set up but, more importantly, it must be kept up-to-date. Indeed, making updating of this information efficient is the basic reason for the architecture of PNNI. Updated information is sent on a timed basis as well as whenever a significant change occurs.

There are three kinds of information flow related to topology updating:

1. Within a PG (on the same level of the hierarchy)

   As mentioned above, this is accomplished by a "flooding" process where Link State Update (LSU) messages are propagated throughout a PG. These PTSP messages do not leave the PG.

2. Up the hierarchy

   The PGL node summarizes the topology of its peer group and then propagates this summarized topology (as an LGN description) to the higher-level PG. In this way the PGL is really a member of two PGs. It is a member of the lower-level PG as a node in its own right and a member of the next-higher level as the processing entity that realizes the LGN appearance.

3. Down the hierarchy

   Reachability and topology information need to be propagated throughout the whole network to every switch. When the LGN sees reachability information arrive at its higher-level appearance, it passes the information to its related PGL which floods the information to every node in the lower-level PG.

5.1.4.17 Stubs and Non-Transit Nodes

Figure 5-11 illustrates two very common but problematic situations.

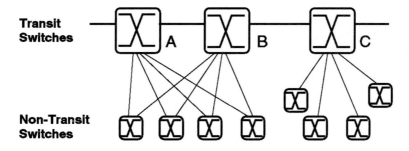

Transit Switches

Non-Transit Switches

Figure   5-11. Dual-Homed Stubs (Non-Transit Nodes)

1. On the right of the figure, Node C has a number of other switches connected to it on single point-to-point connections. In a public network situation, for example, if C was a local exchange switch and the connections were to end users, then we might have up to a few hundred switches radially connected in this way.

2. On the left of the figure, we see the same situation, but every tributary switch is connected to the backbone network by two separate links to different nodes (a common situation for reliability). These are termed "dual-homed stubs".

Both of these situations, while appearing simple, are actually quite difficult to handle in PNNI. Problems relate to the broadcast of reachability information and the sending of too many duplicate topology update messages. In addition, of course, we want to prohibit data flows such as from node A to node B through one of the connected stubs.

In order to improve this situation, in PNNI there is an ability to designate a switch as a "non-transit node". Non-transit nodes do not propagate LSUs and do not allow connections from the transit switches to pass through them.

5.1.4.18 Links between Switches

At the lowest layer, it is possible to have a VP connection as a link between switches instead of a real physical link. This could be a link through an "external" (non-PNNI) network, or it could be through the PNNI network itself. This latter case is illustrated in Figure 5-12.

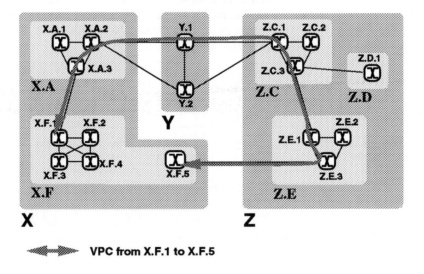

◄━━━━► VPC from X.F.1 to X.F.5

Figure   5-12. Using a VP as a Link between Switches

Switch X.F.5 is physically connected to switch Z.E.3. However, it is a part of PG X.F and is connected to that PG via a VP connection between node X.F.5 and node X.F.1.

5.1.5 Signaling

Signaling is the process used to set up new end-to-end VC or VP connections on behalf of an end user. When an end user makes a request for a connection to be set up that request is sent from the end user to the switch (to which that end user is connected) using UNI signaling protocols. The end-user device communicates with the control point in the switch to which it is connected. PNNI signaling is used to set up the VC in each switch along the path of that connection.

PNNI signaling is very similar to the signaling used at the UNI (specified by the ITU-T in Q.2931). However it has been modified to provide symmetry (Q.2931 is asymmetric) and to include routing information for the call being set up.

5.1.5.1 Setting Up a Connection - Principle

The principle of source routing is illustrated in Figure 5-13. The example network we have been using throughout is here treated as a single peer group without any routing hierarchy (hence, the node numbering has been changed for ease of illustration).

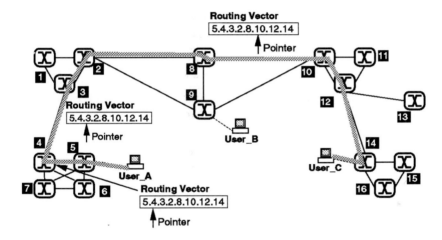

***Figure** 5-13. Setting Up a Connection (Source Routing)*

User_A places a call to establish a connection to User_C. The call request is carried in a signaling message on the UNI connecting the end user to node 5.

1. The switch to which User_A is connected (node 5) looks at its topology database and calculates a route to User_C.

   This route is expressed as a "routing vector" as shown in the figure. This vector is a list of the nodes through which the call being set up will pass. It contains a pointer to the current entry (next hop) which is updated as the message progresses through the network. Because our example has been deliberately constructed as a single PG without hierarchy, the routing vector will be complete. That is, it will contain all the switches along the path.

2. Node 5 sends a setup message (using PNNI signaling) hop-by-hop along the proposed route (from switch control point to switch control point) according to the precalculated routing vector.

   This vector is shown in the figure as the setup message travels from node 5 to node 4. Notice here that the pointer in the routing vector is indicating that the next hop (after the setup message has been received at node 4) is node 3.[11]

3. When the setup message arrives at node 4 the control point sees that the next hop is to node 3, updates the pointer and sends the setup message onward to node 3.

4. This process is repeated at each node along the route until the setup message arrives at the destination switch.

The requested connection is actually a set of table entries within the switching part of each switch (node) along the path. These are set up by the control points when they process the setup request message.

5.1.5.2 Designated Transit Lists

In PNNI the source routing vector is called a *designated transit list* (DTL). The DTL is a Q.2931 information element which is carried in SETUP and ADD_PARTY messages. Each DTL is complete and contains entries for only one level of the hierarchy. The SETUP and ADD_PARTY messages carry a number of DTLs (one for each active level of the hierarchy). This is discussed in the next section.

5.1.5.3 PNNI Source Routing

The rather simple source routing principle described in the previous section applies only to single peer groups. When you have a hierarchical PNNI network the source routing principle has to be modified somewhat. Using the more complex view of our sample network, shown in Figure 5-14 on page 5-25, node 5 of the previous example in Figure 5-13 on page 5-23 is now called X.F.2, and node 14 is called Z.E.1.

As switch X.F.2 does *not* have sufficient information to build the detailed route we built in the previous example, X.F.2 will build a route vector that says:

```
X.F.2,  X.F.1,  X.A,  Y,  Z
```

The route so constructed is called a "partial source route".

---

[11] This is different from source routing in a LAN bridged environment because of the use of a pointer to the routing vector. In LAN source route bridging the destination entry is always the first entry in the routing vector and it is removed as soon as routing takes place.

The route shown above has omitted levels of the hierarchy. In practice, a PNNI route must be *hierarchically complete* (for a number of reasons that are outside the scope of this book). A full, hierarchically complete, source route for the above is:

```
X.F.2, X.F.1, X.F X.A, X, Y, Z
```

The route so constructed is hierarchically complete but not physically complete because it includes no information about the route to be taken through LGNs X.A, Y, or Z. It is clear that X.A, Y, and Z are LGNs and not switches, and to build a real connection through the network, the route must go through real switches not abstractions. What happens is that when the route setup message enters a new LGN, the entry node to the peer group represented by the LGN builds a route through its peer group.

Let us consider the setup for the entire route as shown in Figure 5-14.

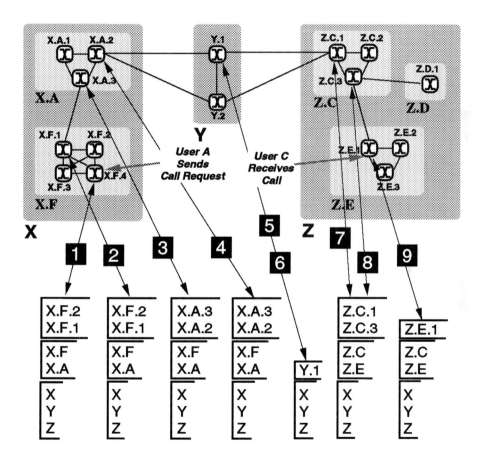

Figure 5-14. Route Setup Example

Operation proceeds as follows:

1. User_A sends a call request to X.F.2 on the UNI interface. X.F.2 builds the hierarchically complete source route vector as shown.

   Notice here that there are three designated transit lists (DTLs) built - one for each level of the hierarchy visible to X.F.2. At each level, we have a complete picture of the route to the end of the particular PG at that level. So, as the list is built we are simultaneously in node X.F.2 (at the lowest level), node X.F (at the level above), and node X (at the top level). So, in a sense we are moving through all three DTLs at the same time but on different levels.

2. When the setup request leaves node X.F.1 the request has finished its transit of LGN X.F and, therefore, the DTL (X.F.1, X.F.2) is deleted from the message.

3. When the setup request arrives in node X.A.3 this physical switch[12] computes the route through its PG (X.A.3, X.A.2) and adds this route (DTL) to the setup request message.

4. When the setup request leaves node X.A.2 it is also leaving LGN X.A and LGN X. We have now completed transit of LGN X.A and LGN X, so both of the DTLs applying to these routes can be removed from the message.

5. On entry to node Y.1, we have the simple case where we must add a single element (Y.1) and then immediately delete it because we are leaving LGN Y.

6. On entry to the switch Z.C.1, we are simultaneously entering LGNs Z and Z.C. At the lowest level, we need to build a route (DTL) across LGN Z.C and at the next level we need a route across Z. Thus two DTLs are added to the transit list.

7. On exit from node Z.C.3, we can delete the top DTL (Z.C.1, Z.C.3) from the route.

8. On entry to Z.E.1, we build an entry for the switch itself and determine that we have reached our destination.

9. Switch Z.E.1 can then forward the call request (without the DTLs because we are now on the UNI interface) to User_C.

As the SETUP message was sent from (physical) switch to (physical) switch the table entries for the resulting connection were set up in each switch along the path.

5.1.5.4 Crankback Protocol and Alternate Path Routing

Let us consider an LGN representing PG_X as shown in Figure 5-15 on page 5-27.

---

[12] Note that the route here is computed by the physical node on which the setup message is received into a particular peer group. This may or may not be the peer group leader. The PGL function does not perform route calculation. It exists solely for topology update and maintenance functions.

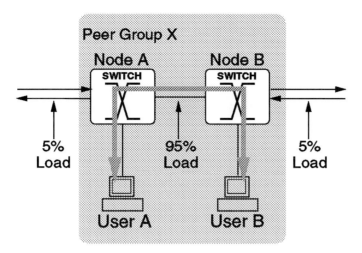

Figure 5-15. *Need for Crankback Protocol*

If such an LGN was situated within a network where traffic could be routed through it, then we get a difficult situation. Both external links (to other parts of the network) are very lightly loaded (5%), but the LGN itself is very heavily loaded with local traffic. Other nodes may *not* know the internal, heavily loaded state of this LGN - from outside it looks fine.

When an LGN such as this is selected for a new route, the connection setup may be refused because of the high local loading. What happens here is that the route is *cranked back*, or unwound, to the entry switch that built this section of the route. The entry switch then has to find an alternate route through its (higher-level) peer group and, if it cannot, then the setup request is cranked back again to the next higher level.

5.1.5.5 Call Admission Control

In ATM, a connection is not set up unless and until the network determines that there is sufficient capacity for the new connection, that is, only if service can be provided with the requested Quality-of-Service (QoS) characteristics. The function that determines whether a call can be accepted is called *call admission control* (CAC). In PNNI, CAC is performed in two places:

1. When a route is calculated (by the entry switch of a PG), the switch determining the route also determines if the call can (probably) be accepted on that route. The criteria of QoS are of course used to determine which route (of many possible) is the best for a particular call. This process is called "Generic Call Admission Control" (GCAC).

2. When the SETUP message is processed in a particular switch (when it transits the switch), the individual switch determines whether or not it can support the call on a local basis. If it cannot support the call it must refuse it and the call is cranked back to the entry switch of that PG. This function is called "Actual Call Admission Control" (ACAC).

5.1.6 Interim Inter-Switch Signaling Protocol (IISP) aka PNNI_0

The IISP (also called the PNNI phase 0) is the ATM Forum's response to the need for a PNNI quickly to enable the construction of early networks. The IISP is not so much a protocol as a technique for using the UNI between switches.

IISP is suitable for small, static environments. Configuration of the network is by manual definition and the network topology is static. Signaling between switches is done using the UNI signaling protocols (Q.2931 and Q.SAAL). In fact, IISP is just the UNI protocol, minimally modified to allow its use for switch-to-switch connection.

IISP will be replaced fairly quickly with PNNI phase 1.

Chapter 6. ATM Physical Interfaces

ATM was defined to make the physical data transport function as independent as possible from the ATM switching function and the things that go on above the ATM layer.

ATM is able to operate over a wide variety of possible physical link types. These vary in speed, medium (fiber or copper), and in structure to suit the particular environment in which the link has to operate. Table 6-1 summarizes link types that have either been accepted by standards bodies or are current proposals. Not all of these will ultimately find wide acceptance.

Table 6-1. ATM-UNI Interfaces

	Rate (Mbps)	Cell Throughput	System	Medium	WAN/LAN	Owner
DS-1 (T-1)	1.544	1.536	PDH	Cu	Both	ANSI
E-1	2.048	1.92	PDH	Cu	Both	ETSI
DS-3 (T-3)	44.736	40.704	PDH	Cu	WAN	ANSI
E-3	34.368	33.984	PDH	Cu	WAN	ETSI
E-4	139.264	138.24	PDH	Cu	WAN	ETSI
SDH STM-1, Sonet STS-3c	155.52	149.76	Sonet/SDH	SM Fiber	WAN	ITU-T
Sonet "Lite"	155.52	149.76	Sonet/SDH	MM Fiber	LAN	Forum
SDH STM-4c, Sonet STS-12c	622.08	599.04	Sonet/SDH	SM Fiber	WAN	ITU-T
FDDI-PMD	100	100	Block Coded	MM Fiber/STP	LAN	Forum
Fiber Channel	155.52	150.34	Block Coded	MM Fiber	LAN	Forum
DXI (RVX)	0-50	0-50	Clear Channel	Cu	LAN	Forum
Raw Cells	155.52	155.52	Clear Channel	SM Fiber	WAN	ITU-T
Raw Cells	622.08	622.08	Clear Channel	SM Fiber	WAN	ITU-T
Raw Cells	25.6	25.6	Clear Channel	Cu UTP-3/5	LAN	Forum
Sonet "Lite"	51.84 25.92 12.96	49.536 24.768 12.384	Sonet Frame	Cu UTP-3/5	LAN	Forum
Raw Cells	100	100	Clear Channel	Cu UTP-3	LAN	Proposed
Raw Cells	155.52	155.52	Clear Channel	Cu UTP/STP	LAN	Forum

The main issues for ATM data transport are:

1. High speed (data rate)

   This almost goes without saying, but if the network is to be made stable by relying on the statistics of aggregated data streams, then link capacity has to be sufficient to support many simultaneous users.

2. Low latency (for some applications)

   ATM will be made to operate over a satellite connection, but the additional latency involved will make some applications (such as interactive multimedia) significantly more difficult.

3. Very low error rates

   This is key. Because of the fact that an errored cell causes retransmission of the whole data block (many cells), some people feel that ATM is likely to be unstable in high-error-rate situations.

There is no doubt however, that ATM systems will be developed to run over radio media (radio LANs) and over satellite connections.

6.1 Structure

The structure of the ATM physical layer is shown in Figure 6-1.

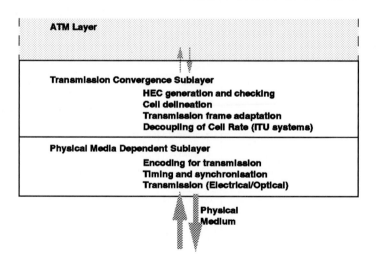

Figure   *6-1.* *Structure of ATM Physical Layer*

- Cells are delivered to the Transmission Convergence (TC) sublayer by the ATM layer.

- The TC sublayer knows about cells and about the logical structure of the transmission medium (if it is framed or not, for example).

- The TC sublayer generates the HEC and builds it into the cell. The cell itself is then placed into the TC sublayer's output data stream which is being fed to the Physical Media Dependent (PMD) sublayer.

- All the PMD sublayer knows about is a stream of bits or bytes and some timing signals.

- The PMD performs coding, timing, and transmission functions.

- The reverse process happens when cells are received.

All currently defined ATM physical interface protocols have three things in common:

1. They are point-to-point.

   That is, they connect an ATM endpoint with an ATM switch, or they connect two ATM switches together. There are no multipoint or LAN type connections defined. (You could say that SDH provides a form of multipointing, but what it really does is to provide a lower layer of multiplexing of multiple, independent, full-duplex connections.)

2. They are all full-duplex (FDX) in operation.

   Data is transferred simultaneously in both directions. This is not an absolute necessity - half-duplex procedures are conceivable with some limitations.

3. Physical link bandwidth *may* be asymmetric.

   That is, a higher data rate may be possible in one direction than the other. There are **no** link protocols yet defined that have this characteristic, but there is no reason why not. It is possible within the current standard to have an SDH connection with 155 Mbps in one direction and 622 in the other. There are some situations where this might be desirable.

   If ATM were to be provided to the home (for multimedia distribution, for example) then the Asymmetric Digital Subscriber Line (ADSL) protocol may well be used. ADSL provides a maximum data rate of 6 Mbps in one direction and 384 Kbps in the other (it is asymmetric). As yet, ATM has not been defined to operate over this kind of link, but for some applications it could make a lot of sense.

6.1.1 Transmission Convergence Sublayer Functions

HEC Generation and Checking

The Header Error Check (HEC) code is capable of single-bit error correction **or** double-bit error detection. This is a type of SECDED (single error correction, double error detection) code.

When an error is detected, there is no reliable way to determine whether the error was a (correctable) single-bit error or an (uncorrectable) double-bit error. If you decide to correct the error, and it was really a double-bit error, then the result you get **is in error!** Some multi-bit (3 and more bits) errors are undetectable.

Some people believe that the instance of double-bit errors will be so low with fiber optical transmission that the single-bit error correction is appropriate. Others disagree and say that we should not take the chance on any error. An error in the cell header could result in mis-routing of the cell (the cell would go to a destination for which it was not intended). If a cell is mis-routed and is received by the wrong destination, then the AAL function "should" detect the error and discard the cell (and perhaps a few others along with it).

The consensus seems to be that for networks using only optical links, then error correction is reasonably safe. But for networks employing high-error-rate copper connections (such as copper T-1 and E-1 links), then the chance of double-bit errors is too high and all errored cells should be discarded.

The HEC is also used for cell delineation (described in the following section).

Cell Delineation

This is the function of deciding where in the data stream (transmitted or received) does a cell start (and finish). In the traditional data network world this function is called "block level synchronization".

There are basically three ways to do this:

1. The transmission level coding can include a delimiter function that marks the beginning and end of cells.

   This is the traditional method used in data networking. For example HDLC link control marks the beginning and end of blocks by using a unique bit sequence (B′ 01111110′). Token-ring LANs perform this function by using a "code violation" within the Differential Manchester line coding as a frame delimiter.

   In high-speed transmission we normally encode a group of data bits into a larger group of bits for transmission on the line. This is called block coding and is described later in this section. Block codes use a unique combination of bits on the line (a combination that does not represent data) to signal the beginning and end of blocks. This is done in many of the "clear-channel" ATM link protocols.

2. Many transmission systems employ framing (as in SDH and PDH systems). In this case, you could get the framing system to locate the cell boundaries for you (for example, with a pointer within the frame overhead section). Alternatively, you can place cells at fixed locations within a frame (although this could cause a loss in efficiency if cells do not fit exactly into a frame). Both alternatives are used in different situations.

3. You can use the cell HEC to locate the cell boundary. This is the most common way of cell delineation. Its operation is summarized in Figure 6-2.

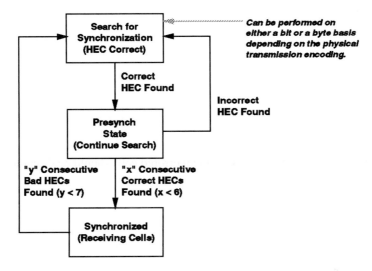

Figure *6-2.* *Cell Delineation by HEC Checking*

What happens here is that as the data stream arrives (either a bit at a time, but more usually a byte at a time), the receiver calculates and checks the HEC as though the last 5 bytes were a cell header. The HEC calculation is such that finding a string of bits (or bytes) that is not a cell header, where the HEC still checks out correct, is a very rare event.

This procedure assumes that cells are sent in a stream exactly one after the other with no gaps (or rather with predictable ones). So, what happens is that you check for a correct cell header, and when you get one you make the assumption that this is a cell header and then check the next cell header (53 bytes later in the stream). When you get a sequence of correct cell headers then you have located the cell boundaries.

Scrambling

In some PMDs it is felt that the transmission coding alone will not guarantee to retain synchronization at the receiver if long strings of 0 or 1 are transmitted. For these PMDs the cell payload is "scrambled" (randomized). This also reduces the chance that the HEC cell delineation will find any false synchronizations.

Transmission Frame Generation and Recovery

In some (most) of the physical transports for ATM there is a framing structure. This is true of all the SDH and PDH based PMDs.

Cell Rate Decoupling

Most ATM PMDs send a constant stream of cells without any gaps. This is true in the framed services (such as SDH) and in some non-framed ones as well (such as the 155 and 622 Mbps SM fiber alternatives).

When there are no cells to send you have to send something. The answer is to send an empty cell (VPI=0,VCI=0). This is inserted on the transmission side and removed on the receiver side.

In fact, things are not quite this simple. Cell rate decoupling was responsible for the failure of a number of early ATM interoperability trials. In the ITU-T standard, an empty cell is coded as VPI=0, VCI=0, DE=1. That is, the cell is marked as discard eligible. In other standards, it is an error for an empty cell to have DE=1. This is in the process of resolution.

At the present time, there is another method of cell rate decoupling in ATM. In this alternative the ATM layer (above the convergence layer) is constrained to deliver a stream of cells at the correct rate such that the convergence layer does not have to insert any. These cells are coded VPI=0, VCI=0, DE=0.

So, right now if an empty cell has DE=1 then it is a convergence layer empty cell and if DE=0 then the cell was inserted (and should be removed) by the ATM layer.

6.1.2 Physical Media Dependent (PMD) Sublayer

The basic function of the Physical Media[1] Dependent (PMD) layer is to take a stream of bits and transport it transparently across a link. In practice, the PMD usually works with streams of bytes rather than bits, because most PMDs encode on a byte or half-byte basis. There is somewhat more than just a stream of bits involved here. Since the TC sublayer builds a framed structure (if needed) there is a timing and synchronization function

---

[1] This is incorrect English. The word in this context should be "Medium". Nevertheless the standard says "Media".

between the TC and PMD sublayers as well as the data stream. Figure 6-3 on page 6-7 summarizes the operation of the PMD sublayer. While this figure applies specifically to the FDDI derived 100 Mbps protocol, the principles are the same for other PMDs.

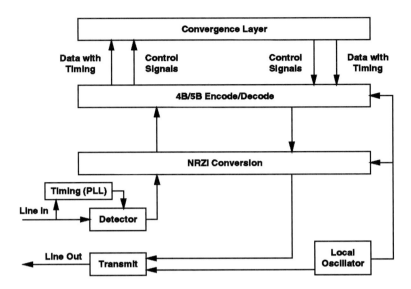

Figure 6-3. Physical Layer Structure ("FDDI" Protocol)

Encoding for Transmission

In most data transmission systems, data is not sent in its original form - it is encoded in some way before transmission. There are generally three reasons for this:

1. When a signal is received either on an optical fiber or on a wire it is necessary to decide where the bits begin and end. In the simple case, if bits are encoded directly as voltages on a wire (or the presence/absence of light), then when a number occurs in sequence it becomes very difficult to know where the boundaries between bits occur. A signal transmitted at x bits per second will vary slightly when it is received (due to distortion in the circuit) and also at the receiver location it is quite impossible to build a clock (oscillator) of *exactly* the same frequency as the transmitter. Thus we need to work out the timing of bits as they are received from the bit stream itself. When the signal changes state, we know that this is a boundary between bits. When there is no change of state, we have to guess where the boundary really is. After quite a short sequence of the same bit we can no longer be sure of that boundary. In order to receive the bit stream reliably we need the signal to change state between 0 and 1 frequently enough for the receiver to maintain synchronization with the incoming bit stream.

Data is encoded to provide sufficient state changes to enable the receiver to derive accurate timing.

2. Some codes allow for additional code combinations that do not represent data. This means that we can have codes to represent the beginning of a cell (or of a frame) and other codes to coordinate the link operation from end-to-end.

3. One of the serious problems of high-speed communications is that electrical technology becomes more and more costly as speed is increased. The electrical circuits that interface to the line must run at the line rate. However, if bits are received in groups then they can be passed to other circuits in parallel at a much slower rate.

In Figure 6-3 on page 6-7 all the functions below the 4B/5B encode/decode box must run at 125 megahertz. But the access protocol gets data passed to it in 4-bit groups at only 25 megahertz.

This means that the link interfacing functions might be implemented in (relatively expensive) bipolar technology and the rest in inexpensive CMOS.[2]

Timing and Synchronization

This layer must generate appropriate timing for signals transmitted and derive correct timing for signals received. This is not always simple.

Transmission (Electrical/Optical)

This function is the actual placement of a signal on a wire or a fiber and reception of it at the other end.

6.1.2.1 Block Coding

Most PMDs use block coding in one form or another. A block code groups data bits into "blocks" and translates each block into another bit pattern before transmission on the line. Block-coded protocols either code 4-bit groups into 5-bit groups (4 of 5 coding) or 8-bit groups into 10-bit groups (8 of 10 code).

The 100 Mbps (FDDI) PMD protocol is a good example:

---

[2] This was partly the reason for the use of this coding type in FDDI, but since that time CMOS has improved to the point where we can build CMOS line tranceivers at up to 200 Mbps. But, of course, the improvement in CMOS has just moved the cost boundary. In a system operating at 622 Mbps we can't use CMOS for the tranceivers, but we would like to (for cost reasons) for the rest of the processing.

Table 6-2. *4B/5B Coding as Used with 100 Mbps PMD.* Four-bit groups are sent as 5-bit combinations to ensure there are at least two transitions per group.

Symbol Type	Symbol	Code Group	Meaning
Line State Symbols	I	11111	Idle
	H	00100	Halt
	Q	00000	Quiet
Starting Delimiter	J	11000	First Byte of SD
	K	10001	Second Byte of SD
Control Indicators	R	00111	Logical Zero (Reset)
	S	11001	Logical One (Set)
Ending Delimiter	T	01101	Terminates Data Stream
Data Symbols	0	11110	B$'$ 0000$'$ (X$'$ 0$'$)
	1	01001	B$'$ 0001$'$ (X$'$ 1$'$)
	...	...	...
		...	...
	...	...	...
	9	10011	B$'$ 1001$'$ (X$'$ 9$'$)
	A	10110	B$'$ 1010$'$ (X$'$ A$'$)
	B	10111	B$'$ 1011$'$ (X$'$ B$'$)
	C	11010	B$'$ 1100$'$ (X$'$ C$'$)
	D	11011	B$'$ 1101$'$ (X$'$ D$'$)
	E	11100	B$'$ 1110$'$ (X$'$ E$'$)
	F	11101	B$'$ 1111$'$ (X$'$ F$'$)
Invalid Symbols	V	00001	Invalid
	V	00010	...
	...	...	...
	...	...	...

Each four data bits is encoded as a five-bit group for transmission or reception. This means that the 100 Mbps data rate is actually 125 Mbps when observed on the physical link.[3] Table 6-2 shows the coding used. This provides:

- Simplification of timing recovery by providing a guaranteed rate of transitions in the data. Only code combinations with at least two transitions per group are valid.

---

[3] It is incorrect to say that the link is operating at 125 Mbps because the rate of actual bit transport is 100 Mbps. The correct term for the line rate is "baud". A baud is a change in the line state. You could say (with equal truth) that the line is operating at 125 Mbaud or at 25 Mbaud (you could consider each 5-bit group to be a "symbol").

- Transparency and framing. Additional unique code combinations (5-bit codes that do not correspond to any data group) are available. These are used to provide transparency by signaling the beginning and end of a block.

- Circuitry simplification as discussed above.

6.1.2.2 NRZI Modulation

The bit stream resulting from the above encoding is further converted before transmission by using "Non-Return to Zero Inverted" (NRZI) procedure. This adds more transitions into the data stream to further assist with timing recovery in the receiver. In NRZI procedure, a "1" bit causes a state change and a "0" bit causes no state change.

A sequence of idle patterns (B' 11111') will result in a signal of 010101 thus maintaining synchronization at the receiver. Some valid data sequences (for example, X' B0' coded as B' 10111 11110') can contain up to 7 contiguous "1" bits and these need to have additional transitions inserted if the receiver is to synchronize satisfactorily.

The net effect of 4B/5B encoding and NRZI conversion is that the maximum length of a signal without state change is 3 baud.[4]

6.2 Physical Connection Types

6.2.1.1 Framed Transmission

The majority of ATM physical interfaces use framed transmission structures. The principle is developed from the Time Division Multiplexing (TDM) systems used to transport digitally encoded voice. The standard voice encoding produces an 8-bit sample 8000 times per second. That is, there are 125 μsec between samples. At a uniform transmission rate this means a regular bit rate of 64 Kbps.

The concept of framing is that you take the transmission link and send a predictable pattern every 125 μsec. This pattern is called a frame. It is just a fixed-length block of data with delimiters arranged such that you can always find the boundary between frames. For example, the European E-1 system, which transmits data at 2.048 Mbps, uses frames of 32 "slots" of 8 bits each. 32 (slots) times 8 (bits) times 8000 equals 2 Mbps. Slots 0 and 16 are used for signaling and framing purposes and this gives 30 voice channels that can be accessed by time-division multiplexing. In the US, the 24-channel T-1 of 1.544 Mbps uses a similar framing concept although it is quite different in the detail.

---

[4] A baud is a state change on the line. Here we are dealing with 4 bits of data already encoded as 5 line states for transmission. The correct term for each line state is "baud" not bit.

As links became faster there was a need to multiplex many T-1s and E-1s into faster and faster circuits. This was accomplished in a hierarchical way (although the US system and the European system use different types of framing and different speeds). This is called the Plesiochronous Digital Hierarchy (PDH). A summary of PDH speeds, etc. is given in B.3, "Plesiochronous Digital Hierarchy" on page B-9.

When optical fiber was developed a need to rationalize and improve the PDH system became apparent and the Synchronous Digital Hierarchy (SDH) system was developed. SDH was derived from a previous US standard called "Sonet". SDH and Sonet are described in Appendix B, "SDH and Sonet" on page B-1.

Sonet/SDH is being installed very quickly worldwide to enable the sharing of optical fiber (multiplexing) and the management of optical fiber links. SDH has very strong system management and cable management facilities.

Most of the proposed (or approved) ATM physical connections use either PDH or SDH. This is done for a number of reasons:

- To enable the use of existing PTT facilities in early ATM implementations.

- To enable the sharing of connections (links) between existing services and ATM. (This will have to continue for a very long time.)

- To enable effective management of the link connections.

- To propagate the network 125-μsec clock. In traditional telephone networks it is immensely important to synchronize the network to a common clock. This is less true in ATM but constant-bit-rate (CBR) AAL services require that identical clocks are available at each attachment to the network. Using a framed link protocol provides an easy way of propagating the system clock throughout the network.

It is likely that in the next few years the PDH-based protocols will get extensive use for early ATM systems. In the longer term, however, this use will diminish and PDH will be replaced with SDH. Many people (in the US) think that SDH protocols will continue forever in use as the link management system for ATM networks.

6.2.2 SDH-Based Connections

In the US, the predominant type of physical channel used for ATM in the public network environment will be Sonet/SDH. This is partly for integration with existing networks and partly because of the excellent OA&M facilities available in Sonet equipment.[5] In Europe, it is likely that Sonet/SDH will not be widely used for ATM transport, but the "clear-channel" approach will be used instead.

---

5 A short description of SDH and Sonet may be found in Appendix B, "SDH and Sonet" on page B-1.

6.2.2.1 155 Mbps STS-3c (STM-1)

Figure 6-4 shows how ATM cells are transported within a Sonet/SDH frame. Notice that within the virtual container, cells are concatenated row by row without regard to row or cell boundaries.

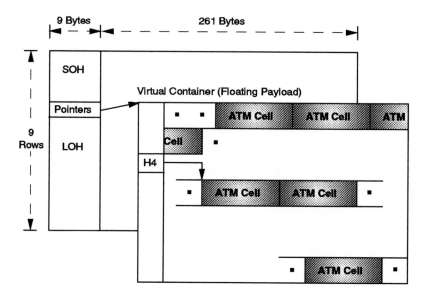

Figure 6-4. *ATM Cells Carried within an SDH Frame*

The figure shows the frame structure for operation at 155.52 Mbps in an STS-3c[6] frame. In the early specifications of ATM, the overhead section of the virtual container contained a pointer (H4) to a cell boundary, so that the system could decide where the stream of cells began. Cells span frames without any gaps. The use of the H4 pointer to locate the cell stream has recently been removed from the standard for all PMDs, except the DS-3 based PMD where its use is optional. Cell delineation is now to be performed only by the HEC method.

In Sonet/SDH and (to a limited extent) in PDH there are a number of end-to-end TDM channels provided across the link quite independent of the main channel carrying ATM cells. This is the *primary* function of the overhead bytes (SOH and LOH in the figure). These additional channels provide for OA&M functions related to operation of the link itself.

---

6 The suffix c after the STS-3 name indicates that the payload is to be concatenated and treated as a single channel. This is to distinguish it from regular Sonet/SDH where the frame carries many TDM channels.

There are *three* variations of this interface currently available (and standardized).[7]

Sonet STS-3c

> This is a US standard developed by the American National Standards Institute (ANSI). It includes very extensive management capability carried in the "overhead" parts of the frame.

STM-1

> This is an ITU-T standard. It uses the same framing as Sonet but is very different in its detail - especially in the management functions.

Sonet "Lite"

> The term "Lite" used here is *not* an official term. It's just a form of convenient slang.
>
> This refers to the Sonet STS-3c over multimode fiber standard adopted by the ATM Forum. Most of the management flows in the "overhead" sections of both STS-3c and STM-1 have been removed and replaced with constants. This is because in the short distance LAN environment (up to 2 km transmission distances) you just don't need the functions provided. Doing this significantly reduces the cost of implementation
>
> It is believed (but not yet proven) that Sonet Lite will communicate with both STS-3c and STM-1 over short distances - provided that the medium (SM fiber, MM fiber, copper) is the same.

All of these may operate over a number of media:

- Single-mode fiber
- Multimode fiber
- Copper coaxial cable (G.703 standard)
- STP (Type 1 cable)
- UTP (Type 5)
- UTP (Type 3) is still under consideration by standards bodies

6.2.2.2 622 Mbps STS-12c (STM-4c)

In principle (although the detail is different), STS-12c is used to transport ATM cells in exactly the same way as STS-3c. Precise mappings are different. The STS-12c facility is treated as a single point-to-point serial link.

It is important to note that *you cannot just take four STS-3c cell streams and merge them into a single STS-12c stream*. ATM does not work like that. VCIs and VPIs are unique

---

[7] This does not include the interface described in 6.2.4.3, "155 Mbps (Fiber Channel) Block Encoded" on page 6-22.

only within the context of a single link, and therefore if cells are arbitrarily mixed, then there is no way to work out which cell belongs where. There *is* an ATM concentrator function that will allow this kind of cell stream merging, but that function requires VPIs in each cell stream to be swapped or translated. The merging cannot be done without logical manipulation of the cell headers.

You *can* still multiplex four STS-3c streams into one STS-12 stream, but this is done by time-division multiplexing and the four STS-3c streams stay logically separate. ATM sees this as just four parallel STS-3c streams and does not know about the multiplexing.

6.2.2.3 51.84 Mbps UTP-3 Physical Layer Interface

This has recently been approved by the ATM Forum. Its principles are as follows:

- The protocol is intended to be used in the local environment with a maximum distance between ATM end user and ATM switch of 120 cable meters over UTP Class 3 cable. This matches the specification of existing UTP-3 LANs. Of course it will operate over UTP Class 5 as well.

- It is defined to operate at two lower speeds (1/2 and 1/4 of the full speed). These are 25.92 and 12.96 Mbps. The reason for this is so that media of a lower standard than the Class 3 UTP specification can be used (but at a lower speed). It also allows for operation over UTP-3 at longer distances than the nominal 100 meters, also by reducing the data rate.

- The link transmission coding is called CAP-16. (At lower speeds CAP-8 or CAP-2 are used.) This is one of a class of advanced "partial response codes" developed by AT&T Bell Labs.

- The line speed is 51.84 Mbps.

- Sonet framing is used. The payload is concatenated to form a single channel rather than a number of TDM channels.

- The Sonet payload consists of 9 rows of 86 bytes each sent every 125 μsec. This gives a cell transmission rate of 49.536 Mbps.

- Cells are located in the data stream by direct mapping and a continuous stream of cells is required. Empty cells are sent when there is no data.

- Cell delineation is done by the HEC method.

6.2.3 PDH-Based Physical Connections

All of the PDH physical layers use framed structures regardless of speed. In general, there are two ways to use the PDH framed services for ATM cell transport.

Direct Mapping

In direct mapping, the bytes within each frame are treated as a continuous unbroken stream of bytes. Frame boundaries are not heeded in any way. Cell boundaries are found by using the HEC. This applies to all the PDH protocols regardless of speed.

Framed Transfer

The frame structure can be used to provide some form of rate synchronization. For example, in the DS-3 framed implementation a floating payload frame is built within the DS-3 frame. The payload frame is synchronized to the system 125-μsec clock, but the link frame structure may not be. Thus, there can be small timing differences between the payload frame and the link frame. This system allows for integration with SDH systems etc.

6.2.3.1 DS-1 (T-1) Physical Layer Interfaces

The simple "direct mapping" approach as described above is used for the DS-1.

Eighteen DS-1 frames are used to carry a single PLCP frame carrying 10 cells each with a 4-byte "overhead" section. The length of the trailer is 6 bytes. This is only trivially different from the structure shown in Figure 6-5 on page 6-16.

The reason for this is that this frame format (and the PLCP frame used in DS-3) is very similar to the frame format used in SMDS and should provide easy interconnection.

It is likely that the framed format will be used for this protocol.

6.2.3.2 E-1 Physical Layer Interface

In principle, this is the same as the DS-1 procedure described above. The differences relate to the length of the E-1 frame. As with DS-1, the direct mapping approach will be used.

6.2.3.3 E-3 and E-4 Physical Layer Interfaces

The ITU-T is developing a frame structure for use of ATM over E-3 and E-4 services. The E-3 frame uses 59 columns of 9 rows each plus 6 bytes of overhead. The E-4 frame has 240 columns, 9 rows, and 17 bytes of overhead.

6.2.3.4 DS-3 (T-3) Physical Layer Interface

This PLCP protocol is intended to carry ATM within existing (standard) DS-3 (T-3) facilities using a transmission speed of 44.736 Mbps. The structure is shown in Figure 6-5 on page 6-16.

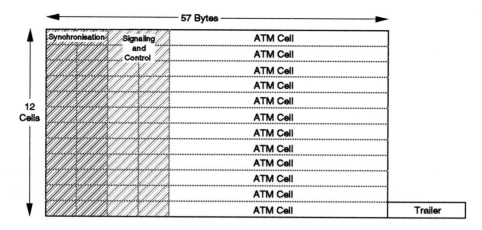

Figure 6-5. DS-3 PLCP Frame

- DS-3 systems use a 125-µsec frame structure. This is retained for ATM.

- Within the DS-3 frame another "PLCP" frame (illustrated) is built.

- This results in 12 cells being sent per frame for a data (cell) throughput rate of 40.704 Mbps.

- The trailer record is nominally 7 bytes long but can vary in half-byte amounts. This allows for adjustment of the frame length to fit exactly within a 125-µsec frame if connected links happen to be running at slightly different speeds.

- Cells fit into a predictable position within the frame and are located by the two synchronization bytes at the beginning of each cell. The HEC is not used for cell delineation.

- The cell payload is usually scrambled to provide a better chance of maintaining synchronization on old-technology equipment.

6.2.4 Non-Framed ("Clear-Channel") Interfaces

6.2.4.1 25.6 Mbps Physical-Layer Interface

This protocol has been approved by the ATM Forum as an interface for local area connection. Sometimes called MUNI (Mid-Range User Network Interface) it uses the same physical signaling (pulse shape etc.) as token-ring. However, the similarity to token-ring stops there as it uses a different data encoding structure. It will, however, operate over any cabling installation that is able to run token-ring protocols.

Cable

One objective of the MUNI is to allow the reuse of existing LAN copper cabling for ATM. The MUNI protocol enables the use of UTP-3, UTP-5, or STP copper cable for distances of 110 meters from the ATM switch (with STP it can be a lot further). These specifications match with the vast majority of installed LAN cabling systems.

Relationship to Token-Ring

The electrical-level signal is the same as for the 16 Mbps token-ring LAN protocol. The token-ring encodes the signal using Differential Manchester coding. The primary reason for this is that for the token-ring to operate properly it must recover a very stable clock signal to synchronize the ring. Jitter adds up around a ring structure and therefore you need an extremely accurate clock recovery mechanism.

This extreme clock stability is provided by the use of Differential Manchester coding. Differential Manchester code gives a minimum of one line state transition per bit but uses two line states (baud) to do it. Thus, a token-ring at 16 Mbps actually runs at 32 Mbaud.

Line Coding

On a point-to-point connection, you do not care too much about jitter at the bit level because the clock does not have to be propagated anywhere. You have to recover accurate data, but after the data is recovered the clock does not matter. This provides us with the opportunity to get a higher data rate without changing the electrical characteristics of the protocol.

MUNI protocol changes the coding to use 4/5 code similar to that used in FDDI (see 6.1.2.1, "Block Coding" on page 6-8). Because we now have 5 line states (bits) representing 4 data bits we end up with 4/5 × 32 Mbaud = 25.6 Mbps (in round figures).

Asynchronous Link Operation

Cells are sent asynchronously. There is no frame structure as with SDH or PDH. That is, each cell begins with a starting delimiter and ends 53 bytes later (there is no ending delimiter). Cells are sent whenever there is a cell to send, but otherwise the link is free. There are no empty cells sent in this protocol.

Idle State

When the line is idle, random data patterns are sent to maintain synchronization between sender and receiver.

Structure

The structure of the adapter is shown in Figure 6-3 on page 6-7. This is the same structure as used in the 100 Mbps multimode fiber PMD described in 6.2.4.2, "100 Mbps (FDDI) Multimode Fiber Physical Layer Interface" on page 6-20. There is one addition and that is that the cells (but not the delimiter characters) are scrambled before encoding.

There are 5 steps involved in sending a cell:

1. Scrambling the cell

2. Block encoding (described in 6.1.2.1, "Block Coding" on page 6-8) including the addition of the start-of-cell delimiter

3. NRZI conversion (described in 6.1.2.2, "NRZI Modulation" on page 6-10

4. Serialization/Deserialisation (SERDES)

5. Physical transmission

The receive process is the same but in reverse with the added need to use a phase-locked loop (PLL) to determine where the bits are in the received signal.

Scrambling

The purpose of scrambling the data is to provide a more even distribution of bit patterns. This assists the transmission by evenly distributing the transmit power over the available frequency spectrum.

The scrambler operates on cell data before (above) the 4B/5B encoding step. Each half-byte (nibble) is separately scrambled.

There is a "pseudo-random" number generator (PRNG) that produces a 10-bit number. The sequence of numbers is called pseudo-random because while it appears to be random in reality it is *exactly* predictable. Once you have the starting number (the seed) and the algorithm used to produce it, you can always produce the same sequence of numbers.

The important thing is that the scrambler must be synchronized (start at the same place in the data) at both ends of the link.

When a data nibble is to be scrambled, the PRNG is used to produce the next 10-bit pseudo-random number. The data nibble is then EORed[8] with the high-order 4 bits of this pseudo-random number.

When the encoded 4 bits are received at the other end of the link, all that is needed is to repeat the encoding process over again. Provided you have syn-

---

8   EOR = Exclusive OR

chronized the PRNG so that the random number used to decode the nibble is the same number that was used to encode it - all you do is EOR the nibble received against the pseudo-random number and you get the original data back.

Scramblers are used in the majority of ATM link protocols.

Code Structure

The code structure used is somewhat different from that used in FDDI. Each data nibble is represented on the line by a 5-bit code. There are 16 data codes (to represent 4 bits) and a single escape code. This escape code produces a unique bit stream which cannot be formed by the concatenation of other codes.

When the receiver needs to synchronize with the transmitter it looks at the bit stream and when it finds a sequence of bits that matches the escape code then it knows that it has nibble (and byte) alignment.

There are three command bytes each of which is composed of the escape nibble concatenated with one of the 17 legal codes (16 data and escape itself). The first half of a command byte is therefore always the escape nibble. There are three command bytes defined:

- X_X Start of cell with scrambler/descrambler reset
- X_4 Start of cell without scrambler/descrambler reset
- X_8 125-μsec timing signal

125-μsec Strobe Signal

Because cells are sent asynchronously, and there is no framed transmission structure, propagation of the system clock is not an automatic by-product of the link protocol. However, for handling many situations involving isochronous or synchronous data transfer, we need to have a reference clock signal propagated throughout the network.

This is done by inserting a special (8-bit) "strobe" character (X_8) into the data stream exactly every 125 μsec. This 125-μsec strobe character can be inserted between any two characters in the data stream (byte aligned).

Rationale

The great benefit of the MUNI protocol is its simplicity and therefore its low cost.

1. The transmission system used is (compared with others) very simple and widely available as it is the same as that used for token-ring.

2. In the ATM switch, the lower data rate and economical transmission system will enable the concentration of many 25.6 Mbps ports onto a single switch port, thus minimizing the per-attachment cost of the ATM switch.

3. Very simple OA&M functions have been defined because in the LAN environment for which this is intended you do not need the kind of OA&M complexity required in the long-line (SDH/PDH) environment.

Relevance

The vast majority of ISA bus PCs (even 486 and above) have no chance at all of being able to sustain a full-duplex data rate of 25.6 Mbps. Only a very few PCs of any kind can make meaningful use of the full rate and this does not look set to change in the immediate future.[9] A 50 Mbps or faster adapter would cost more both on the adapter card and in the ATM switch and provide no greater throughput.

6.2.4.2 100 Mbps (FDDI) Multimode Fiber Physical Layer Interface

At the time of writing, products using this physical link protocol are already available from a number of manufacturers.

The concept here is to use the PMD protocol from FDDI unchanged. A block diagram of the transmitter is shown in Figure 6-3 on page 6-7. This allows the use of available chipsets and means that products can be delivered into the field earlier. The protocol is often referred to as "Taxi" because that is the name of a popular FDDI chipset that implements this protocol.

The protocol is block encoded (as described in 6.1.2.1, "Block Coding" on page 6-8) and does not use framing. When there is nothing to send on the link, idles are sent instead of empty cells. A cell may be sent at any time provided the link is not already sending another cell.

Physical Media: While the protocol is primarily defined for use of graded index multimode fiber, other media types can also be used:

- Multimode fiber

  It is intended that this will be the predominant medium for this protocol type. Using MM fiber, maximum transmission distances will be around 3 km.

- Single-mode fiber

  This is included in the FDDI standard but as yet has had only minor usage - because of the cost. Without repeaters the maximum distance possible will be 20 to 30 kilometers (depending on the equipment specifications and the fiber loss characteristics).

---

[9] Workstations and specialist servers are a different matter.

- Shielded Twisted Pair (STP) copper wire

  The use of STP cable, while it does not have the electrical isolation advantages of fiber, is significantly less than the cost of using fiber. This PMD protocol could be a realistic alternative for the desktop workstation. Over STP this will work at distances of a few hundred meters.

Media Specifications: This PMD is specified to use either single-mode or multimode fiber at a wavelength of 1,300 nanometers. The standard multimode fiber specification is 62.5/125, but the other sizes of 50/125, 85/125, and 100/140 are optional alternatives. The mode field diameter for single-mode fiber is 9 microns. In multimode operation, an LED is usually used as the light source (rather than a laser) and the detector is usually a PIN diode (rather than an avalanche photo diode).

The power levels are expressed in dBm.[10] Two different transmitter power ranges and two different receiver sensitivity "categories" are specified. These are:

Transmit Power Cat. 1 = From $-$ 20 *dBm* to $-$ 14 *dBm*

Transmit Power Cat. 2 = From $-$ 4 *dBm* to 0 *dBm*

Receiver Sensitivity Cat. 1 = From $-$ 31 *dBm* to $-$ 14 *dBm*

Receiver Sensitivity Cat. 2 = From $-$ 37 *dBm* to $-$ 15 *dBm*

A typical transceiver may have the following specification:

```
Input:  -16 dBm
Output: -27 dBm
```

(Input and output here refer to the optical cable.) What this says is that this transmitter transmits at a power level of -16 dBm and that the associated receiver is able to handle a signal of -27 dBm. In this implementation this means that you have 11 dB for loss in cables etc. If this cable loses 3 dB per kilometer, then if devices are two kilometers apart the cable loss will be 6 dB and there is 5 dB left over for losses in splices and connectors etc.

---

[10] This is a measure of absolute power. The signal level in decibels in relation to one milliwatt. Thus 3 dBm is 3 dB above 1 milliwatt (3 dBm = 2 mw). -6 dBm is 6 dB below one mw (-6 dBm = .25 mw).

6.2.4.3 155 Mbps (Fiber Channel) Block Encoded

This transmission system uses the physical components from the FCS (Fiber Channel System). Fiber channel is a fiber-optical I/O connection system designed for computer I/O channel use. It is available in a number of link speeds. Fiber channel tranceivers are now available up to 1 Gbps and beyond. The desire here is to use available components in ATM rather than invent new ones.

The link encoding uses 8/10 code. Eight data bits are coded as 10 bits on the fiber giving a line rate of 194.4 Mbaud.

This is similar in principle to the 25 Mbps system described before except that there is a framing system used. Data is sent in frames of 26 ATM cells and one "overhead" cell per frame. The frame structure is very simple and is shown in Figure 6-6.

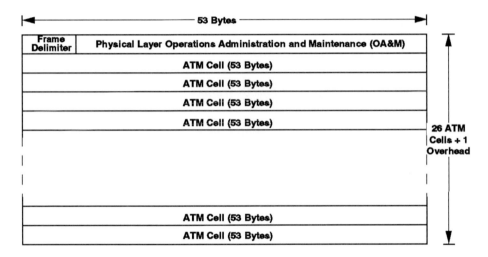

Figure 6-6. 155 Mbps (Fiber Channel) PLCP Frame

Notice that each frame is **not** synchronized to the system 125-μsec clock. In fact, there is a frame every 73.61 μsec. This is done because the amount of overhead in the Sonet/SDH system is exactly 1/27th of link capacity. By using this structure (an "overhead" of 1/27th of link capacity) we get a net cell rate of *exactly* the same (149.76 Mbps) as STM-1. This makes direct connection of the two transmission systems very easy.

However, in many applications it is necessary to propagate the system 125-μsec clock. This is done by inserting a special (8-bit) "strobe" character into the data stream exactly every 125 μsec. (The underlying block coding allows this character to be sent transparently.) This 125-μsec strobe character can be inserted between any two characters in the data stream.

6.2.5 Under Development

There are several new physical-layer ATM interfaces currently under discussion within standards bodies. Two important ones are:

- LAN workstation connection at 622 Mbps

- Plastic fiber in the local area

6.2.5.1 622 Mbps in the Local Area

This proposal is for a very low-cost, short-distance (300 meters maximum) connection at 622 Mbps over multimode fiber (or STP). Its important features are as follows:

- Maximum specified distance 300 meters (but 500 is possible with the current proposal)

- Multimode, graded-index fiber with SC connectors

- STM-4c framing, but no use of the management channels in the TDM structure

- 800-850 nm transmitter wavelength

  This is critical. It enables the use of "CD lasers" (that is, the lasers from CD-ROM players) which are very low in component cost (perhaps 10% of the cost of typical optical tranceivers currently in use).

- Relatively high transmitter power (-4 dBm)

  This allows the use of a low-cost, "pin diode" receiver. You are limited here by the standards set for optical safety. Minus 4 dBm is about 1/3rd of a milliwatt - a tiny amount of power but is currently the maximum power allowed for optical safety without the need for protective measures (these standards are currently being revised).

- Link budget of 10 dB

  This will cover the losses of six connectors (.3 dB each) and 300 meters of cable with quite a wide margin for component aging, tolerances, etc.

This ATM Forum implementation agreement is due for completion by the end of 1995. How long it will be before implementation in real products is an unknown. At the present time, there is no PC and very few workstations that can actually use 155 Mbps, let alone 622 Mbps, but this will come in the future. Since this is a relatively short-distance technology it is felt it will be used for desktop-workstation-to-hub connections but *not* for backbone connections.

6.2.5.2 Plastic Optical Fiber (POF)

This is a very new proposal but looks very promising indeed for applications of ATM where low cost is of prime importance.

POF has a very high attenuation (in the best window around 66 dB per km - many times greater than glass) but it has a very big cost advantage. While the fiber itself costs about the same as glass, the cost of joining connectors to the fiber is very low. A minimally trained person can fit a connector to a POF in about 1 minute with a special tool costing a few dollars. With a bit more skill it can be done in two or three minutes and with a razor blade. Joining a connector to a glass fiber on the other hand requires much more training, an expensive special tool and about 15 minutes. A typical local connection consists of 6 joins (that is, 12 connectors).

Indeed POF promises to be the fiber world's UTP. Low cost, bad transmission environment, but adequate for most purposes.

POF has significantly different parameters from glass fiber:

- The best transmission windows are in the visible light range: around 550 nm and between 620 nm and 650 nm (dark red).

  This means that you have to find transmitters and receivers capable of operating in this range. Existing communications tranceivers used for glass fiber won't work here.

- The fiber itself is about 1 mm in diameter (very thick compared to glass). This means that dispersion is potentialy a significant factor which may limit the possible distance.

- The proposed signal is the 155 Mbps (STS-3c) based protocol as defined by the ATM Forum (UNI 3.1 specification).

- The currently proposed maximum distance is 300 meters.

Communicating over fishing line will certainly be a novelty! Nevertheless this looks to be a very serious contender for ATM in the home environment where low cost and easy installation are overriding considerations.

6.2.6 Data eXchange Interface (DXI)

This identifies not a single interface but a large family of interfaces that are not really ATM interfaces but are ones that we might wish to use for ATM (especially in the short term).

These interfaces are sometimes called "RVX" interfaces. RVX comes from R-series, V-series and X-series interfaces. The most common of these interfaces are V.24 (RS-232), V.35, X.21, and RS-422. Recently, the interface HSSI (High Speed Serial Interface) has been added to the list.

The ATM Forum has released a specification for operation of these interfaces with ATM and it is very likely that V.35, X.21, and RS-422 will get significant use for ATM in the early years as a migration strategy.

Chapter 7. Switching ATM Cells

Perhaps the key factor which makes ATM possible is the ability to build switching devices which will process cells at the extremely high rates required. The "state-of-the-art" data rate for a single channel on an optical fiber in 1995 is 2 Gbps.[1] At 2 Gbps, an ATM link transmits cells at the rate of 4 million per second *in each direction*.

In other parts of this book we have discussed the features of ATM which are intended to make switching cells at extremely high rates possible. This chapter will discuss the switching process and the design of equipment to do this.

7.1.1 An ATM Switching Node

The simplest form of an ATM switch is illustrated in Figure 7-1.

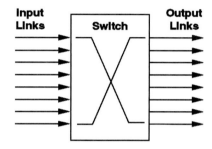

Figure   *7-1.* *ATM Switch Schematic*

A number of communication links are connected with some receiving cells and others transmitting them. These links, while logically separate, are paired such that one inbound and one outbound connection are joined to form a physical full-duplex link. Cells are received by the switch and retransmitted on one of the outbound links according to the routing rules of ATM.

The core of the switching process is as follows:

1. A cell is received on an inbound link and its header is examined to determine on which outbound link it must be forwarded.

2. The VPI/VCI fields are changed to new values appropriate to the outbound link.

---

[1] Laser tranceivers are commercially available at this speed, although significantly higher speeds (such as 12 Gbps) have been achieved in research.

3. The cell is retransmitted towards its destination on an outbound link.

4. During this process the system is constrained to deliver cells to the appropriate output port in the same sequence as they arrive. This applies to each VC (there is no requirement to retain the sequence of cells on a VP provided that on each VC the cells remain in sequence).

There are many other tasks that a real switching node must perform such as:

- While there is no request/response protocol at the link level of ATM, handling the serial link protocol for the attached communication links is still a significant task. For example, links may use framed protocols (SDH or PDH) which require significant logic for transmission or reception.

- When a cell is received, its HEC (Header Error Check) field must be checked and the cell discarded if an error is found (this is necessary to avoid mis-routing of cells). When a cell is transmitted the HEC field must be calculated and inserted into the cell.

- If the ATM links are at the UNI (User-to-Network) interface, then there is a need to enforce rate control protocols on a per VC basis.

- In a real system, attached links will usually run at different speeds. The switching node must be able to handle the switching of cells between links of different speeds.

- The switch must have a mechanism for handling congestion (although this mechanism may well be the simple discard of cells when congestion occurs).

- There must be a control mechanism for updating VPI/VCI connection tables in creating new semi-permanent connections ("cross connects") or real switched connections.

- There must be an OA&M (Operations Administration and Maintenance) system to perform the following functions:

  - Setup, operation, and control of the network

  - Fault diagnosis and reporting

- A system for collecting billing information.

- Many practical ATM switching nodes will provide the ability to attach non-ATM links (such as frame relay or voice). In this case, they will need extensive processing to:

  - Segment long data blocks into cells or to assemble a continuous bit stream (such as a voice conversation) into cells.

  - Provide the ATM AAL processing function.

  - Handle (and terminate) the native link protocol of a non-ATM connection.

Perhaps the most important requirements for an ATM switching node are:

1. They must be able to switch cells at the very high speeds of the attached links. This means cell-switching rates of many millions per second.

2. It must be possible to construct switching nodes with very large numbers of attached links (several thousands).

3. It must be possible to construct quite small nodes in a cost-effective way.

7.1.2 Processing the ATM Routing Header

The process of switching an ATM cell is illustrated in Figure 7-2.

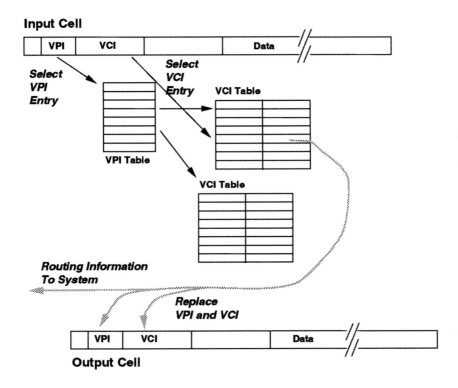

Figure *7-2. The ATM Switching Process*

It is important to note that the process relies on keeping connection tables for each VP or VC connection to be recognized by the switch. *There is a separate set of tables for each inbound link.* (This is because the VPI and VCI fields are only unique within the context of a particular link.)

In the figure, a two-level table structure is shown. This is because you can switch on the basis of the VP only (in which case there is no need to reference the VCI table) or (if the VP terminates in this node) you switch on both VPI and VCI and hence must reference both tables. The objective of the process is to determine the onward routing for the cell and the new VPI/VCI values appropriate to the outbound link on which the cell will be sent.

Operation is as follows:[2]

1. A cell is received and the VPI is used to locate an entry within the VPI table.

2. From the table it is determined whether the VP terminates in this node or not.

3. If the VPC is switched (does not terminate) then the new VPI number and the outbound routing information are fetched from the VPI table. (Only the VPI needs to be replaced here because the VCI does not change). This case is not shown in the figure.

4. If the VPC terminates in this node then the VCI is used to locate the appropriate entry in the VCI table. (Note there is a separate VCI table for each terminating VPC.)

5. The new VPI and VCI values and the onward routing information are then recovered from the VCI table.

6. The cell is then updated with the new VPI/VCI values and routed towards its destination using the routing information recovered from the table.

Some points to note:

- The routing information retrieved from the table will be quite different in nature depending on the design of the switching node.

  - If the node has the "traditional" architecture,[3] then the routing information will most likely consist of the address of a control block on which the outbound cell is to be queued.

  - If the switch is a bus or backplane type of switch, then the outbound link address will consist of an adapter bus address and a link number denoting which outbound link to use on the selected output adapter.

  - If the switch is of the multistage, "self-routing" (source-routing) type, then the information will consist of a path to be followed by the cell through the switch fabric to reach its destination link.

---

[2] A description of logical ID swapping in ATM is given in 2.4.3, "Logical ID Swapping in ATM" on page 2-18.

[3] As described in 7.2.1, "Traditional Approach" on page 7-5.

- The table structure as shown is conceptual. The ATM header at the UNI has 8 bits for the VPI and 16 bits for the VCI. At the NNI the VPI field has 12 bits. You do not have time in any real system to scan a table by software and find the correct entry. However, if you plan to index into the table using the VPI/VCI values then (unless something is done) the space required for the tables could become extremely large (a thousand megabytes or so). The solution is that you are allowed to limit the number of bits used for VPI/VCIs. For example, you could decide on a particular link to use only three bits (the low-order three) for VPI and perhaps 6 bits for VCI (again the low-order bits). Both sending and receiving nodes attached to a link need to use the same limit.

If we were building a very fast VP-only switch (say for trunk line applications), then we could use a hardware table lookup technique called "associative memory". Associative memories compare an input argument to every entry of a table (and retrieve information from the table) on one hardware memory cycle. These are commonly used in the address translation look-aside buffers in virtual storage memory systems and in high-speed buffer memories (to translate a presented main storage address to the real address in the high-speed buffer). The great advantage of an associative memory is that you only need an entry for each *active* VPI or VCI, and there is no wasted table space for unused entries. The technique is also exceedingly fast. However, it is of course more expensive to implement than simple table indexing.

In a real system using switched VCCs, there could be a significant rate of setup and clearing of switched connections. The process of setting up or of clearing a connection involves updating (changing) tables all along the path of the particular connection. There must be a mechanism within the switch to allow the update of these tables without disruption to the ongoing switching of cells.

7.2 Potential Switch Architectures

A major challenge in the implementation of very high-speed networks is in the design of the cell switch itself. There are three general approaches to this but the serial multistage design has the greater potential throughput.

7.2.1 Traditional Approach

In the traditional approach, the switching node is based on a general-purpose computer design (although this is often modified to assist in specialized communications tasks). This approach is not very useful for ATM switching as it has very severe throughput limitations. It is, however, the basis for the overwhelming number of packet switches in existence today.

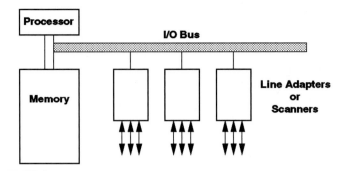

Figure **7-3.** *Traditional Packet Switch Architecture*

The principle is as follows:

- I/O adapters connected to a common bus receive data and place it into the system memory.

- When a block of data is received, the processor is interrupted.

- The processor may have several tasks to perform depending on the detailed switch architecture. For example, it may need to execute the link control protocol, or alternatively this may have already been done outboard.

  However, the processor's main task now is to identify the destination of the data block and direct it to that destination (that is, to perform the switching function). This usually takes the form of requeueing the data block to an outbound link queue.

- When the selected outbound link finishes the task it is doing, another interrupt is received by the processor, the data is removed from the link queue, and transmission is started (by the processor).

The details of this process vary widely between different implementations, but the key points are that the data passes over the bus *twice* and that the processor is required to decide on the destination of the received data block.

The tasks to be performed by either the line adapters or the processor when data is received include:

1. Detection of the boundaries of characters and assembling bits into characters. Associated with this is the task of recognizing control characters and sequences.

2. Detection and synchronization of the boundaries between blocks of data.

3. Transfer of the data and control information into the memory.

4. Processing the logic of link control.

5. Processing the switching logic.

6. Processing control and management logic.

There are similar tasks to be performed when data is transmitted.

Depending on the switch design some (or all) of these functions, except the switching logic, may be performed outboard of the main processor.

The architecture of the IBM 3705/3725/3745 family of communications controllers is a good example of the traditional packet switching approach. In the first IBM 3705 all these functions were performed by the controller program (even assembling bits into characters). All that the link adapter (called a "Type 1 Scanner") did was to send and receive single bits.[4] In the most recent 3745 hardware, everything up to and including the link control logic is performed outboard, either in hardware or in an outboard programmable processor.

While this architecture is very flexible, it is limited by processor speed, contention for the common I/O bus, and contention for the memory. This architecture can and will be used for connection of systems *to* an ATM network (the ATM AAL functions can be performed outboard in the line adapter), but it is unlikely that this architecture will be found useful for high-throughput ATM switching nodes.

7.2.2 Crosspoint Switches

Crosspoint or "space division" switches as illustrated in Figure 7-4 are a very common technology.

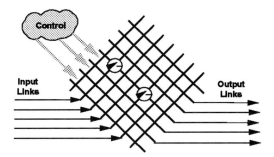

Figure *7-4. Crosspoint (Space Division) Switching*

---

4 The IBM 3705 was a RISC processor by any test - except that the machine was developed many years before the acronym RISC was invented. If you are going to handle several hundred links, a single bit at a time, by program, the processor had better be fast.

For many years this was the predominant technology used in telephone exchanges and in PBX equipment and probably still represents the majority of installed equipment. The term "crossbar" is often used as a substitute for the word "crosspoint"; however, this is incorrect since crossbar switches are merely one type of crosspoint switch. (The IBM 2750 and IBM 3750 line of PBX equipment were crosspoint switches but certainly not crossbar.)

The concept is very simple:

- Inputs are connected to a number of parallel data paths (not connected to each other).

- Outputs are likewise connected to parallel data paths.

- The data paths (in the simple case, they can be just single wires) are connected in the form of a matrix as shown in the diagram.

- At each intersection of data paths (crosspoint) there is a switch.

- Any input can be connected to any output simply by turning on the appropriate switch. Note that this implies the existence of a separate control structure to operate the switch.

- Only one input may be connected to any one output at a time, but (potentially) a single input could be connected to multiple outputs.

It is obvious that this is circuit switching rather than packet switching. When a connection is present there is a synchronous connection between input and output (that is, a circuit).

It would be possible to use such a switch for ATM cell switching. What you need to do is make very short connections, just long enough for a single cell to be transferred. This would have the advantage that there is no blocking within the switch fabric at all (blocking on output is possible when two inputs request connection to the same output). The other advantage is that it is extremely simple. There are a number of problems however:

1. The number of required crosspoints is the square of the number of ports on the switch. As the switch grows in size the cost grows exponentially. This characteristic was a major reason (but not the only reason) for the recent abandonment of crosspoint switches in favor of TDM buses within telephone equipment.

   You can reduce this problem by structuring the switch such that inputs and outputs are not connected directly to each other but through a set of intermediate data paths (almost all "crossbar" telephone exchanges do this). However, when you adopt this structure you remove the main advantage of the crosspoint switch, namely its non-blocking characteristic. What happens is that you have a finite number of data paths within the switch which is less (to be economic it has to be a lot less) than the number of connections to the switch. The net is that you get the possibility of blocking within the switch (the case where an input requests connection to a vacant output but the connection cannot be made due to the unavailability of data paths).

2. The switch must be controlled by a centralized logic function (as shown in the figure). When the switch gets very large, the rate of requests to the control element grows as well. Queueing delay and contention within the control element is considered to be a major problem limiting the throughput of very large (1000 x 1000) switches.

3. There needs to be a complex interaction between each input adapter and the switch to request a connection before a cell is sent.

4. If data paths are to be parallel (to optimize technology cost) then a very large number of switch elements is required.

7.2.3 Bus/Backplane Switches

In this design, there are a number of separate adapter cards each of which connects one or more external links. These cards are really miniature switching nodes in their own right and often have an architecture similar to the "traditional" switch architecture described in 7.2.1, "Traditional Approach" on page 7-5.

All switch functions including routing are performed on each adapter card. Data transfer between adapter cards is done on a "backplane". The backplane is a parallel bus capable of transferring many bits in parallel (typically 64 or 128 bits at a time). As illustrated in Figure 7-5, all adapters connect to this backplane.

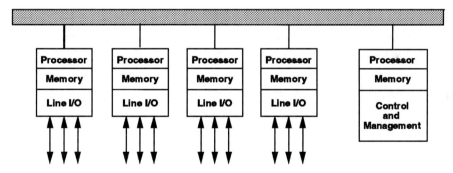

Figure 7-5. *Backplane (Bus) Switch Architecture.* The control processor is not involved in data flow.

The backplane has a high throughput by virtue of the parallelism of data transfer. However, it has significant disadvantages:

- Total system throughput is the throughput of the backplane (because only one adapter can be sending at any one time).

- There is considerable overhead in arbitration (deciding which adapter can use the backplane next).

- Backplanes get slower and less effective the longer they are. You cannot have more than a fairly small number of adapters before the whole system is slowed down.

- Each adapter must be built to handle data transfer at the peak backplane speed (because that is the transfer speed), although the average transfer rate of that adapter may be many times lower than the peak. This serves to increase the system cost.

Structures like this are also used by many devices and, in general, have a higher throughput possibility than more traditional switches, but the throughput limitation imposed by the finite bus speed limits their usefulness.

In 1990/91 IBM developed a backplane switch for use in trial ATM networks. This was named "plaNET". A plaNET switch can have a maximum of 8 adapters each operating at just above 1.1 Gbps simultaneously. Further information about the plaNET research project can be obtained from the publications listed in the bibliography.

7.2.4 Multistage Designs

The simplest form of serial stage-by-stage switching is the "Banyan" switching network shown in Figure 7-6.

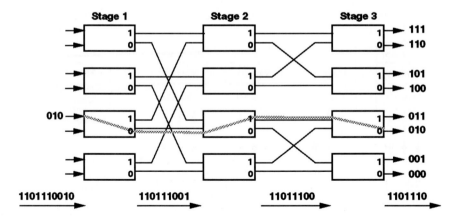

Figure **7-6.** *Banyan Switch*

The concept here is very simple:

1. Each box in the switching matrix represents a single switching element.

2. Each switching element has two inputs and two outputs.

3. The switching elements are connected via serial (one bit at a time) link connections.

4. Input and output links are considered to be quite separate although in a practical switch inputs and outputs are paired to form full-duplex connections.

Operation is as follows:

1. When a stream of bits (block of data to be switched) arrives at an input, then the switching element uses the *first bit received* to determine on which of its two output links the data is to be sent.

2. The bit used to determine the routing is discarded and the block is sent onward to the next switch stage where the same process is repeated.

3. In the figure, the progress of a block of data with a routing header of 010 is shown as it progresses through the switch fabric. *Note that the order of transmission of the bits in the figure is from right to left. So the bit stream "1101110010" is transmitted with the 0 bit first.*

   a. Stage 1 sees that the first bit arriving is a zero, discards it and establishes a (temporary) connection between the input link on which the data is arriving and its 0 output link.

   b. The data is shown leaving stage 1 with the first (0) bit removed.

   c. The process is repeated at stage 2 and then again at stage 3.

   d. Data is output from the switching fabric on the correct output link (destination 010).

   e. Output data has had the routing header (010) removed.

4. Notice here that at each switch stage there has been *minimal* buffering of the data (perhaps 3 bits). This means that switch operation is synchronous from end to end. The beginning of a data block is being output from the switch before its end has been received.

Banyan switching is very simple, modular, and expandable and presents minimal delay in the transit of data through the switch. There is however a significant problem. This is illustrated in Figure 7-7 on page 7-12. If two blocks of data passing through the switch at any time need to use a common link (switch output), then a collision occurs. This problem is severe and has prevented the wide use of pure Banyan switching systems.

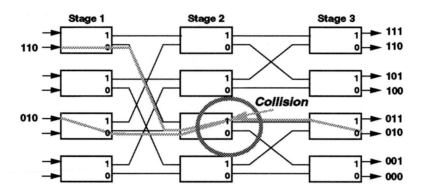

Figure   *7-7. Collision in Banyan Switch*

The obvious solution to the problem of collisions is to buffer the data within each switch element as it arrives and only switch it onwards when its destination link is free. (This usually means waiting for the whole block of data or cell to be received before forwarding it onwards.) A switch element using "input buffering" is shown on the left in Figure 7-8.

Indeed, input buffering as illustrated improves the operation of the switching fabric significantly. However, operation can be improved still further by buffering at the output of the switch element (shown on the right-hand side of Figure 7-8).

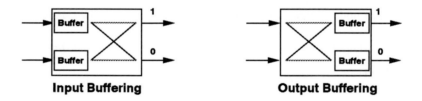

Input Buffering   **Output Buffering**

Figure   *7-8. Buffering in Banyan Switch Elements*

But then the question arises: "How much buffering should we use". Multiple buffers improve the operation of the switch still further, but each additional buffer gives diminishing returns compared to the last one and since they have to be added at each connection point add significantly to the cost. This is discussed in 7.3, "Performance" on page 7-18.

While buffering can alleviate the effects of collisions, some collisions can be avoided entirely and this reduces the need for buffering and provides significantly better performance.

Two kinds of collision (output link blocking) can be distinguished:

1. A collision (as illustrated in Figure 7-7 on page 7-12) can take place within the switch fabric itself. This is called "internal link blocking".

2. A collision can take place at an output port (called "output blocking").

Internal link blocking can be eliminated entirely if the packets presented at the input to the Banyan network are sorted into order by destination address. An elegant solution to this is called the "Batcher Bitonic Sort Network" and is illustrated in Figure 7-9.

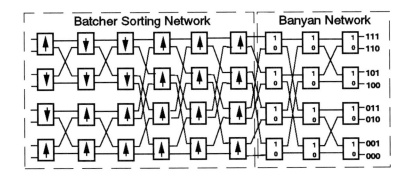

Figure *7-9. Batcher/Banyan Network*

The Batcher network sorts packets into ascending order according to their destination addresses. Each node compares the destination addresses of the two packets sent to it and sends them to their outputs according to which one has the higher (or lower) address. When there is only one packet presented at the input it is sent out on the lower-numbered output. In Figure 7-9, the direction of the arrows shows the sorting order.

Batcher/Banyan multistage networks are quite practical and their use has been reported in the literature for some early ATM switch designs.

7.2.4.1 Principles of Multistage Switching

In the professional literature, there are reported in excess of 50 different multistage switch designs. The paper by Daddis and Torng [5] classifies them into 15 categories. Banyan networks, therefore, are only one possibility out of very many. Other types of network are called "Delta", "Benes", "Omega", "Clos", etc. Many variations on the Banyan network exist, the most famous being the "Batcher Banyan". Variations are called "Parallel Banyans", "Expanded Banyans", "Distributed Network Banyans", and many others.

The general concept is as follows:

- A large switch is built up from many small, identical switching elements.

- Each switching element has at least two inputs and two outputs. It is obvious here that the more inputs and outputs are provided on a single switching element stage the fewer stages will be needed to handle a given number of ports. Fewer stages means lower latency through the network since there is a necessary delay at each switching stage.

- The switching elements are interconnected by (serial or parallel) links in a structure such that data can be routed from any input to any output.

- The header of a data block (or cell) contains routing information to control the path through the switching fabric.

- Most current switches are buffered (either in the input or output) and receive a cell in full before directing the packet to an output port.

- Most proposed multistage switch designs (though certainly not all) specify a short, fixed-length packet (or cell). This simplifies the design of buffering mechanisms within switching elements and has a number of other effects which improve performance.

There are many advantages to this architecture:

1. It leads to a low-cost implementation since a single switch element (indeed many more than one) can be accommodated on a single chip. Individual switch elements can be very simple.

2. Such switches are easy to build and are scalable in regard to the number of attached links. (Not all architectures scale too easily as link speed is increased, however.)

3. It is relatively easy to build multistage switches with a large number of ports. This contrasts with a bus-based design where the physical length of the bus (and the necessary arbitration logic) can be a significant limitation on the number of possible attaching adapters.

4. In a multistage switch design, the switch elements themselves need to operate only at a speed consistent with their own requirements. This should be contrasted with a bus style design where the adapter interface circuitry must run at the speed of the bus, which is many times faster than necessary for data transfer to/from the adapter itself. At the speeds being considered here, this can amount to a large difference in cost.

5. The total switch throughput is very high since (with random traffic) the maximum system throughput is the number of stations **times** the link speed **times** two (links are FDX).

But there are also disadvantages:

1. Congestion control is very difficult in the case where traffic is non-random. That is, if all traffic is to or from a small number of servers, then congestion can become a real problem.

2. Each switch element in a network configuration adds a delay (although a small one) to the cell transit time.

3. Because of the simplicity in switching and routing it is difficult to interface external link connections directly. External link connections often use structured link protocols (such as Sonet/SDH) for control[5] and in any case have the ATM routing algorithm to process. This leads to the separation of the link attachments into external adapters.

7.2.4.2 Architectural Issues

There are four main topics to be addressed when considering multistage switch architecture:

Interconnection Structure

There are many possible alternative interconnection structures.

It is important to remember that one of the principal requirements in ATM is that cells must be delivered by the system in the same order as they were presented to the system (at least within an individual VCC).

Another requirement is that cells must not be duplicated within the system and the loss of cells (through discard) should be minimized.

Routing Data

Depending on how intelligent you can make the switching elements, and how much interaction you want to have with the control processor, you can use almost any routing architecture here. In principle, you could use VPI/VCI label swapping to route within the switch, but this is not really practical. If full routing tables are kept in each switching element, then they will require (potentially) a large amount of storage and continuous updating from the control processor. There is very little time between arriving cells.

Most multistage switch designs use a form of source routing within the switch fabric and isolate the ATM label-swapping operation to the point at which external links are connected. Another issue for the switch architecture is the handling of broadcast and multicast traffic. Some protocols (LAN emulation,

---

5 SDH in itself is not too complex to handle, but it provides excellent OA&M facilities and the interface to these requires software code.

for example) require the ability to broadcast. In addition, the tasks of network control and management can be implemented significantly more efficiently using multicasting. A methodology is needed for the switch to handle broadcast without creating too much congestion.

Contention Resolution and Buffering

No matter what we do there is always a probability of congestion within a packet switch. If all inputs unexpectedly decide to transfer large data files to a single output, there will be congestion and there needs to be some process to handle it.

In very high-speed switches the primary method of relieving congestion is to discard packets. Input rate controls are relied upon to adjust traffic rates to whatever the network can accommodate.

Within a communications system, there will always be places where blocking can occur. This happens for example at each output port on a switching element. In general, it can happen at any point where data can be delivered at a faster rate than it can be forwarded. At each of these points there are four possible alternatives:

1. Discard any data in excess of that which can be forwarded.

2. Provide a "back-pressure" mechanism to allow input to be refused without data loss.

3. Use a synchronous connection-oriented technique (circuit switching) so that a path through the switching network is dedicated to one particular user.

4. Provide buffering so that data can be held in a queue for the output function.

It must be emphasized that queueing is only necessary (or possible) at a blocking point. If data can be forwarded away from a particular point in a network at the maximum rate at which it can be delivered to that point, then there is no purpose in having a queue.

Buffering is a question which has been the subject of a considerable amount of research but cannot be considered in isolation. The method of buffering used is critically linked to the way other aspects of the switching network operate such as its addressing structure, its interconnection system, and its congestion control. It is not easy to separate the question of buffering from discussions about the design of the switching network itself.

Some types of multistage switch and their buffering schemes are examined in 7.3, "Performance" on page 7-18. For each type of switching network there are many questions: Should data be buffered on input (before the switching decision is made) or on output, in both places, or not at all? This depends, of course, on where the points of contention (blocking) are.

Systems that buffer on output are currently believed to offer significant advantages over systems that buffer on input.

The need for buffering in individual switch elements is subject to quite wide statistical variation. If each input or output link needs to have its own buffer space rather than the shared buffer pool of the traditional packet switch case, then you need much greater (three or more times greater) total buffer space. This is because when you use a shared buffer space the variations experienced on individual links tend to smooth out statistically.

Control and Management Processor

In order to set up and control the individual switching elements, and to provide management, an external processor or perhaps multiple processors are needed.

The tasks of the control processor consist of:

- Initializing switching elements
- Activating and inactivating ports
- Keeping routing tables in switching elements up to date
- Monitoring congestion
- Collecting management information

The management system provides a wider system control and management function.

The biggest problem about the control and management processor is how to connect it to the switching elements. The tempting way is through the switching fabric, but for control functions this is not a good idea because a malfunction in the switching process could prevent the control processor from getting in to correct it. The usual resolution is to provide a separate data path from the control processor to each switching element. This is often done by attaching each switching element to a microprocessor bus. The management processor is usually separate and communicates with the control processor through the switching fabric.

7.2.4.3 Characteristics

Multistage switching networks in general have the following characteristics:

- They are capable of very high throughput rates.
- They are very modular and scalable - as you add links the total capacity adjusts.
- They lend themselves to relatively low-cost implementation.
- They need external adapters to interface the external link and routing protocols to the internal routing algorithm of the switching system itself.

7.3 Performance

Figures 7-10 to 7-15 show the results of performance studies on switch designs and queueing principles for a number of possible switch designs. In the performance studies, input cells are generated on each input port for randomly determined destinations. If the input was non-random (for example, if each input had traffic for only one output), and there was no blocking on internal paths within the switch, we would be able to send data at maximum link speed on all inputs without queueing and without the discard of cells. This non-random input case is what determines the maximum possible throughput (in the graphs this is a load of 1.0).

Crossbar with Input Queueing

This is quite a surprising result. Even though the internals of the crossbar switch are completely non-blocking, the maximum throughput (with infinite input queue length and therefore infinite delay) is about .6.

The cause of this result is that when two input queues have data for the same destination, one of them must wait. In the queue for the waiting port there will be cells waiting behind the blocked cell that could have been sent had they been at the head of the queue (because the output they are destined for is free). Thus, much of the switch capacity is wasted. This is called "head-of-queue blocking".

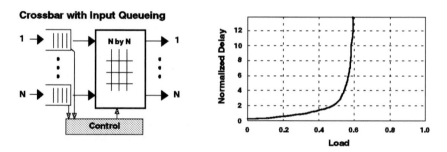

Figure 7-10. *Crossbar with Input Queueing*

Crossbar with Multiple Input Queueing

If we have multiple queues at *each* input port (that is, one queue for each possible destination), then we improve the situation dramatically - in fact we approach an optimal case. (With random input you can never get to 100% throughput.)

At each input to the crossbar there is a selection device such that if a cell directed to a particular output cannot be sent, because the output port is in use, then it will try other waiting cells to see if they can be sent instead.

The problem with this is obvious. You are going to build a very large number of queues and require a very large amount of storage. For example, a 16-by-16 switch would need 256 queues of perhaps 4 elements each.

Crossbar with Multiple Input Queueing

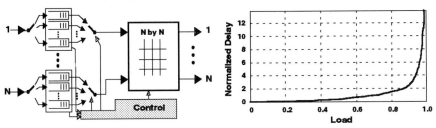

Figure **7-11.** *Crossbar with Multiple Input Queueing*

But now that we have identified each cell and queued it according to its destination, why not share the input queues for each destination? Indeed, why not? This is a sleight of hand - what happens is that now you do not need the crossbar switch at all because there is already a unique queue for each output. To do this you have introduced a *new* switching function on the other side of the queues! So, the crossbar switch disappears, a new input switch is added and the input queues suddenly become output queues. This new case is called "Self-Route with Output Queueing."

Self-Route with Output Queueing

This diagram applies to a non-blocking switch with individual (infinite length) output queues. This case also gives excellent performance.

Self-Route with Output Queueing

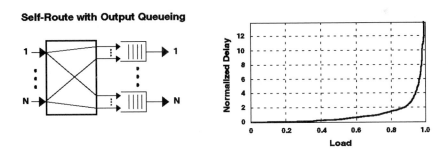

Figure **7-12.** *Self-Route with Output Queueing*

Self-Route with Finite Output Queueing

In the real world, queue memory costs money and we cannot build an infinite queue. The diagram in Figure 7-13 on page 7-20 shows the effect of varying the length of finite (short) output queues. As with most systems of this kind, as the number of queue elements increases there is diminishing benefit to be gained.

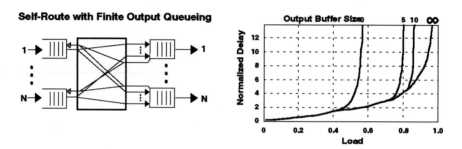

Figure 7-13. *Self-Route with Finite Output Queueing*

Self-Route with Shared Output Queueing

Figure 7-14 shows what happens when you share the output queue. When a single memory is dynamically shared between all output queues you achieve a dramatically reduced total buffer space requirement (a reduction to about 1/3 of the requirement in the case of no sharing). Another way of looking at it is to say that for the same amount of buffer space, performance is significantly enhanced in the case of a shared queue.

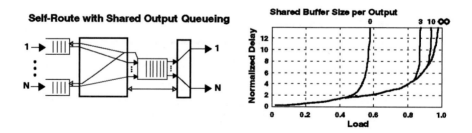

Figure 7-14. *Self-Route with Shared Output Queueing*

The single-stage switch-on-a-chip described later in this chapter is an example of shared output queueing.

Multistage Queueing

This is the case where several switching elements of the "shared-output-queueing" type are interconnected into a multistage network. Note that the graph lines apply to the number of buffers in each stage of the switch (previous diagrams referred to the number of buffers *per output port*).

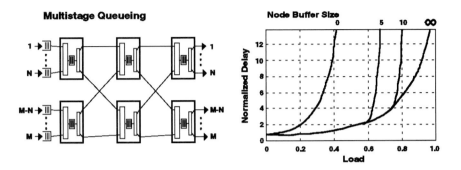

Figure   7-15. *Multistage Queueing*

7.4 A Practical Multistage ATM Switch

In order to use the multistage switch principles discussed above in a real ATM switching node an architecture such as the one illustrated in Figure 7-16 is required.

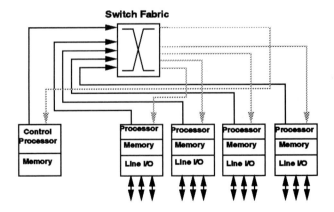

Figure   7-16. *A Practical Multistage ATM Switch Design.* This is very similar to the bus/backplane design except that the bus has been replaced by a multiway switch.

The key parameter in this design is that the switching fabric itself does *not* interface directly to any external ATM link. This is for a number of reasons:

External Link Protocols

In the Banyan multistage network described in 7.2.4, "Multistage Designs" on page 7-10, each connection between switch stages is a single-wire physical link, in principle the same as the external link connections. (The majority of multistage networks are envisaged as having single bit-serial connections between the stages.) In practice, things need to be quite a bit different.

External links are different from internal ones because they are subject to much more distortion than inter-chip connections. There are practical problems in receiving the signal and recovering its timing on external connections that do not exist on internal ones. Furthermore, even though there is no interactive link protocol in ATM there is usually a complex physical-layer protocol involved (such as PDH or SDH).

Technology Speed and Cost

The big issue is technology cost.

1. If you build each switch in CMOS technology, then you will certainly get one (and possibly many) switch elements on the one chip. But CMOS technology has a practical maximum system clocking limit of between 60 and 100 MHz.

2. When the speed is increased you can use a "bipolar" technology, but that is significantly less dense and therefore considerably higher in cost than CMOS.

3. Increasing the speed further, there comes a point when you need gallium arsenide chips. This is an order of magnitude more expensive than bipolar technology.

Cost is optimized if we keep the clock speed down by using parallel connections.

External links are serial by their nature and we cannot do much about that,[6] but connections between chips on a board can be parallel (to a limit imposed by the number of wires you can attach to the chip). In practice, a multistage switch can be built in CMOS technology with serial internal connections up to a maximum speed of around 50 or 60 Mbps (on all links). Above that speed, it is much more

---

[6] Perhaps we can. There has been some research on the possibility of using multiple light wavelengths on the same fiber (WDM) to provide multiple parallel channels and therefore a parallel connection. Watch this space.

cost effective to use parallel connections between switching elements (chips) than it is to use faster logic.

Connections between Adapters and Switch Fabric

This is an area that requires careful design. For reasons expressed above, we want to use parallel connections as much as possible because this keeps the chip cost down. However, a number of factors limit our ability to use parallel connections:

- When you want to build a switch with a large number of I/O connections (which often happens to be the case with very fast switches) then you come up against the problem that parallel connections create a very large number of connections (wires) to handle both on the backplane and attaching to the chip.

- As you increase the link speed you have to increase the number of wires in each parallel connection (if you cannot increase the basic clock rate). This again can result in having just too many wires to handle.

- As you increase the basic clock speed, and as you increase the number of wires in each parallel connection, you start to get problems with skew. That is, the signal on some paths (wires) arrives at a different time from the parallel signal on a different path. Skew is a serious limitation on our ability to use parallel connections and its control is a key design issue.

In medium-size switches parallel connections will likely be used, but in very large switches serial ones may need to be used because of the number of connections becoming unmanagable.

ATM Routing

It would be very difficult for the switching fabric to use the ATM label-swap form of routing - or even to interface to it. This is because of the large amount of table space required and because of the continuous need to update the tables.

It is better to use self-routing within the switch fabric and confine ATM label-swap routing to the line processor.

Manufacturing Economy

If the switch stages are implemented as a single, standard chip (perhaps many stages on one chip) without the need for external link connections, then economy of scale in design and manufacture can be achieved. If we had external link connections on the switching chip, then we would need many different versions of it for the many different types and speeds of link connection.

By having a single switching element chip that can be used in a wide variety of situations we can have greater manufacturing volume and thus lower unit costs.

This leads to the design shown in Figure 7-16 on page 7-21. It is essentially the same as the bus/backplane design shown in Figure 7-5 on page 7-9 except that there are now multiple paths between the adapters. The multistage switch fabric has replaced the bus. A separate control processor is required to perform OA&M (Operations Administration and Maintenance) functions.

Very high-speed adapters will need to be implemented largely in hardware logic in order to achieve full throughput speed. At least the main data flow part of the adapter will need to be a completely hardware design.

At lower speeds the use of a RISC-based control processor offers the possibility of significant additional function and flexibility. For example:

- If the ATM switching node is to have UNI connections, then the input adapter must enforce the input rate control protocols (on a VP and/or a VC basis).

- In practical switches, it will be necessary to connect to non-ATM protocols (such as frame relay or even voice) directly. This means that the adapter needs to convert from the external (non-ATM) protocol to ATM. At minimum this means breaking the input data stream up into cells (and perhaps reassembling at the destination) and processing the adaptation layer (AAL) protocols.

The external adapters are called either "I/O adapters" or "switch fabric adapters".

7.5 The IBM Switch-on-a-Chip

The IBM switch-on-a-chip is an integrated cell-switching chip developed by the IBM Research Laboratory[7] in Zurich, Switzerland. It is used in the first two IBM products to implement ATM, the IBM 8260 Multiprotocol Intelligent Switching Hub and the IBM 2220 Nways BroadBand Switch. In the latter, it is used to switch packets of *any* length (up to a certain maximum) including, of course, ATM cells.

7.5.1 Characteristics

The switch-on-a-chip is a multiport, single-stage switching element. Its major characteristics are as follows:

- The switch-on-a-chip has 16 input ports and 16 output ports.

- Each port can operate at speeds of up to 400 Mbps. The actual speed depends on the clock rate selected in the specific piece of equipment within which the switch-on-a-chip is used.

---

[7] The research team was lead by Dr Antonius Engbersen. A list of published technical papers describing the switch-on-a-chip research project may be found in the bibliography.

The 400 Mbps data rate assumes a clock rate of 50 MHz (20-ns cycle). Products using the switch-on-a-chip are free to clock at a lower rate if desired and it is likely that the first products will use a clock rate of 33.213 MHz (30-ns cycle) resulting in a per-port throughput of 266 Mbps.

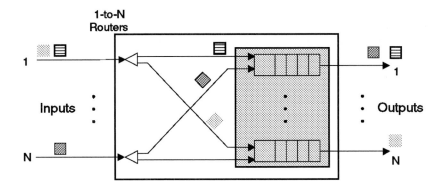

Figure 7-17. *Switch-on-a-Chip Logical Structure.* In the current implementation N=16.

- Each port may run at the full 400 Mbps simultaneously with each other port. This results in a total module throughput (depending on how you measure it) of either 6.4 Gbps (if you measure the amount of data being processed through the switch) or 12.8 Gbps (if you measure the total I/O rate). It is all in your point of view.

  It is very important to consider this (quite valid) difference in perspective when comparing different switching architectures and/or products. When system throughput is quoted it is not always clear which figure is being used. This can lead to very wrong conclusions being reached.

  6.4 Gbps corresponds to roughly 15 million packets per second.

  In the initial implementations this will be 4.224 (or 8.448) Gbps.

- The switch latency (assuming no queueing) is around one microsecond.

- The switch-on-a-chip is a self-routing cell switch *not* an ATM switch per se. That is, the switch-on-a-chip does not understand the ATM header structure or meaning - it treats the ATM header as just plain data. The switch-on-a-chip is a general-purpose cell switch and it could (and is in the IBM 2220) be used for many applications unrelated to ATM.

- In ATM usage, the switch-on-a-chip switches data blocks of 53 bytes (plus the self-routing header) but it can switch data blocks of any length from 14 to 64 bytes. A single-stage switch-on-a-chip will use a 2-byte routing header, so for a 16-port switch configuration the length of the data block handled is 55 bytes.

- As shown in Figure 7-17 it is a 16-way non-blocking switch with a shared (128 position) output queue.

- There is an input "back-pressure" mechanism to allow the switch to refuse input when buffers are full. This avoids the discard of cells and allows for additional buffering of input within the attaching adapters.

- All switch-on-a-chip input and output data paths use 8-bit parallel connections (plus control signaling). This results in a module with 472 pins!

- The chip itself is built on a 14.7 mm square die using .7-μsec CMOS technology and contains around 2.4 million logic elements (transistors).

- The design allows for the interconnection of multiple chips (all switch-on-a-chip chips are identical) to increase the number of ports, provide modular growth in port speed, allow for load sharing and to support modular growth in aggregate throughput.

- A practical switching-node design using the switch-on-a-chip will be similar to that described in 7.5.1, "Characteristics" on page 7-24.

7.5.2 Structure

An overview of the switch-on-a-chip structure is shown in Figure 7-18.

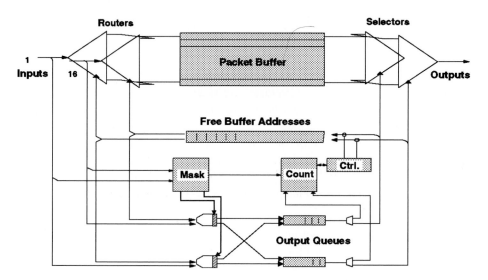

Figure   7-18. Switch-on-a-Chip Structure

The key elements are as follows:

Packet Buffer

The packet buffer is *not* a conventional storage.[8] It consists of 128, 64-byte active storage registers. Even though the switch-on-a-chip is a CMOS chip this is not the common CMOS type of storage - they are active registers that can be read or written in a single clock cycle. Regular CMOS memory (which stores data in small capacitors) requires three storage cycles of perhaps 60 ns each to access or store data.

The active storage registers are used in a similar way to shift registers - except that the data does not really shift - the storage address pointer is moved.

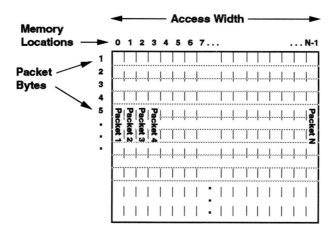

Figure 7-19. *Packet Buffer Structure (Conceptual).* Packets are stored such that a single storage access reads or writes the same byte of each packet simultaneously.

The packet buffer is accessed in parallel. That is, byte x of each buffer is accessed on the same cycle. From an access perspective therefore it can be thought of as a memory of 64, 128-byte words. Each storage word (128 bytes) contains one byte of each packet in the buffer. So, storage word 4 would hold byte 4 of each packet in the buffer. This is quite different from the usual way of storing packets in a switching element.

The packet length is the same for all packets and cannot be changed during operation (it is set up by software to any value between 14 and 64 bytes at initialization time).

---

8   The design of the packet buffer is new and quite unique. Patents covering the design have been applied for.

Storage Access Modification Table (Not Illustrated)

Within the control section there is a table that controls the order of storing bytes into the packet buffer. This could be used for a number of purposes, but is primarily used to reorder the bytes of the routing header so that they are correct at the input of the next stage of the switch.

Input and Output Ports

There are 16 input ports and 16 output ports (unrelated to one another). Each port transfers 8 bits of data in parallel in a single clock cycle (20, 25, or 30 ns).

Routers

There are 16 input routers (one for each port). Each router can direct input to any of the 128 packet buffers.

These routers can together be thought of, conceptually, as being similar to a 16 by 128 position crosspoint switch. Data is routed from an input port to its position in the allocated packet buffer one byte at a time in parallel. Potential output blocking in this 16 x 128 crossbar will never occur because the 16 ports are guaranteed to have mutually exclusive destinations (1 of 128).

Selectors (Output Routers)

These are very similar to the input routers except that they operate in the other direction.

Control Logic

The key element in the control logic is a set of output queues (one per output port). After a cell is received, the control logic analyzes the first byte of its routing header (the current routing tag) and places the address of the packet buffer holding that cell into the correct output queue for its destination port. Each output queue controls the selector for one specific port. When an opportunity comes for a cell to be transmitted the packet buffer address at the head of the queue for each port tells the selector from which port to take its input.

In a similar way, when an input operation is about to commence, each input router is fed with a free buffer address from a common queue of buffer addresses.

Additional logic copies the current routing tag from each packet to the control section while the packet is being received.

Modification of the routing header (described in 7.5.4, "Switch-on-a-Chip Self-Routing Mechanism" on page 7-31) is also accomplished by the control section. This involves discarding the destination address of the packet (the first byte) and adding the input port address at the end of the address vector.

7.5.3 Operation

The key to understanding the switch-on-a-chip operation is to realize that operation is synchronous at the packet[9] (cell) level.

- There is a packet cycle. Packet reception and transmission on all ports is synchronized.

- On any particular input cycle, the same byte position of every input packet is received from every input port.

Figure 7-20 shows the principle: Three active ports are shown (ports 4, 9 and 15). Each is sending byte 7 of a cell to the switch. Port 4 is receiving into packet buffer 2, port 9 into packet buffer 8, and port 15 into packet buffer 117. For this example let us assume that the switch-on-a-chip is connected in a three-stage configuration and thus the length of the routing header prepended to the cell is 4. In this case, the packet length set in the switch-on-a-chip at initialization will be 57 bytes (53-byte ATM cell and 4-byte routing header).

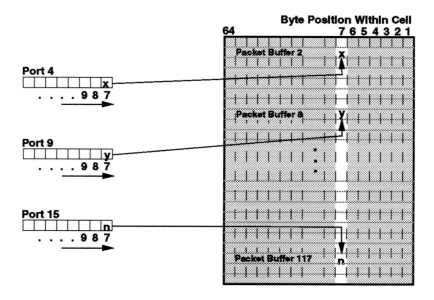

Figure 7-20. Switch-on-a-Chip Operation. Byte ordering is shown in the opposite order from the usual convention. This is done to clarify the method of operation and to emphasize the similarity to the operation of a shift register.

---

[9] The word "packet" is used here rather than cell to emphasize the fact that there is an additional self-routing header present and that the ATM cell (including its routing header) is processed as data by the switch.

Operation proceeds as follows:

1. Before the start of a cell cycle, each port router is allocated a free packet buffer (cell buffer) by the control section.

2. The first cycle in a packet is unique. On this cycle:

   - The first byte from each port is routed to the control section. This byte is called the current routing tag and specifies the packet's destination.

     This routing information causes the control section to place a pointer entry in the output queue corresponding to the destination of this cell. The pointer entry is the packet buffer address.

   - The input port identification number is sent by the router to the packet buffer - instead of the current routing tag.

   - The Storage Access Modification table has been set up so that this byte is not stored in position 1 of the packet buffer but in position 4 (the last byte of the routing header).

3. During the next cycle, the second byte received from the port (byte 2 of the incoming packet) is placed in byte 1 of the packet buffer.

4. The rest of the routing header is received on subsequent cycles into consecutive positions in the packet buffer (bytes 3 and 4 of the received cell header are received into bytes 2 and 3 of the packet buffer).

5. The above sequence of operations has had the effect of stripping the first byte of the routing header and adding the origin identifier onto the back of the routing header.

6. During the next cycle, the next byte of the cell data is stored into its position in the packet buffer (byte 5 of the received packet into position 5 of the packet buffer).

The reverse operation takes place on output. Immediately before a cell cycle begins each selector obtains the packet buffer address of the next cell in its output queue. Output is performed in a similar way to input, the same byte from each packet buffer is sent to its appropriate output port on the same output cycle. There is a difference from input however in that there is no reordering of bytes as they are output from the packet buffer.

The use of a cell cycle has very little impact on the latency of the switching element but significantly simplifies operation.

A number of points should be apparent from the above description:

- The input and output adapters (switch fabric adapters) send and receive cells in exact synchronization with the switching element. (If one was delayed then the next byte would go into the wrong position in the packet buffer.)

- There is no possibility of blocking within the switch-on-a-chip switch itself. Provided there is buffer space available, cells will be accepted and switched towards their destination. Of course, there is output port blocking when many cells arrive which are addressed to the same output port - resolving this situation is what the queue is for.

- This is an output queuing switch design since the cell is switched to its destination output before it is logically queued.

7.5.4 Switch-on-a-Chip Self-Routing Mechanism

Figure 7-21 illustrates a three-stage network (switching fabric) consisting of switch-on-a-chip switching elements.

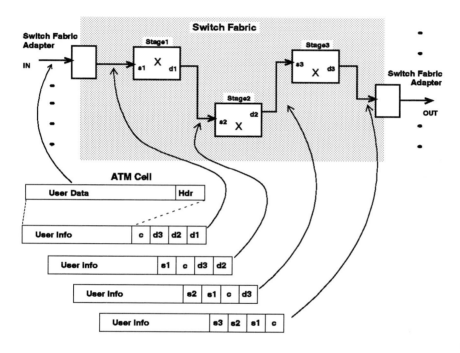

Figure 7-21. *Switch-on-a-Chip Self-Routing Mechanism*

The method of routing within a multistage switch-on-a-chip switching fabric is called self-routing or source routing. The route that a cell is to follow through the switching fabric is specified by a routing vector prepended to the cell itself.[10] This routing header is *not* the ATM header. The ATM header is just data to the switch-on-a-chip.

---

[10] This is exactly the same principle as is employed in IBM Token-Ring bridges.

Operation is as follows:

- The external adapter (the switch fabric adapter in the figure) receives the ATM cell from an external link.

- The adapter then uses the ATM VPI and VCI fields to locate the correct entry for this VC in its routing table.

- When the correct entry is found the VPI/VCI values that will be correct on output from the node (output adapter) are updated into the cell. This process was described in 7.1.2, "Processing the ATM Routing Header" on page 7-3.

- The routing vector specifying the route that this cell must take through the switching fabric is retrieved from the VCI table and prepended to the cell.

- The cell is then queued to the first switch-on-a-chip (called "stage 1").

- Before receiving the cell, the switch-on-a-chip allocates an empty packet buffer to the input port.

- As the cell is received within the switch-on-a-chip, its current routing tag is copied into the control section.

- As previously described, as the packet is received the routing header is rotated such that the first byte of the received packet is stripped (this is the current routing tag).

- Another byte is added at the end of the header specifying the number of the input port from which the cell arrived. (This feature is present to assist in fault diagnosis.) Thus, the length of the packet does not change on its transit through this switching stage.

- The data of the cell is received into the remainder of the packet buffer.

- The switch-on-a-chip then uses the routing tag to determine to which output port this cell belongs.

- Notice the routing vector element called C in the figure. This is not used by the switch-on-a-chip at all. It is the routing information to be used by the destination adapter to determine to which of its attached links this packet belongs. In fact, this byte has just been included for the example. Since byte "C" is meaningless to the switch-on-a-chip, its use (and its presence) depends solely on the design of the switching node of which the switch-on-a-chip is a part.

  The process of reordering the header is controlled by the Storage Access Modification table (not shown in the figure).

- The cell is then sent to stage 2 where the routing process is repeated.

- The same thing happens at stage 3.

- The cell is now sent to the output adapter (switch fabric adapter in the figure).

- This adapter then removes the routing vector and transmits the cell on the link specified by the last element (the C) in the routing vector.

7.5.4.1 Broadcast and Multicast

The switch-on-a-chip has the ability to handle broadcast and multicast traffic in an optimal way. This is achieved as follows:

- The switch-on-a-chip allows the specification of a number of special routing tags which are not output port identifiers.

- Each of these special routing tags identifies a list of output ports.

- When a packet is received by the switch-on-a-chip it only occupies a single packet buffer, even if its routing tag specifies multicast. *The packet is not duplicated in the packet buffer even though multiple copies will be transmitted.*

- The address of this packet buffer is placed into each output queue on the list of port addresses pointed to by this routing tag. Thus, a single packet buffer address is placed in multiple output queues.

  For example, if the list of output ports for a particular routing tag identified ports 3, 8, and 17, then when a received packet specified this particular routing tag the packet buffer would be queued separately to queues 3, 8, and 17.

- The problem here is one of housekeeping. Since some queues will already have cells in them awaiting transmission while others will not, the particular packet buffer will be output on different ports on different cycles. When do you return the packet buffer to the queue of free buffers? The switch-on-a-chip keeps a count of the number of copies on a packet that need to be transmitted. The count is decremented when a packet has been transmitted. When the count reaches zero the packet buffer is returned to the free buffer queue.

It is very inefficient to broadcast or multicast by copying the data many times at the input. (It also has bad performance effects on the network since it produces very heavy intermittent loads). With this mechanism we can delay copying the data until the last moment, so that only one copy of broadcast or multicast data ever appears on any given link.

The switch-on-a-chip's internal mechanism for dealing with multicast has the great advantage of saving packet buffer space (the packet is never duplicated within the switch-on-a-chip).

Using this feature with ATM is not completely straightforward. Broadcasts in ATM use different VPI and VCI values along different segments of their path. (See 2.3.4, "Broadcast and Multicast" on page 2-11.) This means that each copy of a broadcast cell can/will have different VPI/VCI values.

The mechanism described in 7.1.2, "Processing the ATM Routing Header" on page 7-3 shows the VPI/VCI numbers being swapped *before* the cell is copied!

The resolution of this is to allocate a special identifier (called a Broadcast Channel Number) to the broadcast cell instead of the output port identifier. When the cell arrives in the output adapter the adapter discovers that it is a broadcast cell and swaps the VPI/VCI itself.

7.5.5 Expansion Capabilities

The switch-on-a-chip is designed in such a way as to allow multiple chips to be used to expand the capacity of the switch. The most obvious requirement here is to provide a capability for expanding the number of ports. However, in addition to this switch-on-a-chip chips can be interconnected in such a way as to increase port speed (without increasing the speed of the clock) and to increase overall performance by allowing extra buffering.

The ability to expand the switch-on-a-chip in many dimensions without changing the chip itself results in significant economies in manufacture (you get a long production run of a single design rather than many short production runs of slightly different designs).

Performance Expansion

> In some applications it may be found that the shared 128-cell buffer in a single switch-on-a-chip may not provide sufficient buffering to allow the target level of performance. (This situation could arise with heavily skewed (non-random) traffic loads, for example.) Figure 7-22 illustrates how switch-on-a-chip-based systems may be designed to handle this.

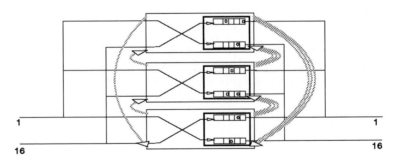

Figure 7-22. Switch-on-a-Chip Performance Expansion. Interconnection of multiple chips to provide additional buffering.

> Chips can be connected in parallel (inputs and outputs paralleled) such that the system behaves as though it was a single chip with a larger buffer memory.

It is easier to illustrate the principle when only two chips are paralleled. On the input side, when one chip signals that its buffers are full then the second chip immediately begins to accept input on all connections. At this moment, in the chip which stopped accepting input, the end of each output queue is marked with a bit. On each individual output port, packets are sent out until this marker is detected. Then, for this specific queue, the next packet will be sent by the next chip. This enables cells to stay in sequence even though multiple chips are used to hold the buffer queues.

Expanding the Number of Ports

There are basically two ways to expand the number of ports. They are illustrated in Figure 7-23.

1. Multiple switch-on-a-chips can be connected in a single-stage parallel configuration.

2. Multiple switch-on-a-chips can be connected in a cascade (the multistage case in the figure). This is called a Benes network.

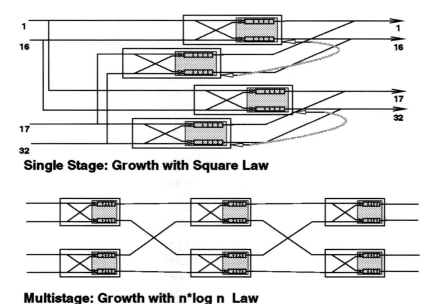

Single Stage: Growth with Square Law

Multistage: Growth with n*log n Law

Figure   *7-23. Switch-on-a-Chip Port Expansion*

The single-stage case requires more chips in large configurations but only has the delay of one switching stage. The multistage case is more conventional and requires fewer chips but at the cost of a delay within each stage.

Operation in a multistage configuration has been discussed in 7.5.4, "Switch-on-a-Chip Self-Routing Mechanism" on page 7-31.

Single-stage expansion is achieved as shown in the figure (when reading the figure N=16).

- The top two chips feed the first 16 outputs and the bottom two chips feed the outputs numbered 17 to 32.

- The top chip gets inputs 1 to 16. The next chip in the pair gets inputs 17 to 32.

- The lower pair of chips in the figure also get inputs 1 to 32 (16 each).

- This means that all input goes to *both* sets of chips.

- Since the top pair of chips only feed outputs 1 to 16, any input they get addressed to other outputs (17 to 32) is immediately discarded.

- The lower pair of chips operates in the same way. Input specifying output ports 1 to 16 is immediately discarded.

- On the output side, each pair of chips feeds the *same* set of output lines. External logic is used to resolve the conflict such that only one chip is allowed to output on a particular port at a particular time. (This mechanism can be quite simple since there is no problem in keeping cells in sequence.)

Port Speed Expansion

There are two methods of increasing the speed (throughput) of a port as illustrated in Figure 7-24.

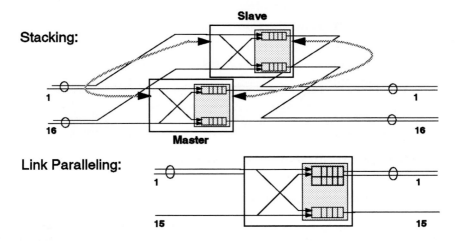

Figure **7-24.** *Switch-on-a-Chip Speed Expansion*

1. Two switch-on-a-chips can be connected together with concatenated inputs and outputs.

   In this technique the 8-bit parallel I/O data path between the switching chip and the I/O adapter is doubled to 16 bits. The adapter presents 16 bits of data at a time to two switch-on-a-chips connected in a master/slave arrangement. The first byte is sent to the master switch-on-a-chip and the second byte to the slave. Each byte of the routing header is duplicated so that each switch-on-a-chip gets a complete routing header. (This is necessary for each switch-on-a-chip in a multistage configuration to get a correct current routing tag.) Operation of the two chips is locked together and controlled by the master.

   This technique doubles the speed of all 16 ports.

2. Two ports on a single switch-on-a-chip can be grouped together such that a new port is created with twice the data throughput.

   This technique is used when a single port on a switching element needs a higher throughput, but the rest of the ports need only a lower rate. By reducing the total number of ports by one, we are able to provide a single port at double speed. It is important here that the port speed is *not* actually doubled. Two ports are strapped together such that they form a single logical port, but each port sends/receives complete packets at the same speed as every other port on the chip.

   So there are two parallel connections (ports) that are used as one logical port. The potential problem with this is that cells may get out of sequence on the connection. There is logic built into the switch-on-a-chip so that the sequence of cells is maintained.

7.5.6 Congestion Control

Back-Pressure Mechanism

When the switch-on-a-chip is unable to accept input from a particular port (for example, as a result of not having a free packet buffer) it is able to block input. This does *not* result in any loss of packets but allows the sending adapter (or preceding switch-on-a-chip stage) to build a queue for that port.

This can be thought of as a form of input queueing or (more correctly) as output queueing in the previous stage.

Maximum Queue Length per Destination Port

There is a possibility that the queue for a single output port may become very large and monopolize the packet buffers so that the whole system chokes up. This could be the result of the random occurrence within a varying traffic pattern, or it could be the result of an output stage being blocked for a period of time.

To alleviate the effects of this problem, the switch-on-a-chip has a programmable maximum queue length which applies to all output ports. No queue is allowed to get longer than the set limit.

When the switch-on-a-chip cannot accept input packets they are not lost or discarded. As a packet is received in the packet buffer the control circuits check to make sure that the packet will not cause the output queue length to be exceeded. If the packet would cause its destination output queue to exceed the limit, the switch-on-a-chip aborts the packet reception at the input port and exerts the back-pressure mechanism. The sending adapter recognizes this condition and should retry sending the cell on the next available cycle.

Cell Discard

The switch-on-a-chip does *not* discard packets unless an output port becomes non-operational.

Prioritization

The switch-on-a-chip does *not* implement any form of priority scheme either in queueing or in cell discard. Experience with packet switches in the past indicates that both of these functions are best done in the attaching adapters (the switch fabric adapters).

Queueing Model

The queueing model appropriate to a single-stage switch-on-a-chip is that shown in Figure 7-14 on page 7-20. The multistage case is shown in Figure 7-15 on page 7-21.

Operation at Less than Maximum Rating

The switch-on-a-chip will usually be used at somewhat less than its possible maximum throughput. This is because standardized ATM link speeds are not the same as the switch-on-a-chip's link speeds.

For example, in the case where the switch-on-a-chip is clocked at 33 MHz it has an I/O data rate of 266 Mbps on all ports. But currently planned ATM link speeds are 25, 50, 100 and 155 Mbps. So, an I/O adapter supporting two 100 Mbps links will feed the switch-on-a-chip at a maximum rate of 200 Mbps. (This should not be confused with the switch-on-a-chip's I/O rate. The adapter will still transfer cells to/from the switch-on-a-chip at 266 Mbps but for a proportion of time there will be no cells to transfer.)

This has a similar effect to increasing the number of packet buffers within the switch-on-a-chip because cells can be delivered out of the switch-on-a-chip faster than they can be presented. The result of this is that potential queueing delays are significantly reduced. The effect here can be quite dramatic. If an switch-on-a-chip's throughput capacity is as little as 15% greater than the maximum I/O rate of the attaching adapters, the benefit is much the same as *doubling* the number of packet buffers. (Although in some situations what is actually happening is that packet buffers move out of the switch-on-a-chip into the output function in the adapters.)

7.5.7 Further Reading

The best sources of information in this interesting area are the professional journals. Some papers relating to this chapter are:

Switching Architectures

"A Taxonomy of Broadband Integrated Switching Architectures" [5], "A Survey of Modern High-Performance Switching Techniques" [1] and "Fast Packet Technology for Future Switches" [7] give good overviews of possible switching architectures.

Performance

The question of performance in switches and switching networks is addressed in "Performance of a Packet Switch with Shared Buffer and Input Queueing" [15] and "Performance of Packet Switches with Input and Output Queueing" [16].

The Switch-on-a-Chip

The switch-on-a-chip design is discussed in "A Highly Modular Packet Switch for Gbps Rates" [8].

Switching Node Design

The design of a prototype ATM switch using the switch-on-a-chip as its switching element is discussed in "Flight of the Falcon" [4].

Chapter 8. Traffic Characteristics

In ATM we wish to integrate many kinds of network traffic onto the same network and share the network's facilities between them. Each type of network traffic has its own peculiar characteristics and, therefore, needs to be treated differently from the others. The traffic types may be summarized as follows:

- Traditional data traffic
- Voice and high-quality sound
- Full-motion video and interactive multimedia

Traditional data networks were built to handle both interactive and batch data but were not built to handle image, voice, or video traffic. The new types of traffic put a completely new set of requirements onto the network.

8.1 Throughput Demand

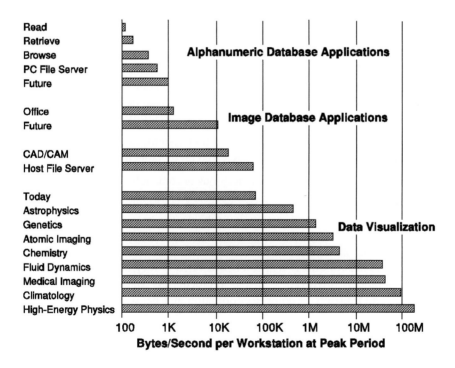

Figure   8-1. *Application Throughput Requirements*

One of the most important factors in considering traffic is the amount of throughput required. Some of the computer applications for high-speed communications can be seen easily from Figure 8-1. (Note that here the x-axis is using a logarithmic scale.)

8.2 Traditional Data Traffic

At first thought traditional data traffic should not be much of a problem in an ATM network environment. Traditional data networks were built with internal congestion controls, flow controls, and error recoveries, but ATM networks have none of these. Data traffic in an ATM environment deserves some study.

Interactive Transactions

Interactive transactions are those used in the day-to-day processing of business information. This includes banking teller transactions, airline reservations, insurance processing, etc. What happens is that you get large numbers of identical fixed-format transactions.

For example, in the traditional banking teller environment a transaction consists of about 30 bytes of data sent to the host (server) system and a response of about 100 bytes. In peak processing times, the rule of thumb is that you get a maximum of three transactions per hundred terminals per second. So a 1000 terminal banking network produces a maximum of around 30 transactions per second. During a business day the peak will be something around 4 times the average (the rate quoted above is a peak). As the number of terminals employed (to do the same job) is increased (such as when you increase the number of terminals per bank branch from one to four), the variability of the traffic increases.

Fixed transaction profiles for fixed-function systems aggregate very well and in large networks can provide very stable and predictable traffic patterns.

In recent years, the size of transactions has become a lot larger, but the principle is unchanged.

Interactive traffic of this nature is probably the most demanding of the data traffic scenarios and yet a network end-to-end delay of 200 to 300 milliseconds will provide excellent performance in this environment. The amount of end-to-end network delay that can be tolerated is very dependent on the higher-layer protocols involved. If the protocol has only a few "handshakes" (end-to-end transfers of control information and data) per transaction, then we can tolerate a much longer network delay than we can when the transaction involves a large number of handshakes. Typical SNA application systems use 2 or 3 exchanges of information per transaction (although you can get down to only one if you try). There are protocols and systems in use which require as many as 18 end-to-end exchanges of information per transaction.

Interactive Office

This type of traffic is where you have a utility host-based system supporting a number of screen/keyboard devices (often/usually PCs). Users have a wide range of freedom in the transactions performed and programs run. This kind of operation tends to produce an average input transaction of perhaps 100 bytes with an output of 1000 to 3000 bytes, but the transaction rate is quite slow (on average one per terminal per 5 minutes or so). Once the response time becomes less than one second, further improvements in response are hard to justify.

A complication of this type of traffic today is the increasing use of the terminal/host connection for file transfer (in the case where the terminal is a PC).

ASCII Emulation

This is probably the least efficient form of data transmission ever invented. ASCII emulation is where single ASCII characters (to/from a character-based terminal) are sent on a LAN (or even through a network) as individual characters (with the LAN or network header appended). Depending on the system used this gives a transmission overhead of between 25 to 1 and 70 to 1. *Nevertheless, this form of transmission is still in wide use on LANs - even from PCs to servers.*

This kind of traffic will run extremely well over an ATM network. You send one cell for every character in the terminal-to-processor direction at keyboard speed and the character is echoed back through the network. Network delay, jitter, etc. are so small in the ATM environment as to be no problem here. However, this is not very efficient in its use of network bandwidth.

File Transfer

File transfers vary widely in their characteristics. They can be from requester to server (PC to server on a LAN for example) or mainframe to mainframe and can send any amount of data from a few thousand bytes to a few hundred million.

The characteristics of importance to ATM are:

- Data is sent (usually) in long blocks or frames.

- Some form of rotating-window, end-to-end flow or error recovery control is usually used.

- The rate at which data is sent depends almost solely on the speed of the sending processor and its disk access.

- A file transfer is a uniform, regular transmission of frames of data usually sent at a constant rate (determined by the speed of the host system).

- End-to-end delay and jitter in the network are not usually a problem except in the sense that any rotating window protocol in use must be adjusted to take account of the amount of delay.

LAN Network Data Traffic

LANs are the big problem. Not only do they carry interactive traffic, but they also carry large file transfers intermixed. In addition, there is the protocol "overhead" traffic created by the various LAN higher-layer protocols in use.

LAN systems were created with the conviction that LAN transmission capacity was infinite and free and had no errors. Most of the widely used LAN protocols were never properly designed.

Studies of LAN traffic (see the papers by Leland et. al. [18] and Fowler [12]) have shown that traffic does not easily "smooth out" when you add it up statistically (at least over time scales of a few minutes).

Some LAN protocols require an interactive response for every data block sent and hence are relatively sensitive to network delays.

The interface of the higher-layer LAN protocols to the LAN dependent ones is called the MAC (Media Access) layer. LAN systems have been built to include end-to-end error recovery at the MAC layer (because LAN systems do not recover errors - like ATM they discard data). This makes the interface between existing LAN system software and an ATM system very clean and easy.

Multiprotocol Networks

These are usually interconnected LAN networks and have all the traffic problems of normal LAN traffic. The presence of a router that understands many of the protocols has a calming effect on the traffic and tends to induce better traffic behavior than you see directly on the LAN itself.

It can be seen from the above descriptions that the real issue for data in ATM networks is flow, rate, and congestion control.

8.3 Voice Traffic

It is attractive to think that when voice is digitized, it then becomes in some way "the same" as data. Or it "becomes" data. Up to a point this is true, but there are many differences between traditional data traffic and digitized voice, which make the integration of the two a challenging technical problem.

8.3.1 The Conflicting Characteristics of Voice and Data

Length of Connection (Call)

Traditionally, the most important difference between voice and data has been that voice calls are (on average) around three minutes and data calls can last for many hours. In the past, telephone exchanges were designed to have large numbers of external lines but relatively few "paths" through the exchange for calls. So it was possible, when the exchange was busy, for calls to "block." That is, for the caller to be attempting to make a connection and the called interface to be free, but the call cannot "get through" because all paths are "blocked" (in use by other calls).

Therefore, when data connections are established through a traditional telephone exchange, all the paths can be used up very quickly and the rest of the exchange will become unavailable because all paths are blocked. Modern digital PBXes have solved this problem by providing the capacity to handle more calls than there are interfaces. For example, an exchange with 500 telephones can have a maximum of 250 simultaneous calls but an internal capacity for perhaps 400 calls. This is because the internal data path equipment in a digital PBX represents only 2% or 3% of the total cost of the exchange, whereas, in the past, the function accounted for perhaps 30% of the cost. Nevertheless, while this difference is solved for the time being, in the future, the problem will appear again as the sharing of voice and data on the tails becomes more common. Hence, the number of connections to be made increases and the internal limitations imposed by bus speed become a factor.

Flow Control

The bandwidth required for voice is dictated by the digitization technique and the circuit is either in use (using the full bandwidth) or not. Data can go at any speed up to the access line speed. Voice does not need (or want) flow control. Voice must be either handled at full speed or stopped. You cannot slow it down or speed it up. Data, on the other hand, must be controlled since a computer has an almost infinite capacity (at least with "traditional" link speeds) for generating data traffic.

Data has another problem, in that a data device, such as a terminal, can and will establish a connection and use it in a very "bursty" manner. There may be minutes or hours with no traffic at all and then a few minutes of data at the maximum transmission rate. Added together statistically the traffic does *not* "average out." What happens in large data networks is that interactive traffic tends to "peak" at different times of the day, and on particular events (for example, after a computer system has been "down" and has just recovered).[1]

Voice exists in bursts (talk spurts) also and, in general, only one party speaks at a time. Statistically it poses quite a different problem for a switching system than does data. In fact, voice is a lot better than data in a statistical sense. If you statistically multiplex (merge) a large number of compressed voice calls (with silence suppression) into a single carrier the variations smooth out and you get an extremely stable load. In the case where you have (say) 10 000 active calls in a single carrier there will be only a very tiny variation in the load placed on that carrier. This suggests that ATM networks carrying voice may be able to utilize trunk routes at 95% and above!

In the past, there have been several levels of flow control available to data devices. For example, link-level controls (which are aimed at optimizing the use of the link and not at network flow control), and network-delivery type controls (like pacing in SNA or packet-level flow control in X.25).

Delivery Rate Control

In data networking equipment in the past, there has also been another very important control, that of the link speed itself. Most equipment is designed to handle data at whatever speed the link can deliver (at least at the link connection level). At the "box" (communication controller, packet switch) level, the switch is never designed for every link to operate simultaneously "flat out," but any individual link attachment must have that capability. Link speed provided an implicit control of the rate at which data could be sent or received.

But the new technology allows link speeds which are very much faster than the attaching "box". For example, a link connected to a terminal (personal computer) might run at 64 Kbps, but the device, while handling instantaneous transmission or reception of blocks at this speed, may not allow for aggregate data rates much faster than (say) 500 characters per second. The same device might also be connected to a local area network at 4 Mbps with the same restriction

---

[1] Another peculiarity here is that the difference between the peaks and the troughs in data traffic becomes greater as the network gets larger. This is not due to network size per se but rather is an effect that follows from the same cause. Networks get larger because terminal costs decrease. As the cost of terminals and attachments decreases, users are able to afford many for dedicated functions. An example is in the development of banking networks. In the early networks there was only one (expensive) terminal per branch and work was "queued" for it. It was in use all of the time with a dedicated operator (with others taking over during lunch). Thus, there was very little variance in the traffic over time (though the mixture of transaction types changed quite radically). Now, with cheaper terminals, most bank branches have many terminals and they are operated by their direct users not by dedicated operators. Thus, in midmorning for example, after the mail arrives, there is a processing peak with every terminal in use. At other times, there can be little or no traffic.

that only a few hundred characters per second can be handled by the device. The same characteristic at higher speeds applies to the data switching processor itself.

This leads to the observation that if link speed is no longer to be a flow limiting mechanism, then others (adequate ones, such as those shown in 9.3, "Flow and Rate Controls" on page 9-16, exist) will have to be used.

Blocking Characteristics

Data exists in discrete blocks.[2] It is transmitted through the network in blocks. The two block sizes can be different (logical blocks can either be split up or amalgamated for transport). Telephone traffic is continuous or effectively so. It can be considered as very long indeterminate length blocks but the "real-time" characteristic does not allow the network to receive a burst of speech as a single block and treat it that way.

Acceptable Transit Delay Characteristics

An acceptable network delay for even the most exacting real-time data network is about 100 milliseconds (one way). More usual is a data interactive traffic delay of 500 milliseconds or so. Batch data does not have a problem with transit delays. Voice traffic, however, is marginal on a satellite where the transit delay is 250 milliseconds one way. For first-quality voice, the transit delay should be no greater than 50 milliseconds.

Further, variable transit delays (variations in response time), while an annoyance in data traffic, make voice traffic impossible. Voice cells must be delivered to the receiver at a steady, uniform rate. They must not "bunch up" and get delivered in bursts (a characteristic of today's data networks).

A short interruption to the circuit (for example, caused by an airplane flying between two microwave repeaters) which could result in a one-second outage of the link will have quite different effects for voice than for data. For data, it is nearly always preferable to have a delay of a few seconds rather than losing the data. With voice, a cell that is one half a second old is just garbage. It is much better to discard delayed voice cells quickly, thus allowing the circuit to return to normal, than it is to build up a queue, particularly due to the fixed speed of the receiving (and of the transmitting) device.

---

[2] There is an unfortunate conflict here in the usage of the word "block." In the telephone world it describes the action of preventing a call being set up due to lack of resources. In the data world a "block" is a logical piece of data which is kept together for transport through the network.

Error Control

The most important thing about data traffic is that errors must be controlled, which means either detected or (preferably) detected and corrected. This correction mechanism can often only be done by context[3] (since you do not know who the sender is until you are sure there are no errors in the block), and will require retransmissions for recovery. Voice, on the other hand, cannot tolerate the time delays inherent in recoveries and does not care about occasional errors or bursts of errors. (Voice and human language are very redundant indeed.)

Power Demands

Problems caused by fluctuations in the demand for power, should not happen in modern digital systems.

Statistics show us that when many variable (or varying) things are added up then the mean (average) becomes more and more stable (has less and less variation). For example, if one takes the power demands on a trunk amplifier for a large number of voice calls, then the requirement is very stable indeed and well known. The dynamics of speech, when added up over many calls, produces remarkably stable system demands.

When data is used instead of voice, many things change. Call duration is usually cited (data calls are generally much longer than voice), but there are other problems. When modems are used for data communication over a telephone channel there are no "gaps between words." The modem produces a constant, high-level signal. If too many modem calls happen to be multiplexed on a single interexchange (frequency-division) trunk, then the additional electrical power required by the multiplexers and amplifiers can be so great as to cause the device to fail. (Power supplies are designed to supply only enough power for voice calls.) This restriction will go away with the advent of digital systems, but it was the cause of PTT hesitancy about allowing modems to be connected arbitrarily around the telephone system without consideration of their effects on that system.

Volume of Data

If telephone calls are to be regarded as 64 Kbps full-duplex, then not even the largest organization today transmits enough data to be more than 10% of its telephone traffic. Most organizations transmit less than 5%, and of all the communications traffic carried over public communication lines perhaps 1% or 2% percent is data. This is very important because whatever you do to the network

---

3 At the link level, the sender is always known regardless of the content of the block. Later, when released from the context of the link, the only identification for the block is the routing information within the block itself.

to help it handle data adequately had better not add too much cost to the voice part of the system. If it does, it will be very hard to justify because of the large cost added to the total system to benefit only a minority part.

It is perfectly true that data traffic is growing rapidly and voice traffic is not, but there is a very long way to go. Particularly in that the number of interfaces to the public networks being used for voice versus the number of interfaces being used for data is a more important criteria than the number of bits sent. This ratio of the number of interfaces is even more biased in the direction of voice traffic.

Balanced Traffic

Most voice calls involve a two-way conversation (although some people talk more than others!). This means that for voice transmission, the traffic is usually reasonably well balanced.

Not so for data. Even without the obvious example of file transfer (which is one way), traditional (IBM 3270 style) interactive data traffic involves very short (perhaps 30 to 50 bytes) input and large output (typically 500 bytes but often 2000 bytes or more). In graphics applications the inbalance is even greater than this.

Echo Cancellation

In traditional (analog) voice systems, the problem of suppressing echoes is extremely important. In a digital full-duplex system, it would seem that echoes were no longer a consideration.

This is not completely true. Some echoes can be generated within a telephone handset and though this is a small problem compared with the problems of the past, it must still be considered. In a system where voice is packetized, the size of the packet (cell) determines the length of time that it takes to fill a packet before transmission (64 Kbps equals one byte per 125 µsec). As the delay in the circuit increases, then so does the problem caused by echoes.

These facts have fueled a debate over the optimal packet size for packetized voice. Some people contend that a packet of around 80 bytes or so will produce problems with echoes where packet sizes of 32 bytes will not. (This is because of the time needed to assemble a packet.)

There is a significant problem with echoes in the situation of a digital, full-duplex backbone network with analog subscriber loops.

8.3.2 Encoding Voice

According to the international standard, when voice is converted to digital form, the analog signal is sampled at the rate of 8 000 times per second (one sample every 125 µsec) and each sample is represented by 8 bits. This gives a constant bit rate of 64 000 bits per second.

The coding system is called "Pulse Code Modulation" (PCM). The basic concept of PCM is that each eight-bit sample is simply a coded measure of the amplitude of signal at the moment of sampling. But this can be improved upon by a system called "companding" (compressing/expanding). It happens that the signal spends significantly more time in the lower part of the scale than it does at the peaks. So, what we do is apply a non-linear coding, such that the lower-amplitude parts of the waveform are coded with more precision than the peaks. (In basic concept, this is just like the "Dolby" system for improving the quality of tape recordings.) In practice, PCM is always encoded this way but the standard is different in different parts of the world. One system is called "μ-law" [4] and the other "A-law".

In order to transport this across an ATM network individual samples must be assembled into cells. The principle is described below.

8.3.2.1 Basic Principle

Figure 8-2 illustrates the principle of sending voice over a cell-based network.

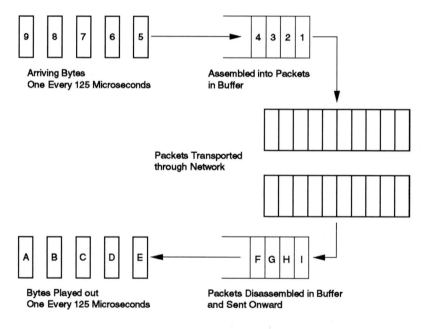

Figure 8-2. Transporting Voice over an ATM Network

---

4 Pronounced mu-law

1. The telephone handset generates a stream of 8-bit bytes of voice information at the rate of one every 125 µsec.

2. The digitized voice stream is received into a buffer until a block the length of a cell has been received.

3. When the cell is full it is sent into the network.

4. Once the cell is received at the other end it is disassembled and sent to the destination at the rate of one byte every 125 µsec.

A number of points should be made about this principle.

- The end-to-end delay as experienced by the end users will be the time taken to assemble a cell *plus* the transit delay through the network.

- If the network delivers cells to the destination cell disassembler at an uneven rate, then buffering will be needed at the destination to smooth out irregularities in the cell delivery rate.

- ATM networks deliver cells at an uneven rate.

- What must happen is that when the circuit is established the receiving cell disassembler must hold the first cell for some length of time sufficient to overcome the largest possible variation in transit delay before sending anything on to the receiver.

  This increases the end-to-end delay significantly.

8.3.2.2 Transit Delay

The transit delay in a network is the time it takes a cell to travel through the network. This is made up of transmission time, propagation delay, and node delay (processing and queueing delays within a node).

Transit Delay Variation (Delay Jitter):

The problem with most cell networks is that the transit delay varies with the instantaneous load on the network. Figure 8-3 shows the regular arrival of cells into a network and the irregular rate of delivery of those cells.

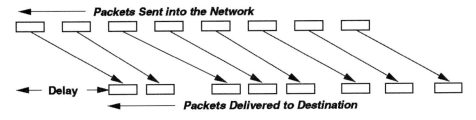

Figure 8-3. *Irregular Delivery of Voice Cells*

As mentioned earlier, to overcome these variations in network transit time we need to have a deliberate delay at the receiver and a queue of arriving cells, so that the delays are not apparent to the receiver.

There is another problem here and that is that the bit timing of the "playout" operation cannot ever be quite the same as the timing of the transmitter - unless of course, there is a universal worldwide timing reference available. In continuous transmission, there will be occasional overruns or underruns at the receiver (clock slips) due to this lack of clock synchronization.

The Effect of End-to-End Network Delay on Voice Traffic:

The end-to-end delay experienced in a voice situation is made up of three components:

1. Cell Assembly Time

   This is the time it takes to assemble a packet or cell. Using the ATM standard 48-byte cell payload, we will need a 1-byte header (in addition to the cell header) leaving 47 bytes. At 64 Kbps (PCM code), this gives a cell assembly time of almost 6 milliseconds. For 32 Kbps the assembly time is 12 milliseconds.

   As more exotic coding schemes are employed, the cell assembly time increases as the required data rate decreases.

2. Network Transit Time

   This depends on the structure of the network but should be less than one millisecond per node traversed *plus* propagation delay at about 5.5 μsec per kilometer.

3. Delay Equalization

   This is the deliberate delay inserted immediately before the receiver in order to smooth out the effects of transit delay variation (jitter). Depending on the characteristics of the network this delay could be set somewhere between two and ten milliseconds.

The delay characteristics of the network are very important for two reasons:

1. Long transit delays cause the same effect subjectively as the well-known "satellite delay". (This is 240 milliseconds one way.) Most people find holding a voice conversation over a satellite circuit difficult. The effect is one that many people never become accustomed to.

   There is some argument over what is an acceptable delay. Some academics say 100 milliseconds others 150. But all agree that a one-way delay of 90 milliseconds or so causes no subjective loss of quality to most people.

2. The problem of echoes. Experience shows that when the delay is 45 milliseconds or more there is a potential problem with echoes.

The primary source of echoes is the "hybrid" device where the connection to the end user is carried over a two-wire analog circuit. Another source is reflections on the two-wire line itself.

In the case where the connection is fully digital from one end to the other the situation is controversial. In a recent paper on the subject (Sriram et al. 1991) the authors argue that echo cancellation is not needed in situations where the circuit is fully digital from end to end. Other people say that there is mechanical feedback caused in some telephone handsets and that this is a source of echo that cannot be eliminated by the fully digital circuit. This is an important and unresolved issue.

The importance rests in the fact that while echo cancellation technology is very good indeed, echo cancellers cost money.[5] In small countries where distances are short, network providers have only installed echo cancellers on international connections. A requirement for echo cancellation could add significant cost to their networks. In larger countries (such as the US or Australia) propagation delays are so great that echo cancellation is a requirement anyway.

8.3.3 Voice "Compression"

There are various ways available to reduce the data rate required in a voice circuit from the 64 Kbps standard rate. A coding scheme which reduces the data rate to 32 Kbps without measurable loss of quality is called Adaptive Differential PCM (ADPCM). In concept, ADPCM encodes each sample as the difference between it and the last sample, rather than as an absolute amplitude value.

There are many ways of voice compression which rely on the fact that a voice signal has considerable redundancy. (You can predict the general characteristics of the next few samples if you know the last few.)

PCM and ADPCM are very good indeed in terms of quality. It is very difficult for a listener to detect the difference between an original analog signal and one that has gone through encoding and later decoding. And because digital transmission is perfectly accurate, there is no loss in quality no matter how far the signal travels.

Nevertheless, even though we cannot hear a quality loss, a small loss does take place. This was the reason that the 64 Kbps standard for digital voice was adopted in the first place. In large public networks (such as in the US), the transition between the existing analog system and a universal digital system was (is) expected to take a very long time. During that transition, a call across the network may go through the conversion from

---

[5] Papers in the technical literature suggest that to build a digital echo canceller for this environment using a digital signal processor (DSP) requires a DSP of about 5 MIPS. This outweighs all the other functions performed in a digital packetizer/depacketizer (PADEP) by a ratio of five to one.

analog to digital and back again many times. Quality loss adds up, little by little. The standard was chosen because it was felt that there would need to be as many as *seven* conversions from analog to digital and back again along the path of some calls.

8.3.3.1 Variable-Rate Voice Coding

One of the ways of encoding voice looks to see when there is no actual speech and just stops sending data during the gaps.[6] This is not a new principle - it was used in the past over long distance analog circuits but is much improved using digital techniques. Speech does occur in "talk spurts" and it is half-duplex (most of the time only one person is talking). This means that about 60% of any (one-way) voice conversation, consists of silence. Why transmit silence?

There are many techniques available for encoding voice in this way. In the encoded form the conversation consists of short bursts of cells. A device called a *voice activity detector* (VAD) is used to turn the encoding process on or off (you must not compress when the voice channel is used, for example, to transmit a fax). It also should be noted that even within a period of speech the encoded information rate is variable.

One characteristic of the VAD is that it suppresses echoes. Provided the echo is at a relatively low level, the detector will stop encoding the signal. However, this is not perfect because when both parties talk simultaneously (a not unknown phenomena) each party could hear an echo of his/her own speech mixed up with the voice of the other speaker.

A reasonably good-quality, variable-rate voice coding scheme should result in a peak data rate of around 20 Kbps or a little more during talk spurts and an average rate (in each direction) of around 10 Kbps.

Thus, variable-rate voice puts a statistical load onto the network, but variable-rate coding does *not* remove the need for fast and uniform network transit delays.

8.3.3.2 Encoding Priority Schemes

In ATM, the only available method of alleviating congestion is to discard cells when there is a problem. If the cells can be coded in some way such that there are "essential" and "discardable" cells we can hope for a situation where all that happens when the network becomes congested is a graceful degradation in quality of service.

One suggested method is to code the voice cells in such a way as to put "essential" and "quality improvement" information (samples, etc.) into different cells. This is conceptually shown in Figure 8-5 on page 8-21. The most-significant bits of each sample are

---

6   An excellent discussion on this subject may be found in "A Blind Voice Packet Synchronization Strategy".

placed into the same cell and the least-significant bits into a different cell. The cells are marked in the header to say which cells may be discarded and which ones may not.

When the cells are presented at their destination for playout (after buffering for a time) if a low priority cell is missing, the decoder can extrapolate and, although the voice quality is affected, the signal is still understandable.

The example shown above is intentionally very simple. In practice, the coding schemes used in this way will be variable-rate ones and the algorithm will be much more complex than just a selection of bits by their significance. Nevertheless, the principle is still the same.

8.4 Image Traffic

Image traffic is conceptually similar to traditional data traffic with one major difference - images are very large compared to traditional character screen images.

A traditional IBM 3270 character screen showing multiple fields and many colors averages about 2500 bytes (the screen size is 1920 bytes, but other information relating to formatting and field characteristics is present). The same screen displayed as an image could be as much as 300 KB.

Images are therefore transmitted as groups of frames or packets (in SNA, as "chains"). Response time is important but only within normal human response requirements. Less than a second is goodness, up to perhaps five seconds is tolerable, above five seconds users become more and more seriously inconvenienced.

Nevertheless, because image traffic is typically initiated by a human operator entering some form of a transaction, display will be relatively infrequent - because systems are such that a user typically needs to spend time looking at the display before looking at the next image. In the future this may not hold true. Online books (with illustrations) for example may encourage users to "flick through" the pages looking for the information they need. "Flicking through the pages" of a book involves the consecutive display of many images perhaps a second or two apart. This could put a substantial unplanned load onto a data network.

8.4.1 Transporting Images

Image traffic is really not too different from traditional data traffic. Images range in size from perhaps 40 kilobytes to a few megabytes. If the user happens to be a real person at a terminal, subsecond response time is just as valuable for images as it always was for coded-data transactions.

In the "paperless-office" type of application, image users tend to spend more "think time" looking at the screen once it is displayed. That means that the transaction rates per terminal tend to be lower, but perhaps that is because most of the experience to date is with systems that are very slow in displaying the image and the user is thereby encouraged to get all the information possible from one display before looking at the next.

In engineering graphics (CAD) applications, interaction can be as often as once a minute and the user demands subsecond response time for megabyte-sized images.

Of course, images can be compressed and ratios of four to one are about average. This reduces network load and speeds up transmission time.

An open question for the future is "what will be the effect of very high-quality displays". It is possible today to buy color displays with a resolution of 4,000 points by 4,000 points with 256 colors and excellent quality. (The main use of these to date has been in air traffic control, military applications, and in engineering design.) The picture quality is so good that it rivals a color photograph. The point here is that images with this level of resolution are many times larger (even compressed) than the typical formats of today.

If these high resolution systems become popular then there will be significantly higher requirements for the network.

8.5 Full-Motion Video

At first thought, video traffic appears to share many of the characteristics of voice traffic (you set up a connection and transmit a continuous stream of data at a more or less constant rate until you no longer need the connection). In reality, while there are many similarities, transporting video in an ATM network is a quite different problem from transporting voice.

Video systems display information as a sequence of still pictures called frames. Each frame consists of a number of lines of information. The two predominant broadcast television systems currently use 625 lines at 25 frames/sec (PAL) or 450 lines at 30 frames/sec (NTSC).

Data Rate

If a PAL signal is to be digitally transmitted we could perhaps break up a line into 500 points and encode each point in 12 bits (color, intensity, etc.). This becomes quite a high transmission rate:

```
625 (lines) × 25 (per sec) × 500 (points) × 12 (bits) = 93,750,000 bits/sec
```

In fact, for reasonable resolution we probably do not need 500 points in each line and maybe we can code each point as 8 bits, but whichever way you look at it the data rate is very high.

This is altogether the wrong way to look at video. Over history we have broadcast video (a PAL signal requires about seven MHz bandwidth) over a fixed-rate channel. Every point in the picture was sent (although via analog transmission) in every frame. **But the information content of a video frame is inherently variable.** The point about video is that the majority of frames are very little different from the frame before. *If a still picture is transmitted through a video system, all we need to transmit is the first frame and then the information content of each subsequent frame is* **one** *bit. This bit says that this frame is the same as the one before!*

If a video picture is taken of a scene such as a room then only a data rate of one bit per frame is necessary to maintain the picture (that is, 25 bits/sec for PAL). As soon as a person enters and walks across the room, then there is much more information required in the transmission. But even then much of the picture area will remain unaffected. If the camera is "panned" across the room, then each frame is different from the one before *but* all that has happened is that the picture has moved. Most pixels (picture elements - bit positions) move by the same amount and perhaps we do not need to retransmit the whole thing.

There are many examples, such as the typical head and shoulders picture of a person speaking where most of the picture is still and only the lips are moving. But in a picture of a waterfall many pixels will be different from ones before *and* different in non-systematic ways. A video picture of a waterfall has a very high information content because it contains many non-systematic changes.

What is being discussed here is something a little different from what we traditionally regard as compression. When a still picture is examined, much of the picture area contains repetition. Any particular line (or point) will very likely have only small differences from the one either side of it. Within a line, there will be many instances of repetition such as when crossing an area of uniform color and texture. There are many algorithms available to compress a single image to a much smaller amount. So, although one can look for redundancy and compress it, a still picture contains a fixed amount of information (from an information theory viewpoint). A sequence of video pictures is different in the sense that, from an information theory standpoint, each frame can contain from one to perhaps a few million bits!

The net result of the above is the conclusion that video is fundamentally variable in the required rate of information transfer. It suggests that a variable-rate channel (such as an ATM network) may be a better medium than a fixed-rate TDM channel for video traffic. Consider the figure below:

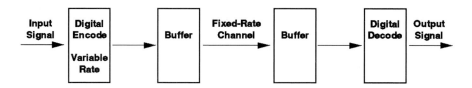

Figure *8-4.* *Transmitting Video over a Fixed-Rate Channel*

This is typical of existing systems that transmit video over a limited, digital transmission channel. Systems exist where quite good quality is achieved over a 384 Kbps digital channel. When the signal is digitally encoded and compressed, the output is a variable rate. But we need to send it down a fixed-capacity channel. Sometimes (most of the time) the required data rate is much lower than the 384 Kbps provided. At other times the required data rate is much higher than the rate of the channel. To even this out a buffer is placed before the transmitter so that if/when the decoder produces too much data for the channel it will not be lost. But when the data arrives at the receiver end of the channel data may not arrive in time for the next frame, if that frame contained too much data for the channel. To solve this, a buffer is inserted in the system and a delay introduced so there will be time for irregularities in reception rate to be smoothed out before presentation to the fixed-rate screen.

Buffers, however, are not infinite and if the demands of the scene are for a high data rate over an extended period of time, then data will be lost when the buffers are filled up (overrun). This is seen in "full-motion" video conference systems which typically operate over a limited channel. If the camera is "panned" too quickly, then the move-ment appears jerky and erratic to the viewer (caused by the loss of data as buffers are overrun).

It is easy to see from the above example that it is quite difficult to fit video into a limited-rate channel. Always remember however that the average rate required in the example above will be perhaps ten times less than the 384 Kbps provided and that most of the channel capacity is wasted anyway!

The extreme variation in information transfer requirement means that if a fixed-rate channel able to handle the fastest rate is used, then there will be a large amount of wasted capacity. If a limited channel is used then there is less (but still significant) waste of capacity but more important, there is loss of quality when a high transfer rate is used for a longer time than the buffers can hold. (Typically, existing systems buffer for a few seconds of high activity in the picture - if something such as the stereotype television car chase sequence occurs, then the system cannot handle it.)

Thinking about the matter statistically, if a number of video signals were able to share the same communications resource, then it is likely that when one video channel requires a high bandwidth, others will require much less. The statistics of it say that the more signals there are sharing a resource the less variation there will be in the resource requirement.

When there are only two users sharing a resource, there is a reasonably high probability that there will be times when both signals will require a high transfer rate at the same time. When 50 signals share the resource there is still a finite probability that all 50 will require a high transfer rate at the same time, but that probability is tiny.

This all leads to the conclusion that high-speed cell networks and LANs are the natural medium for digital video transmission.

Timing Considerations

Video traffic is like voice in one important respect - it is isochronous. Frames (or lines) are scanned at a constant rate and when displayed at the other end must be displayed at the same rate. But cell networks tend to deliver data at an uneven rate (this is also called "delay jitter"). Something needs to be done at the receiver end to even out the flow of cells to a constant rate. As with voice, this can be done by inserting a planned delay factor (just a queue of cells) at the receiver.

Redundancy

Even more than voice, video is very redundant indeed. The loss or corruption of a few bits is undetectable. The loss of a few lines is not too much of a problem since if we display the line from the previous frame unchanged, most times the loss will be undetected. Even the loss of a frame or two here and there does not matter much because our eyes will barely notice. Of course, it must be noted that when video is digitally coded and compressed loss or corruption of cells will have a much larger effect (because the data is now a lot less redundant).

Video Applications

Very often video applications are for one-way transmission (as in viewing television or a movie). In this case, the amount of delay that we may insert into the system without detriment can be quite great (perhaps ten seconds or more).

Interactive video is a little different in that this is the "videophone" application, that is, people talking to one another accompanied by a picture. In this case, although the voice communication is logically half-duplex (that is, hopefully only one person talks at one time), the video portion is continuous. Delay is still less stringent than for voice - although the voice component has all the characteristics of regular voice (without video). It appears that synchronization of voice with the movement of lips is not too critical.

Most people do not detect a difference of 120 milliseconds between the image and the sound in this situation.

8.5.1 Digital Video in an ATM Network

The discussion above concluded that packet or cell-based networks are a natural medium for video transmission. But certainly we do not mean "traditional" packet networks. Many, if not most, existing packet networks do not have sufficient total capacity to handle even one video signal! In order to operate properly, a packet network processing video must have a number of important characteristics:

1. Sufficient capacity. The throughput capacity of the network must be sufficient to handle several video signals together - otherwise the benefit of sharing the resource is lost.

2. End-to-end delay appropriate to the application. This varies quite a bit with the application. One-way traffic does not care about network delay too much. Interactive video needs a transit delay approximating that of voice (because voice accompanies it) but does not need to be exactly synchronized to the voice.

3. Minimal cell jitter. Irregularities in the cell delivery rate need to be smoothed out by inserting a buffer and a delay.

In addition, there is the question of what to do when the network becomes congested and how to handle errors.

8.5.1.1 Hierarchical Source Coding

All networks of finite capacity encounter congestion at various times. But with video (as with voice) you cannot slow down the input rate to the network in order to control congestion (as we do in data networks) because a video frame arriving too late is simply garbage. If the network is congested, the best we can do is to throw some cells away until the network returns to normal. If this happens only very infrequently, then video and voice users will not get too upset, but if it happens often, then the system can become unusable.

One approach to congestion is to code the information (video or voice) into cells in such a way that the information is split up. Information essential to display of the frame is coded into a separate cell from information that merely improves the quality. This means that some cells contain essential information and others less-essential information. The cells can be marked in the header so that the network will discard only less-essential cells during periods of congestion. This technique (originally invented for handling packet voice) is called "Hierarchical Source Coding" (HSC) and has the obvious advantage of allowing the system to continue basic operation during periods of congestion.

The concept is very simple. Imagine that a particular byte of encoded data represents the intensity level of a particular point on the screen. A simple HSC technique might be to take the four high-order bits and send them in one cell (marked essential) and the four low-order bits in a different cell (marked less-essential). In the normal case, when the cells arrive at the destination the byte is reconstructed. In the case of congestion, perhaps the cell containing the less-important, low-order bits has been discarded. The receiver would then assume the four low-order bits have been lost and treat them as zeros. The result would be to give 16 levels of intensity for the particular point rather than the 256 levels that would have been available had the less-important cell not been discarded. In practice, HSC techniques need to be designed in conjunction with the encoding (and compression) methods. These can be very complex indeed.

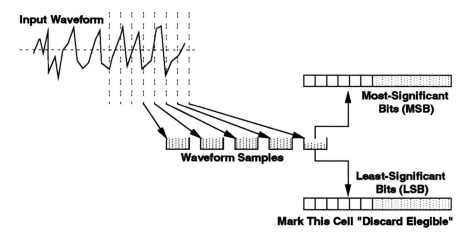

Figure **8-5.** *Hierarchical Source Coding for Priority Discard Scheme*

In principle, this is not too different from what we do in the analog broadcasting environment:

- Most color TV sets contain a circuit called a "color killer". When the received analog TV signal is too weak or contains too much interference the circuit "kills" the color and displays the picture in black and white. This enables a viewer to see a picture (although only a B+W one), which, if displayed in color, would not be recognizable.

- In radio broadcasting of FM stereo an ingenious system is used such that two signals (left channel plus right channel and left channel minus right channel) are transmitted. The two are frequency-multiplexed such that the L+R signal occupies the lower part of the frequency band and the L-R the upper part. When the signal is received strongly, the channel separation can be reconstructed by addition and subtraction of the channels. When the signal is weak, the L+R signal dominates because it occupies the lower part of the band. What you get then is only L+R (mono) reception. So when the signal is weak, you lose the stereo effect but still get a basic signal.

Hierarchical Source Coding will probably become a basic technique for processing both voice and video in ATM networks.

This depends a bit on the standards allowing it. At the present time the endpoint must not set the Cell Loss Priority bit - some people feel this should be the prerogative of the network. However, the issue is not yet resolved.

8.5.1.2 Error Control

The worst problem in processing video is delay jitter (erratic delays in cell delivery). Recovery from link errors by retransmission of data is not usable within a cell network containing video for this reason. The best thing to do with errored cells is to discard them immediately. Misrouting due to errors in the destination field in the header can have catastrophic effects. ATM cells have a frame check sequence field (the HEC, which protects the header, not the payload) which is checked every time the cell travels over a link and the cell is discarded if an error is found.

There is a question about what to do at the receiver when an expected cell does not arrive due to errors or congestion in the network. It has been suggested that using a very short cell size with an error-correcting code might be a useful technique. Unfortunately, while this technique would overcome random single-bit errors, it is not a satisfactory way to overcome the loss of many cells in a group. This is because an error-correcting code capable of recovering from this kind of situation would be so large that the overhead would be unacceptable.

The best technique for handling errors in video involves using the information from the previous frame and whatever has been received of the current frame to build an approximation of the lost information. A suitable strategy might be to just continue displaying the corresponding line from the previous frame, or if only a single line is lost, extrapolating the information from the lines on either side of the lost one.

8.5.1.3 High-Quality Sound

High-quality sound (CD-quality stereo) involves a very high bit rate. Encoding sound is, in principle, the same problem as for voice but with a few differences for the network:

- High-quality sound (such as a film soundtrack) is continuous - unlike voice transmission where talk exists in "spurts".

- The data rate is much higher (but the same compression techniques that worked for voice also work here).

  20 (KHz) x 2 (samples) x 8 (bits) x 2 channels = a data rate of 640 Kbps for minimum-quality stereo.

- Delay through the network does not matter as much - this depends on the requirements for the video signal the sound accompanies.

- The major requirement is that (like video and voice) high-quality sound be delivered to the network at a constant rate and played out at the receiver at a constant rate.

8.5.1.4 Summary

The transmission requirements of digital video were discussed in 8.5, "Full-Motion Video" on page 8-16. As far as the network is concerned, video traffic is very similar to voice in the sense that both require a timing relationship to be maintained between the sender and the receiver. Packets or cells must arrive at a regular rate if the receiver is to maintain a stable picture.

There are some differences from voice however:

- The absolute amount of bandwidth required is enormous compared with telephone-quality voice transmission.

- The quality required of a video transmission varies widely with the application. Broadcast quality requires a significantly greater bandwidth than does remote education or videoconference applications. Videophones require even less (as low as 128 Kbps).

- While a raw video signal is a very high constant rate, the characteristics of video make variable-rate coding schemes significantly more effective than they are for voice. The problem is that the amount of variation is extreme. A still picture, properly coded, has an information content of 25 bits per second. A piece of very fast action may require an instantaneous rate of over 100 megabits per second.

  Voice traffic occurs in spurts, but the extremes of variation in throughput requirement are not at all the same.

- Video is much more redundant than voice and a "glitch" is perhaps less significant. A missed frame here and there will hardly be noticed.

- The natural coding of video (because of the amount of information) is in large blocks (in excess of a thousand bytes).

- Most video is not interactive. Broadcast-quality video is almost never so. For one-way video we do not have the strict network delay problems that exist with voice. We can afford to have a large reassembly buffer and a playout delay of perhaps several seconds to compensate for transit delay variations in the network.

- Interactive video is usually accompanied by voice and so tighter transit delay requirements are needed, but video does not need to be exactly synchronized to the voice in any case. A 100 millisecond difference is quite acceptable. Thus, we can afford a 100 ms playout buffer for video traffic even if it accompanies a voice signal.

- Encoding priority schemes such as described earlier for voice are also available for video traffic (see 8.3.3.2, "Encoding Priority Schemes" on page 8-14). This enables cells carrying "less-essential" parts of the signal to be discarded by the network during periods of congestion.

The biggest problem with video is just the enormous data rate that is required. If the peak data rate required by a single video user (or even a small number of users) is a significant percentage of the total capacity of the network, then there is potentially a serious congestion problem. For example, if a broadcast-quality signal fully variable-rate encoded required a peak data rate of 50 megabits per second (even though the average might be say 10 megabits per second) and the base network uses 140 Mbps internode links, (that is, a single user can take up 30% of one resource) then there is a potential congestion problem. The safe planned utilization of a network (for stable operation) in this situation might be as low as 30%.

As the number of users increases and the capacity of the network increases the problem becomes less and less significant. One hundred broadcast-quality video users with characteristics as described above will require perhaps 1000 megabits per second, *but the maximum total peak requirement might be no more than 1200 megabits per second.* In the previous example, the peak requirement of a single user was four times the average requirement. In the case of a hundred users, the peak (for practical purposes) is only 20% greater than the average.

8.5.2 Characteristics of Multimedia Applications

Many people believe that the ability to provide a coordinated mixture of data, voice, and video services to the desktop will provide major productivity enhancements for business. Indeed, some people believe that this ability is the key to a whole new way of living and working for large numbers of people because it will mean the final removal of distance as an inhibitor to intellectual interaction between people. Proposed applications may be classified as follows:

- Multiparty video conferencing

- Real-time audiovisual collaboration (one on one)

- Interactive training

- Enhanced personal videoconferencing

There are several important points to note here:

1. Communication requires a large amount of bandwidth.

2. Communication must be to each user's desktop (or home).

3. Multiple types of information are involved (voice, data, video, image).

4. The presentation of this information to the end user must be coordinated. That is, *presentation of the different forms of related information must be synchronized.*

8.5.3 Quality of Service (QoS)

The above discussion leads to an important conclusion: *Different kinds of network traffic require different service characteristics from the network.* These service characteristics[7] may be summarized in three critical parameters of which two are illustrated in Figure 8-6.

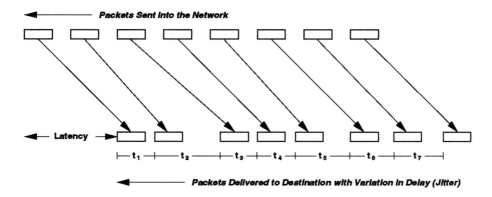

Figure 8-6. *Latency and Jitter*

Latency is the delay in time between when the stream is transmitted and when it is presented to the end user. This is more than propagation delay because of staging delay within transit nodes, the need for buffering, etc. at the end-user device.

Jitter is variation in latency over time. This causes erratic presentation of information to the end user. When you introduce buffering in the receiver to smooth out the presentation, then the presence of the buffers increases the network latency.

Skew is the difference in time of presentation to the end user of related things (such as a video of someone speaking and the related sound).

This is *the critical problem* for multimedia in ATM. The synchronization between voice and video streams within a receiving workstation.

Overrun and Underrun are perhaps not predominantly network issues. This is where the video or voice signal is generated at a different rate from the rate at which it is played out. In the case of overrun, information is generated faster than it can be displayed and, at some point, information must be discarded. Underrun is where the playout rate is greater than the rate of signal generation and therefore "glitches" will occur when data must be presented but none is there.

---

[7] See "Multimedia Networking Performance Requirements" by James D. Russell in bibliography.

In order to avoid these effects you need to provide end-to-end network synchronization. This involves propagating a network clock throughout the ATM network. This is discussed in Appendix C, "Synchronization" on page C-1.

To an extent, depending on the application, a good system can mask the effects of overrun and underrun.

The importance of each of these factors varies with the application, but skew is both the most important for the multimedia application and the greatest challenge for the network (and incidentally for the workstation itself).

Interactive Applications

Applications such as videoconferencing (personal or group) have the same requirements as regular voice. That is, a maximum latency of about 150 ms is tolerable.

Jitter must be contained to within limits that the system can remove without the user knowing (perhaps 20 ms is tolerable).

Skew (between audio and video) should be such that the audio is between 20 ms ahead and 120 ms behind the video.

One-Way Video Distribution

In this application a delay of several seconds between sender and receiver is quite acceptable in many situations. This largely depends on whether the user expects to watch a two-hour movie or a 20-second animated segment in a training application. The delay really only matters because it is the time between the user requesting the information and when it starts being presented. For a movie, perhaps 30 seconds would be tolerable, but for a short segment, one second is perhaps the limit.

Jitter and skew, however, have the same limits as the interactive applications above.

Audio with Image Applications

These are applications such as illustrated lectures and voice-annotated text where still images are annotated by voice commentary. Depending on the application, latency may need to be less than 500 ms (between the request for the next image and its presentation), but the skew (audio behind the image) could be perhaps as long as a second or so.

Figure 8-7 on page 8-27 shows a summary of jitter and cell-loss tolerance for various application types. These requirements place a significant demand on the network as discussed above.

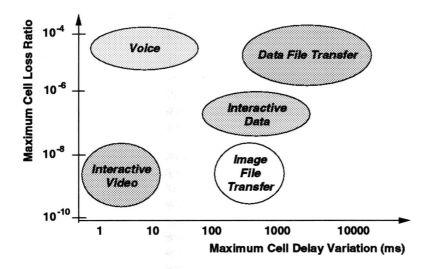

Figure 8-7. Jitter and Cell-Loss Tolerance of Some Application Types

You need:

1. Adequate (high) data rates (to keep latency low and to allow sufficient capacity to service the application)
2. Low latency
3. Very low jitter
4. Very low skew
5. End-to-end control through propagation of a stable clock

All of this must be delivered to the workplace (desk or home)!

8.5.4 Quality-of-Service Classes

Quality of service in an ATM network is a concept that attempts to describe the important parameters of the network service provided to a given end user. These parameters include:

- End-to-end delay
- Delay variation (delay jitter)
- Cell loss ratio

This is a very difficult thing to guarantee in a network that handles any kind of bursty traffic. These characteristics vary quite widely with the load on the network. In some situations, tight control of these parameters is a major issue. Voice, video, and CBR traffic need to know these parameters so as to decide on the size of playout buffer queues, etc.

The following QoS classes have been defined in the standards:

QoS Class 1 (Service Class A Performance Requirements)

> This QoS class applies to circuit emulation and constant bit rate traffic (CBR video and voice for example).[8] These are to be set such that the result should provide performance comparable to current digital private lines.

QoS Class 2 (Service Class B Performance Requirements)

> This is not yet fully defined but should provide suitable conditions for packetized video and audio in teleconferencing and multimedia applications.

QoS Class 3 (Service Class C Performance Requirements)

> This is intended for interoperation of connection-oriented data services such as frame relay.

QoS Class 4 (Service Class D Performance Requirements)

> This is intended for connectionless services such as LAN emulation, IP, or SMDS services.

A particular QoS class has specified performance parameters attached to it, and it may have two different cell loss ratios. A different cell loss ratio is appropriate for cells with CLP=0 to that for those cells with CLP=1. There is also a QoS class with no specified performance parameters (unspecified QoS class). Each connection may have its own unique QoS class attached to it.

Practical networks may support one or many specified QoS classes, as well as traffic with unspecified QoS.

---

8   Service classes were discussed in 3.1.1.1, "AAL Service Classes" on page 3-2.

Chapter 9. Traffic Management

Traffic management is probably the most controversial (and important) aspect of ATM. The original concept of ATM included the idea that network congestion would not be controlled by mechanisms within the network itself. It was (and still is, by many) felt that detailed flow controls cannot be successfully performed within the network.

9.1 ATM Service Categories

The ATM Forum has specified five "service categories" in relation to traffic management in an ATM network. These are similar to but are not the same as the AAL service classes discussed in 3.1.1.1, "AAL Service Classes" on page 3-2. These categories are:

Constant Bit Rate (CBR)

> CBR traffic includes anything where a continuous stream of bits at a predefined constant rate is transported through the network.

> This might be voice (compressed or not), circuit emulation (say the transport, unchanged, of a T1 or E1 circuit), or some kind of video. Typically you need both short transit delay and very low jitter in this service class.

Real-Time Variable Bit Rate (rt-VBR)

> This is like CBR in the sense that we still want low transit delay but the traffic will vary in its data rate. We still require a guaranteed delivery service. The data here might be compressed video, compressed voice with silence suppression, or HDLC link emulation with idle removal.

Non-Real-Time Variable Bit Rate (nrt-VBR)

> This is again a guaranteed delivery service where transit delay and jitter are perhaps less important than in the rt-VBR case. An example here might be MPEG-2 encoded video distribution. In this case, the information may be being retrieved from a disk and be one-way TV distribution. A network transit delay of even a few seconds is not a problem here. But we do want guaranteed service because the loss of a cell in compressed video has quite a severe effect on the quality of the connection.

unspecified bit rate

> The UBR service is for "best effort" delivery of data. It is also a way of allowing for proprietary internal network controls. A switch using its own (non-standard) internal flow controls should offer the service as UBR class. You send data on a UBR connection into the network and if there is any congestion in any resource, then the network will throw your data away. In many cases, with

appropriate end-to-end error recovery protocols this may be quite acceptable. This should be workable for many if not most traditional data applications such as LAN emulation and IP transport.

Available Bit Rate (ABR)

The concept of ABR is to offer a guaranteed delivery service (with minimal cell loss) to users who can tolerate a widely varying throughput rate. The idea is to use whatever bandwidth is available in the running network after other traffic utilizing guaranteed bandwidth services has been serviced. One statement [2] of the primary goal of the ABR service is for *"the economical support of applications with vague requirements for throughputs and delays"*.

In an operational network, there may be bandwidth "allocated" to a particular user but in fact going unused at this particular instant in time.

Either by providing feedback from the network to the sender or by monitoring the network's behavior, the ABR service can change the bit rate of the connection dynamically as network conditions change. The end-user system must be able to obey the ABR protocol and to modify its sending rate accordingly.

Many people believe that ABR service requires the use of complex flow and congestion controls *within* the network. Others disagree very strongly.

9.2 Congestion

However, while there are disagreements about complexity and whether controls should be done inside or outside the network, the control of congestion is an essential aspect of any communication network.

9.2.1 The Problem of Congestion

Congestion is perhaps the most significant problem in communication network design. When too much data is sent into the network many things happen - most of which are very undesirable to network operators. The exact effects always depend on the architecture of the network itself, but in ATM networks the effects include:

- Large (uncontrolled) cell jitter
- Very long network transit times (and response times)
- Loss of data

Within a network, any shared resource is a potential point at which congestion may occur. If you consider the prototype of a communication network, it consists of a number of nodes (switches, routers...) interconnected by communication links (in this context, often called "trunks"). End-user devices are connected to the nodes through other communication links.

In Figure 9-1 on page 9-3, there are two places where information flows *share* network resources:

1. Links (trunks)
2. Nodes (switches or routers)

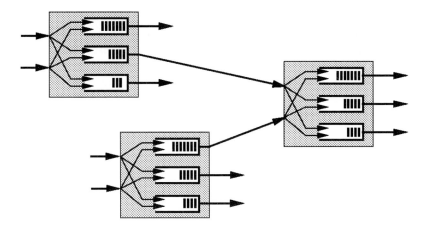

Figure 9-1. *An ATM Network with Infinite-Capacity Switches.* It is possible to build an ATM switch as an almost completely non-blocking device with no significant internal queues except for queueing for outbound links.

Depending on their design, there are different aspects of a node which are shared:

- Memory (packet buffer pools)
- I/O processors (scanners, etc.)
- Internal buses or switches
- Central processors
- Network management processors
- Many other things depending on the particular node's design

Whenever there is sharing of resources between data flows, there is usually (notably not always) the temptation for designers to overcommit resources. For example, in the traditional packet switch architecture of the 1970s and 1980s a shared memory was used as a "pool" for intermediate storage of data as it passed through the node. This was done because of the immense cost benefit (20 to 1, perhaps 100 to 1) by taking advantage of the statistical characteristics of network traffic. There are actually many aspects to this, for example, the use of a single memory (implying the sharing of access to that memory) instead of multiple small memories and the total size of that memory. Another example is the universal use of shared trunks, the capacity of which is usually significantly less than the total capacity of connected links to end users.

Whenever there is a shared resource where there is the possibility of contention for the use of that resource you have to do something to resolve who gets it. The usual "something" is to build a queue in front of the resource. Indeed, a communication network can be seen as a network of queues.

The presence of a queue implies a delay (a wait for service). Because queues vary in length, sometimes very quickly, their presence also implies a variation in delay (jitter). It also implies a cost (for storage to hold the data, for example). But what do you do when the queue gets too long? You could throw the data away, you could tell the input devices to stop sending input, you could perhaps keep track on the length of the queue and do something to control the input rate so that the queue never became too long. These latter techniques are flow controls.

In the networks of the 1970s and 1980s there were usually flow controls built into the network protocols. This was (in some contexts still is) a very important issue. It was the superiority of the flow controls in IBM SNA that enabled SNA to utilize trunk links to very high utilization while maintaining stable network operation. This meant that users saved cost on trunk connections. It was this aspect that underwrote the enormous success of SNA.

9.2.1.1 Queue Behavior
Figure 9-2 shows a very famous (but not intuitive) result.

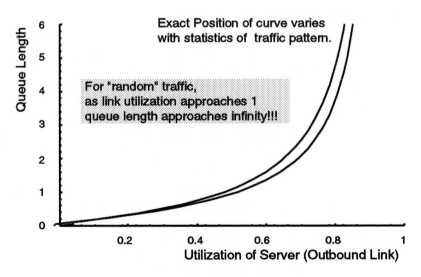

Figure *9-2.* *Queue Length versus Resource Utilization*

This applies to queueing in general, not only in communications. If you have a shared resource (such as a supermarket checkout) where transactions (customers) arrive randomly (whatever definition of randomness you like to use) you get a queue forming. A critical aspect of this is the rate of arrivals at the shared resource (server) and the rate at which transactions are processed.

There is a surprising (and critical) result here: *As the average rate of arrivals approaches the average rate of transaction processing the length of the queue will tend to infinity.* This hinges on randomness of arrivals and is influenced by randomness in service times (that is, the number of items in the basket in a supermarket or the length of a block of data in a communication network). Another way of stating the above is to introduce the concept of utilization of the server. Utilization is just the average arrival rate multiplied by the average time it takes to service a transaction expressed as a proportion of total time. Utilization is usually quoted as the percentage of time that the server is busy.

Many books have been written on queueing theory! An important thing to note is that there are many variables here that affect the position of the curve in Figure 9-2 on page 9-4. The precise arrival pattern is very important. If arrivals are at exact intervals and all transactions take exactly the same time to process, then the curve shifts to the right so that there is almost no queue at all until we reach 100% utilization. Different patterns of randomness [1] result in the curve shifting to the left of where it is shown.

The point is that as you increase the loading on any shared facility you reach a point where, if you add any more traffic, you will get severely increased queue length and problems with congestion.

9.2.1.2 Effect of Network Protocols

Figure 9-3 on page 9-6 shows what happens in different kinds of networks when the load offered to the network (potential traffic that end-user devices want to send) is increased beyond the network's capacity to handle it. The curve on the left is typical of Ethernet (and ATM with some traffic types). As load is increased, the network handles it fine until a point is reached where the traffic can no longer be handled. Network throughput actually *decreases* very quickly when this point is reached. In fact, in the case of Ethernet, the network collapses and no data at all gets through. This is because collisions take capacity away from the network, as load increases collisions increase and capacity decreases which itself increases the probability of more collisions!

It must be pointed out that Ethernet works perfectly well in many situations, mainly as a result of the flow controls imposed by network protocols at higher layers (that is, external

---

[1] There are many different random distributions.

to Ethernet itself). The same is true of IP (TCP flow control stabilizes it) and (many would assert) will be true of ATM.

The curve on the right shows what happens in well controlled networks. Once full throughput is reached, the network continues to operate at full capacity. There are queues, of course, but these are mainly in the end-user devices to avoid an overflow of the queues in the network. This comes at the higher cost of token-based access control (in TRN and FDDI) or extensive flow controls and the necessary processing hardware (in SNA). "Ya pays yer money and ya takes yer choice."

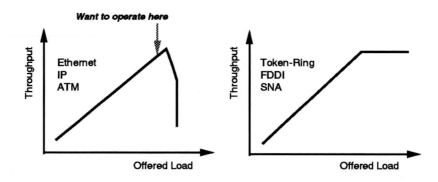

Figure *9-3. ATM Network Throughput under Increasing Load Conditions*

9.2.2 Congestion in ATM Networks

In an important sense, ATM networks don't ever get congested. Small parts of ATM networks experience congestion, but this seldom spreads very far within the total network. The most obvious resource that can become congested is a link. That is, a queue forms for the link and exceeds a "normal" value. In addition, parts of switches (but seldom whole switches) can also become congested:

- You could develop a queue for the internal switching element or bus. This might occur if its total capacity was less than the amount of traffic.

- Depending on how it operates you could get a queue within the internal switching element. It could also occur, for example, if many inputs to the switching element were all directed to the same output. Another way might be if there was a large amount of multicast traffic which causes duplication (expansion) of the amount of data within the switching element.

- You can certainly have congestion on one link affect other links if there is a shared buffer memory (a number of links statistically share the same memory).

- You could queue for a control process (again if that process was shared among a number of links). For example, this might be the process that translates the VPI/VCI, if this process was shared between many links.

- And in many other places depending on the design of the particular switch.

However, ATM switches accept all the input that is sent to them. There are no window-based (credit-based) flow controls (although these have been proposed). So, congestion in one part of the network will not easily spread to the rest of the network, and congestion on one link will not easily cause congestion on other links. This is basically because people have much less sharing of resources within an ATM switch than in older architectures.

There are a number of considerations that apply particularly to ATM networks (or other high-speed architectures) when it comes to consideration of potential congestion control and avoidance strategies.

High Speed (Bandwidth× Delay Product)

Contrary to popular belief, when a link gets faster it doesn't really get faster! A link running at 35 Mbps does send more bits in a given space of time than one running at 9.6 Kbps. However, *nothing* goes any faster! The speed of electricity in a wire or light in a fiber hasn't changed. What we have done is pack the bits closer together on the medium. Propagation delay is still 5 μsec per kilometer or thereabouts.

On a link between New York and Los Angeles you have a one-way transit delay of about 20 ms. This means that at 620 Mbps you have 620 000 000×20/1000 bits in flight (1.6 mega*bytes*) at any one time. If you are sending from NY to LA and the LA node gets congested and signals NY to slow down, then the LA node will receive 3 megabytes more data even if the NY sender stops immediately upon receiving the request.

This can be generalized to say that the amount of data outstanding on a link at any time is the product of its bandwidth and its delay (the so-called bandwidth×delay product). If traditional link control protocols are used for controlling a link such as this, then enormous buffers will be needed at each end of the connection.

High Speed (Processor Speed)

Link speeds have increased much faster than processor speeds (at least recently). In the original concept of ATM many people felt that a switch could only handle the speed if processing was minimal. At 622 Mbps you have less than one microsecond per cell to do all the needed processing. If you go to 2.4 Gbps you have a quarter of a microsecond.

Whatever protocols are adopted for the switch, they should be able to be realized in hardware so that cells can be processed at full rate.

Guaranteed Quality of Service

Traditional data networks regard transit times of .5 second as quite good. Jitter in transit time of perhaps .5 of a second is acceptable in most conventional data networks. However, in ATM networks we wish to guarantee transit delays and to guarantee jitter performance, because we wish to handle voice, video, and constant-bit-rate traffic. This is a new requirement for any kind of packet network.

New Uses

Traditional networks (even the much touted LAN client/server networks) have traffic patterns that are dominated by host-terminal interactions (client/server is only a new name for host/terminal). That is, data transfer is between a single host (server) and many terminals (clients). There is almost no client-to-client traffic. This means that the total network load is regulated and a maximum is set by the power of the server (host). You can't get more traffic than the servers can process. This is why Ethernet works!

But we now conceive of many new applications where there still may not be too much client-to-client traffic, but where the number of servers and things that can act as servers has increased dramatically.

Low Error Rates

One significant benefit of the new fiber links is that error rates are very low. Indeed, error rates on fiber are typically a hundred million times better than error rates on copper media. So, you don't need complex link error recoveries any more (but you don't get flow control as a by-product of link control either).

Network Collapse

This is the situation illustrated on the left-hand side of Figure 9-3 on page 9-6. Error recovery in an ATM network is *always* performed from end to end (from adaptation layer to adaptation layer). When an ATM network detects an error on a link or becomes congested the only mechanism it has for resolving the situation is to discard cells (data). For example, in a congestion situation a node might discard all the data queued for transmission on a particular link or group of links.

The problem is that cells are very short. Cells do not have the space to contain additional header overheads to enable error recovery (by retransmission) of individual cells. Error recovery is done by retransmission of whole user data blocks. For example, when a 2 KB (kilobyte) block is sent through a cell network, it is sent as 43 cells. If an individual cell is lost (or discarded by the network) then the error recovery operation is to *resend the whole logical data block!* That is, resend all 43 cells.

This does not matter too much for cells lost due to random errors on internode links (error rates are extremely low). But, in the case where the network discards data due to congestion there is a potential problem.

When a node discards, say, 1000 cells it is *extremely unlikely* that these cells will come from a small number of logical data blocks. It is very likely that the 1000 cells will be from different logical blocks of user data. If the average user data block length is 2 KB (a low estimate), then the amount of data that must be retransmitted is 43 000 cells. *So, discarding 1000 cells has caused the retransmission of 43 000 cells.* And this only happens when the network is already congested!

Traditional Flow Control Methods

The flow and congestion control mechanisms used in existing software-based packet networks are not adequate for the high-speed environment. Some types of traffic, voice or video for example, cannot have their delivery rate slowed down. You either have to process it at its full rate or clear the circuit.

Also, traditional "rotating-window" (credit-based) flow controls such as are used within traditional packet networks require complex processing in software within the network nodes. Processing in software would prevent a totally hardware-based switching operation. It thus conflicts with the need for very fast routing performed by hardware functions.

LAN or WAN Environment

While ATM is a technology that is equally applicable to the LAN and WAN environments[2] it has very different characteristics in each environment.

In the LAN we just don't care about the bandwidth×delay product (distances are very short) or about propagation delays. In the LAN we also have almost limitless bandwidth potential because the user owns the links and they can run at (almost) any speed we like. Bandwidth is essentially free in the LAN.

In the WAN we must buy link capacity from a carrier and this is very expensive. So, in the WAN, we want to optimize bandwidth usage; in the LAN this is only a minor objective.

Other requirements have different levels of importance. It is unlikely that we will want to use an ATM switch to replace a voice PBX within a building in the short term (though in the long term this is a serious application). In the WAN

---

[2] Also the HAN - Home Area Network

most user "data" is still voice. In the WAN, the carriage of voice traffic is perhaps the major cost benefit item in ATM.

It is these different environments, and the different operational characteristics implied by these environments, that give rise to most of the controversy about ATM flow and congestion controls. Different people are focusing on different environments.

It is quite clear that unless there are very effective protocols in place to prevent congestion, and to limit the effects when congestion occurs, ATM networks are just not going to work at all!

9.2.3 Controlling Congestion

9.2.3.1 Detecting Congestion

In the preceding section the point was made that an entire ATM network will experience congestion very seldom, if at all. However, individual parts of them (especially links) can become congested very easily. The question is "how do we know when we have congestion"? In traditional packet networks this was easy - you almost always had a shared buffer pool for all links connected to a node and when that started to fill up you knew you were in trouble!

In ATM it is not so easy. Because of the granularity of ATM equipment it is quite likely that there could be severe congestion in one direction of an end-to-end connection and no congestion at all in the other direction. This is because there may be very little sharing of resources between data flows in one direction or the other within an ATM switch.[3] An obvious response to congestion on a connection might be for a switch to send a warning message back to the sender when it sees traffic from that sender arriving at a point of congestion. But the fact that there is little or no commonality between send and receive paths makes this quite difficult to do in practice. It is also logically complex to implement.

There are no standards in place or proposed that define what constitutes congestion or how it is to be detected. What has to happen is that you need to monitor the length of every queue in the system (individually) and perhaps have a number of different states depending on the individual situation.

---

[3] Both of IBM's ATM Switch products - the IBM 2220 Nways BroadBand Switch and the IBM 8260 Multiprotocol Intelligent Switching Hub have only minimal sharing of this kind.

These might be for example:

1. Uncongested
2. Slight congestion
3. Congested
4. Extreme congestion (start cell discard algorithm)

IBM's Networking BroadBand Services (NBBS) architecture uses an interesting technique for the detection of congestion from outside the network. It uses measurements of change in network end-to-end delay to detect the onset of congestion. This is discussed in 9.3.1.1, "Enhanced Adaptive Rate-Based (eARB) Control" on page 9-17.

9.2.3.2 Infinite Capacity

One obvious way to avoid congestion is to decide not to have any! That is, make sure that all the components of the network have more capacity than it is ever possible to use. This is *not* silly.

A good example is the experimental video-on-demand network built by Time-Warner in Orlando, Florida. In this case they deliver MPEG (1) video streams to homes and process the AAL (5 in this case) within the set-top box. These MPEG video (including sound) streams are all a constant rate (around 3 Mbps) but they are not isochronous (MPEG contains its own timing information independent of the network). The system is designed such that each link (and switch) knows how many simultaneous streams it can handle and will accept no more connections. Hence they can run at very high utilizations with *no flow or congestion control at all!*

It might be said that if you don't take advantage of the potential bandwidth saving, then why bother to use ATM? But in fact, ATM has many more advantages than bandwidth optimization. Even with CBR streams it is significantly more cost-effective to switch ATM streams than TDM streams.

Even with varying streams, if bandwidth cost is very low why not just allocate the maximum for each connection? In the LAN environment (where bandwidth cost is exceedingly low) this may not be a bad idea.

In practice, however, people want to buy something that sounds faster. 155 Mbps is faster than 100 Mbps (isn't it?) even if the device attached to it can't do 50 Mbps! Current activity in the ATM Forum suggests that we will soon have a very low-cost 622 Mbps desktop link protocol defined. The realities of marketing suggest that everyone will want this even if there is little of no chance they can make use of it any time soon. Thus, we can't easily know just what actual data rate we will receive from an attached link. It would not be practical to plan everything for the maximum link speed attainable.

But the real issue here is what to do about LAN client/server traffic. A client requests a file from a server (perhaps 100 megabytes). The client makes a request like that perhaps

3 or 4 times per day (but stays logged on). The user would like the data immediately but, in practice, will be happy with a few minutes. It is clearly impractical to allocate capacity in this environment or to provide for the total of all the peaks.

9.2.3.3 Statistical Techniques

Many traffic types that vary significantly nevertheless add up to a very stable traffic characteristic. Often referred to as the "law of large numbers", this principle is illustrated in Figure 9-4. The figure shows computer-generated random numbers but will make the point. In this case we have taken 50 sets of random numbers where each number varies between 1 and 2 (with a mean of 1.5). Adding these sets up (think of them as signals varying over time) we might expect a total that varies between 50 and 100. But this is not what happens at all. True, the mean is 75, but the variation is only between 70 and 80. Thus, as a proportion of the total, the amount of variation in the stream has become very much less!

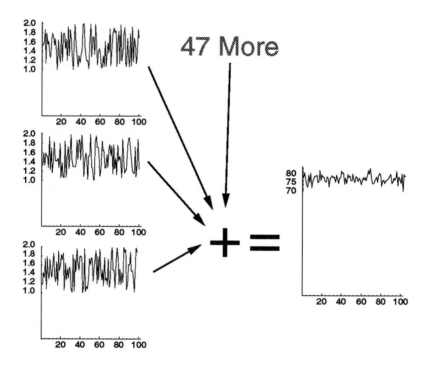

Figure 9-4. The "Law of Large Numbers". When you add up many varying things with similar characteristics the amount of variation in the total becomes proportionally smaller as the number of things is increased.

If we take (say) 1000 variable-rate, compressed voice signals including silence suppression we can expect the total to be very stable indeed. Given this, on a high-speed ATM link connection where we might be able to put several thousands of compressed voice streams, we could quite safely plan the maximum link utilization for over 95% or very close to it.

In a traditional banking teller network with only transaction traffic, there is a rule-of-thumb: you get 3 transactions per second for every 100 terminals in the network. So, a network of 3000 terminals can be safely planned for 90 transactions per second even if there is some remote probability of a greater instantaneous rate. In planning such a network we might plan capacity such that at 90 transactions per second the maximum utilization on any resource would not exceed (say) 70% (to keep queues short).

We can generalize this observation. The law of large numbers will produce stable traffic (with little variation) for us if:

1. There is a large number of similar traffic streams.

2. These streams are combined onto a single path.

3. They all have similar (random) traffic characteristics.

4. No stream is a significant portion of the total.

5. They are unrelated (this is most important).

These characteristics apply to VBR traffic such as compressed voice and video (if you can get sufficient similar streams onto a single path) and some types of traditional data traffic (such as banking or airline reservations traffic).

Sadly, this will not work for LAN client/server traffic. Or rather that the variations are so large and the traffic so sparse that we would need to get an enormous number of streams together before we experienced the stabilizing effect.

9.2.3.4 Implicit Controls

In traditional data networks, end-user devices were connected to data switching nodes typically by 2400 bps and 4800 bps links (and in many parts of the world they still are!) The data switching nodes themselves were connected perhaps by "fast" 64 Kbps links. The speed of the attaching links and the internal processing speed of the end-user devices themselves provided a limitation on the rate at which data could be sent to the network. In addition, these links were typically operated using "polled" link protocols. The networks could (and many did) control the rate of data input by controlling the polling process. In the emerging high-speed environment, devices are typically connected to the network through a link that is many times faster than the processor to which it is attached. Thus, there is no longer the implicit rate control provided by the slow speed of the attaching link. And, there is no more polling.

Implicit rate controls exist in many places:

- The speed of attaching links
- The throughput of servers

  If the majority of traffic is client/server (or host/terminal) the total potential load that could be placed on the network is limited by the total throughput of the servers. Install a fast server and watch your network go down!

- Unintended side effects of link controls (*not* with ATM)

  Traditional link controls have credit-based flow control built into them.

- The throughput of client devices

9.2.3.5 Network Equipment Design

Careful design of the network switches can go a long way in helping mitigate congestion within the network. The key here is to minimize the use of shared resources. This topic is discussed further in Chapter 7, "Switching ATM Cells" on page 7-1.

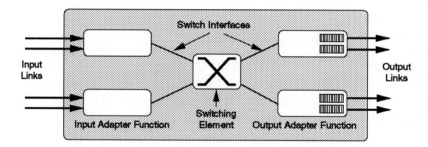

Figure *9-5.* *ATM Switch Design for Performance*

Figure 9-5 shows a typical ATM switch design. Careful design and implementation can result in minimal queueing in any part, except for the queues ahead of output links which are inevitable. Thus, you do get a network like the one illustrated in Figure 9-1 on page 9-3. To achieve this:

- The switching element should have greater capacity than the total of all connected links.
- Each switch interface (between the switch and the input/output adapters) should be faster than the total of all links connected to any adapter.
- Each adapter should be fast enough to process input and output at full rate for all connected links.

- There should be minimal sharing of link buffers within an adapter (or at least there should be a way of preventing one link developing a queue so long that it interferes with other links on the same adapter).

In fact, this is not perfectly achievable and you do need some buffering at input to the switch element and some buffering within the switch element. For practical purposes however, this structure is achievable. The IBM 2220 Nways BroadBand Switch has this structure and characteristic. In order to handle traffic of many different types and QoS characteristics within the same network, it is necessary to provide priorities wherever significant queues may develop. This is one reason for keeping the queuing to output links only.

An ATM cell doesn't contain a priority. It contains a discard priority, but discarding cells is a bit extreme. However, ATM is a *connection-oriented protocol*. When a cell arrives in an input adapter the first thing we must do is use the VPI/VCI to look up a table to find the destination (and new VPI/VCI because we have to change it). That table is in the input adapter, but it can contain as much information as we like about the connection. For example, it can tell us which priority queue to use in the output adapter. This information must then be switched to the output adapter along with the cell.

As illustrated in Figure 9-6, we could have in the output adapter, for example, a top-priority queue for traffic with a guaranteed, very short end-to-end delay. Such a queue might have a *maximum* length associated with it. If the queue exceeds the maximum length, then start throwing cells (arriving in this queue) away. With some types of transfer, late delivery of information is worse than none - better to throw some away and stay within the agreed transit delay.

All of the above can be performed in hardware at full speed.

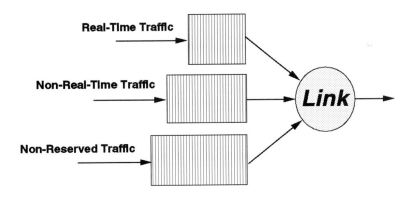

Figure *9-6. Transmission Scheduling*

9.2.3.6 Explicit Control of Data Flows

As stated in a number of places above, if we want to process "available-bit-rate" (ABR) traffic then we need some form of explicit rate control. This is discussed in the next section.

9.2.4 Congestion Actions

In 9.3, "Flow and Rate Controls" we will discuss what can be done to control the flow of cells to mitigate or prevent the occurrence of congestion. Congestion is still going to occur. What can we (or should we) do about it? We cannot just shut down input links (as some early networks did) because this shuts off necessary control flows. In any case, when using the ATM link protocols the sender doesn't get to know it should stop sending. This would just be a non-selective discard of cells.

When congestion becomes severe we must discard cells, but we can be quite selective about it.

1. Since we have (or can have) a number of priority queues for each link we should perhaps discard all arriving cells for UBR (unspecified-bit-rate or best-effort) traffic first.

2. Then we should start looking at the CLP (Cell Loss Priority) bit in the cell header. Cells arriving for other priority queues marked with CLP=1 could be discarded next.

3. A strategy that makes a lot of sense is for the discard of whole frames of data rather than individual cells. This mitigates the problem explained above that discard of a single cell causes re-transmission of many cells and therefore contributes to the problem of congestion rather than solving it.

   The problem here is how to do it. Detecting the beginning and end of a frame is possible in AAL-5, but this means keeping track of frames on a per-VC basis - a processing task that many do not want to contemplate within a switch. Nevertheless, some ATM switches on the market today do perform whole frame discard (the IBM 8260 Multiprotocol Intelligent Switching Hub, for example).

It is clear that there are many possible strategies for cell discard. Different equipment suppliers will adopt quite different strategies. There is no standard for this and none is planned.

9.3 Flow and Rate Controls

Perhaps the first question in controlling the rate of data in an ATM network is precisely which flows should be controlled.

- We could control the flow on physical links between switches (say) by a credit-based technique or even by a simple ON/OFF command.

This is relatively simple to do but has a big problem. As discussed above, an ATM switch (as a whole) rarely becomes congested and congestion on the input side of a switch should be very rare. On a 16-port ATM switch, when there is congestion on one outbound port which input link do you slow down? It could be that every input link has some connections going to the congested output but that only one or two of them are sending a very high data rate. Deciding which link to close down is a big problem because there are relatively few shared resources in the switch. In addition, you would be slowing down flows which don't need to be affected (that go to other destinations).

- This leaves us with controlling individual connections. It is clearly the best and fairest way to do it, but it involves processing on every connection through a switch (in both directions). This is a lot of overhead and something we would like to avoid because it potentially adds a significant cost to the switch.

9.3.1 External to the Network

There are many ways to perform flow control external to the network. For example, in TCP/IP networks, the IP switches do not participate in complex congestion control procedures. Congestion control is performed through a rotating-window protocol operating between end users (TCP entities). This works to a point but the network cannot enforce this on the end users and it is quite possible for individual end users to adopt a non-conforming protocol (for example, UDP). In addition, the protocol involves substantial overhead and has problems with fairness in certain situations. However, for data transport in high-speed networks there will be some form of rotating-window, end-to-end protocol which will perform a flow control function.

9.3.1.1 Enhanced Adaptive Rate-Based (eARB) Control

This mechanism is a part of IBM NBBS but, at this time, is not a part of any standardization activity.

This mechanism operates outside the network without the knowledge or cooperation of the switches within the network. When we think of detecting congestion within a network we usually think of measuring the transit delay across it. This would be good but it's very difficult to do especially from an external device. You can measure the roundtrip delay, but then you don't know in which direction (forward or backward) the delay occurred. There are lots of proposals for measuring one-way transit delays, but none of them are really satisfactory. The best system would be to synchronize the time-of-day clocks in all attaching devices to some very accurate broadcast time reference. Sadly, this is not a possibility yet.

In eARB we detect congestion by looking at short term changes in the network transit delay. If a transit delay is getting longer, then this is being caused by a queue somewhere getting longer. The sender puts special cells into the transmitted data stream interspersed among the data cells. These cells are sent at precise, measured, intervals. In the second cell of a pair of these measurement cells there is the time *difference* (the interval) between the sending time of the two cells. The receiver measures the difference in arrival times of the cells and compares that with the difference in their sending times. If the difference in times at the receiver is greater than the difference at the sender then we know that somewhere a queue is getting longer. (Of course, there is normal jitter throughout the network. When deciding if we have congestion we must look for large changes in transit delay or consistent ones.)

The receiver then decides if congestion is present on this connection and rates it on a scale of 1 to 4. This estimate is then sent back to the source and the source uses the information to modify its sending rate.

The sender also "times out" responses from the receiver so that in cases of extreme congestion it can stop altogether.

It should be noted that the eARB protocol could be performed either in the switches at the entry points to the network or in the end user devices. It does not need to be completely external.

9.3.2 Entry to the Network

An important method for control of flows in an ATM network is to control the rate of entry of packets to the network and not have controls within the network itself. In the high-speed environment, at very high loadings, when congestion does occur the network will recover by simply throwing some data away.

By control at the entry point of the network here we mean at the UNI. That is, the flow of cells is controlled by interaction between the network and the end-user over the UNI.

This area is not yet fully defined or standardized. The issues are as follows:

Use of Generic Flow Control (GFC)

In the ATM cell header at the UNI (but not the NNI) there are 4 bits defined to be used for Generic Flow Control. In general, it is intended that GFC be used to control traffic flow in order to alleviate any short-term overload conditions that may occur. At this time, the precise way in which the GFC may be used to achieve this is not defined in the standards.

Whether or not the ATM endpoint uses the GFC field is an option.

- If the GFC field is used the transmission is said to be "controlled".

- If the GFC bits are set to zero the transmission is said to be "uncontrolled".

There is a current proposal in the standards to further define the GFC field to allow its use as a subaddress. This would allow a point-to-multipoint capability quite similar to that used in the ISDN passive bus. It would also prevent the use of the GFC field for admission flow control. At the present time this is a subject for discussion.

Call Admission Control

When a new connection is planned either by subscription (permanent connection) or by switched call setup, the network must decide if the connection is to be allowed. The traffic descriptors provide information about the peak and average cell rate required and the QoS characteristics requested.

The problem for the network engineer is how to decide when a new connection is to be allowed. You could add up the peak requested throughput rates for every connection that uses a resource (such as a link). Then you could make sure that this maximum is less than the throughput capacity (link speed) of the resource. This policy would guarantee that there would never be any congestion. Unfortunately it would also guarantee extremely inefficient use of the network.

Another policy could be to take the sum of the average requested rates and ignore the peaks. This would almost work in some situations but would guarantee congestion problems in the majority of cases.

Traffic Policing and Shaping - Usage Parameter Control (UPC)

At the entry point to the network (at the ATM switch connection to the UNI) there must be a function that checks the rate of arriving traffic and ensures that it meets the traffic profile allocated to this user (VC or VP connection). A "leaky bucket" will be used to perform this policing function. (See 9.3.2.6, "Leaky Bucket Rate Control" on page 9-26.)

When cells are received in excess of the allowed rate the network may either:

1. Discard cells immediately.

2. Mark the cells in excess of the agreed rate as discard eligible (DE).

It should be noted that the leaky bucket mechanism is not a queue. No data is stored or slowed down. Leaky bucket is just a mechanism for checking the flow rate of cells.

The problem is how to set the depth of the leaky bucket and what rate to allow. What we are doing here is not shaping the traffic to a profile so much as fitting the profile to the traffic. We have to ensure that the actual traffic meets the profile given to the network; otherwise, the network may experience problems with congestion.

- Variable-bit-rate (VBR) voice traffic has relatively predictable characteristics and a very stable set of statistics when many streams are aggregated. If the network operator was sure that the endpoint was really always sending VBR voice only, then policing would hardly be necessary.

- VBR video traffic is much more variable and much less predictable.

  We do not know if the picture is going to be a talking head or a high-speed car chase. What about the occurrence where the video has quite a low rate for perhaps half an hour and then a very high one for say 15 minutes. We could conceive of an average traffic rate of perhaps 200 Kbps changing to a rate of perhaps 5 Mbps and staying there for perhaps 15 or 20 minutes (quite long enough to disrupt the network).

- Data traffic can be more difficult in a sense. Traditional interactive transaction traffic is relatively easy. Transactions are small and are spaced apart because human interaction is required as part of the process. Statistically these traffic flows aggregate quite well into relatively stable traffic. Client/server traffic is very different. It is quite normal for an engineering workstation to request the immediate download of the current CAD files an engineer is working on. This may well be 20 to 30 megabytes. A user logging on to an office workstation typically causes the download of 1 or 2 megabytes of data immediately. But at other times both the engineer and the office worker may only send sporadic electronic mail.

This raises the question "what should the network do". How should we set the leaky bucket parameters?

The easy way is to treat the maximum rate allowed for a particular device as though it was a constant rate. In this case the leaky bucket algorithm would throw away anything in excess of the agreed rate. This rate would be used to decide whether a new connection would be allowed simply by adding up all the rates along the path of the new connection and refusing it if capacity was already allocated. This is the easy way but extremely wasteful.

In order to make intelligent use of ATM you really need to overcommit the network's resources and make use of the fact that the average data transfer rate of many devices will be perhaps 1/100th to 1/1000th of their peak rates.

Use of the Cell Loss Priority (CLP) Bit

At the present time the standards say the CLP bit may only be set by the network. It would be set to indicate traffic in excess of the agreed leaky bucket parameters.

Some people, however, want to use hierarchical source coding schemes (see 8.5.1.1, "Hierarchical Source Coding" on page 8-20) to help shape their traffic. This is currently not allowed in the standards but is under discussion.

Explicit Forward Congestion Indicator (EFCI) Bit

There is a congestion notification function available in the Payload Type (PT) field of the cell header. Unlike the similar function in frame relay, ATM congestion notification is only presented one way (in the forward direction). The detailed operation of congestion notification has not yet been fully defined by the standards. How it should be used by an ATM endpoint is another issue entirely.

In short-term congestion situations some devices may not be able to react in time to make the usage sensible. In fact, you could make the situation a whole lot worse. For example, let us assume that a short-term congestion situation has occurred on a particular node.

- Traffic passing through that node has been marked that there is congestion.
- Endpoint devices take notice of the notification and slow down their data transmission rate.
- After a minute or two the congestion goes away and the system stops marking cells.
- Devices can now go back to their originally agreed-on behavior.
- This will work for some types of devices and some types of traffic.

But there is a problem. If, for example, endpoints have just stored up their traffic (or requests) logically they will all now be able to send at their maximum agreed rate.

What happens is that in many situations a logical queue of unsatisfied requests builds up in the end-user devices.

- When the congestion situation is removed they can all go back, *not to their average traffic patterns, but to their peaks.*
- The additional traffic now causes the network to become congested again.
- The network notifies congestion, etc.
- This causes the buildup of bigger waiting queues in the end-user devices.

Early data networks used to go into uncontrolled oscillation (in and out of congestion) with the peak congestion becoming worse on every cycle (cycles could be as long as 20 minutes). The end result was that the network became so congested that further operation became impossible. An ATM network will not throttle its input in congestion situations. It will discard cells. After a few seconds the endpoints will try to retransmit those cells *and* a whole lot of additional cells (because we retransmit entire frames - not just errored cells).

This is not a hypothetical situation. In the early days of data networking (the late 1960s and early 1970s) data networks were built without any internal flow or congestion control procedures. These networks were mainly airline and banking networks. The scenario described above (the oscillation effect and the disruption caused by it) was observed many times in practical real-life situ-

ations. In the late 1980s there was a major event on the Internet which had a similar effect and the same cause.

Another point about congestion notification is that it penalizes users that obey the notification and rewards ones that do not. In frame relay networks, where there is a similar notification protocol, it has been proven that a "misbehaving" device which ignores the notifications gets much better network service than devices that obey the notification. When data must be discarded to alleviate congestion it is impossible to identify data belonging to the misbehaving device and so data from orderly devices also is discarded.

9.3.2.1 Bandwidth Reservation

When a user requests a connection through the network a contract is established with the network about agreed throughput and QoS. This is done regardless of whether the connection is set up by OA&M procedures (permanent connection) or through a signaling process (switched connection). There is a set of traffic descriptors and quality-of-service descriptors that formally describe what these characteristics are.

There are two classes regarding bandwidth reservation:

Reserved Bandwidth (RB)

> If the network is to be able to establish a connection by reserving bandwidth along the path of that connection, then we need to know reasonably accurately the characteristics of the traffic (average cell rate and variability). The network can then apply some statistical judgment on whether to admit the connection or not.

> An RB connection is one on which the bandwidth has been reserved and which should offer the best network service. We can have as many different types of RB traffic and as many different priority queues as we desire. This is a question for the designer of the switch and is not standardized.

Non-Reserved Bandwidth (NRB)

> A non-reserved bandwidth service class would apply to very bursty traffic where the peak and average traffic rates are essentially meaningless. This applies to the vast majority of LAN client/server traffic. Cells arriving on a connection using NRB would automatically be marked with the CLP bit as eligible for discard.

> This is fine until congestion occurs. Then there are serious problems. What is needed is a mechanism (under discussion in the standards but as yet undefined - see the following section) for control of NRB connections without affecting the RB connections.

9.3.2.2 Generic Flow Control at the UNI

The need for flow control can be considered from a number of different viewpoints. The discussion above on bandwidth reservation considered the demands for bandwidth that a particular type of traffic places on the network. Another way is to consider the capacity of the network for traffic as a varying thing. That is, looked at from the perspective of a single end user the network has a variable capacity depending on what other traffic happens to be there at that moment in time.

Figure 9-7 shows bandwidth availability and demand varying over time on a single UNI link to the network.

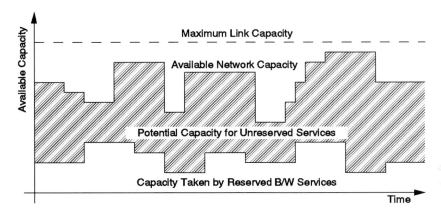

Figure *9-7.* *Available Non-Reserved Capacity*

- The horizontal dotted line shows the maximum link capacity (this is just the link speed).

- The lower line on the graph represents the actual amount of bandwidth used by traffic that has made bandwidth reservation. This will usually be less than the absolute amount of reserved bandwidth. It varies because many types of devices that reserve bandwidth do not use all that they reserved.

- The upper line shows the amount of capacity that is available from the network's point of view.

- Between the two lines the shaded area shows the amount of capacity that is available on the link if only we could find a good way to control its use.

9.3.2.3 Status

The ITU-T Study Group 13 has agreed on a proposal to control the flow at the UNI such that much of this non-reserved network capacity can be used without the danger of catastrophic flooding of the network. This is currently in the process of being finalized.

9.3.2.4 GFC Operation

The principle of operation is very similar indeed to the link-layer flow control in X.25 and SDLC/SNA. In detail it is quite different.

- GFC flow control operates *only* in one direction: from the ATM endpoint to the ATM switch over the ATM UNI. The flow of data *to* the network is controlled, while the flow of data *from* the network to the endpoint is *not controlled*.

- The flow control is for traffic on the physical link viewed as a whole.

- The flow control mechanism is performed at the ATM layer, but it does not know about nor take any notice of VCs and VPs.

The aim of the whole process is to provide a control mechanism for *unreserved traffic*. However, since the GFC flow control mechanism does not take account of VCs or VPs it cannot know which ones are using reserved bandwidth and which ones are not. The GFC flow control mechanism understands two classes of traffic:

Controlled Traffic

> This is traffic to which the GFC mechanism is applied. It would/should usually be all of the non-reserved traffic on an interface. Controlled traffic is distinguished in the cell header by the presence of a non-zero GFC field (GFC ≠ B′0000′).

Uncontrolled Traffic

> This traffic is not subject to GFC control and is treated as having a higher priority than controlled traffic by the GFC mechanism. This would normally be traffic for which there is a bandwidth reservation.

> This traffic is identified by the fact that all four bits of the GFC field are set to zero.

The concept is illustrated in Figure 9-8.

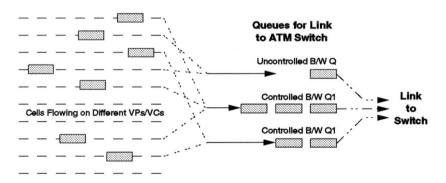

Figure 9-8. GFC Operation

- Cells to be sent from an ATM endpoint on a particular UNI are queued on one of three queues. (There are always logical queues present here, but real queueing would only occur in times of congestion.)

- One queue is for uncontrolled traffic (traffic with a bandwidth reservation) and the other two are for controlled traffic.

  The reason for having two queues for controlled traffic is not to give any particular queue priority but to provide separate control for different types of traffic if needed.

- The presence of two "controlled traffic" queues is optional and in default there is only one queue.

- When a cell is to be sent to the line, if there is anything on the uncontrolled queue it is sent immediately.

  If the uncontrolled queue is empty, a cell is sent from one of the controlled queues (if a cell is waiting). Sending priority of the two controlled queues "flip-flops" between the two queues so that when a cell is sent from one queue the next cell (if there is one) is sent from the other queue.

Halt Mechanism

There is an overall halt mechanism. The HALT command is a command from the network to halt all input (controlled and uncontrolled). This is something that should be used only as a last resort since it halts also the bandwidth-reserved traffic which may have constant-bit-rate requirements.

Flow Control

Each queue has a "window" of cells that it is allowed to send before the network must respond to give permission to continue. The window is just a simple counter.

When a RESET is received from the network the counter is set to a specified value. Each time a cell is sent, the counter is decreased by one. When the counter reaches zero, the endpoint is not allowed to send any more traffic until the counter has been reset.

In normal operation, the network would send RESET to the endpoint fairly often so that the counter never reached zero.

Each queue has a separate counter and a separate reset value so that the window size allocated can be different for the two queues.

The reset value (the value to which the counter is reset) starts at one (on link initialization) and may be dynamically changed by command from the ATM switch.

The process operates using the GFC field in the (bidirectional) cell stream. Any cell may be used to carry the necessary information. The GFC is used as follows:

Towards the Network

In cells traveling from the ATM endpoint to the network the GFC bits have the following meanings:

- Bit0 is unused.

- Bit1 indicates that this cell belongs to a flow controlled by Q1.

- Bit2 indicates that this cell belongs to a flow controlled by Q2. (In the case where only one queue is used then this bit is always 0.)

- Bit3 indicates if the equipment is controlled (1) or uncontrolled (0).

Away from the Network

In cells traveling from the network to the ATM endpoint the GFC field has the following meanings:

- Bit0 means HALT (1) or NOHALT (0).

  This means that when the network is holding up traffic all the traffic from the network to the endpoint will have the HALT bit set. Traffic may restart when the HALT bit is reset (0 again).

- Bit1=1 means RESET on Q1. Bit1=0 is a null operation.

  This allocates a new window of cells that the endpoint can send.

- Bit2 means RESET on Q2 (if Q2 exists). Bit2=0 is a null operation.

- Bit3 is reserved for future use.

9.3.2.5 Switch Control
In order to make the GFC mechanism work, the controlling ATM switch must have information about the load (and amount of congestion) present in the network. This requires the network to use internal signaling procedures to distribute information about network loadings. The information will be required at each link adapter.

9.3.2.6 Leaky Bucket Rate Control
In the high-speed environment, an input rate control system is needed (perhaps in addition to end-to-end user flow controls) which will apply to all (data, voice, video...) types of traffic.

When a connection is set up its throughput demands are assessed by a node that allocates capacity to the individual connection (call). These demands are things like average packet throughput rate, maximum allowed peak rate, priority (if any) and loss priority (the tendency for the network to throw away the packet when congestion occurs).

The method of operation suggested is that the attaching user node should control its rate of data presentation to the network through a system called "Leaky Bucket Rate Control" and *that the network should monitor this traffic at the network entry point to make sure that the end user node does not exceed its allowance.* This mechanism is a control on the rate at which data may be sent *into* the network rather than a control of data flow *through* the network. Once data has entered the network there is no proposed control of flows except the implicit throughput capability of the links and nodes involved.

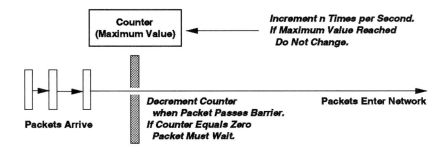

Figure 9-9. Leaky Bucket Rate Control

In concept, leaky bucket rate control operates as follows:

- A packet entering the network must pass a "gate" called the leaky bucket. This is really just a counter, which represents the number of packets that may be sent immediately on this path.

- In order for a packet to pass and enter the network the counter must be non-zero.

- The leaky bucket counter has a defined maximum value.

- The counter is incremented (by one) n times per second.

- When a packet arrives it may pass the leaky bucket if (and only if) the counter is non-zero.

- When the packet passes the barrier to enter the network, the counter is decremented.

- If the packet has been delayed it will be released immediately after the counter is incremented.

The leaky bucket is really an analogy to what happens and is in many ways misleading! When the packet (cell) fails the test (that is, the counter is zero when the cell arrives) then we have a choice:

- The cell could be immediately discarded.

- The CLP bit in the cell could be set to 1 to signify that this cell is outside the traffic contract and may be discarded if necessary. But the cell would then be allowed immediate entry to the network.

- The cell may be queued.

The problem with using the leaky bucket analogy is that to many people it always implies queueing.

In fact, the problem goes further than that: the idea of a leaky bucket implies that data will arrive in a bursty fashion and will be smoothed out and fed to the network at a relatively constant rate (poured into the bucket and then leaked out into the network).[4] In fact, what we are doing is allowing short bursts of cells into the network without hindrance (to the counter's maximum value) but enforcing an average delivery rate over time.

Leaky bucket rate control may be operated on individual connections or it may operate on a group of connections such as all the connections on the same link or all the connections on the same virtual path (as in ATM). In addition, there may be a number of leaky buckets implemented in series to give a closer control of rates. In some variations of the leaky bucket scheme there is no input queue to the leaky bucket! A packet arriving at the barrier is either allowed immediate passage or is discarded. From a network perspective, it does not matter whether there is a queue or not. The choice of whether or not to have queueing here depends very much on the type of traffic being carried and the design of the particular adaptation layer involved.

This scheme has the effect of limiting the packet rate to a defined average, but allowing short (definable size) bursts of packets to enter the network at maximum rate. If the node tries to send packets at a high rate for a long period of time, the rate will be equal to "n" per second. If however, there has been no traffic for a while, then the node may send at full rate until the counter reaches zero.

A refinement of this method uses two leaky buckets in series with the second one using a maximum bucket size of 1 but a faster clock rate. The total effect is to limit input to a defined average rate but with short bursts allowed at a defined higher rate (but still not the maximum link speed).

The scheme can be dynamic in that the maximum value of the counter and/or the rate at which the counter is incremented may be changed depending on current conditions within the network (provided that the network has some method of signaling these conditions to the end user).

---

4 Indeed there are times when you want to do exactly this - at the entry point to a public network for example.

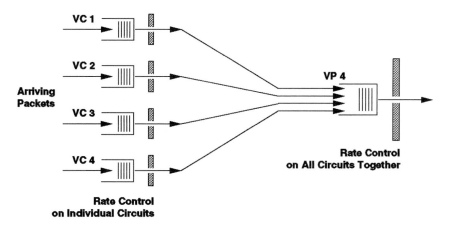

Figure 9-10. *A Cascade of Leaky Buckets.* Leaky bucket rate control is applied to individual circuits and then to the total of a logical group. Leaky buckets are not necessarily queues. They can be just a rate limitation mechanism.

Figure 9-10 shows one potential configuration such that individual circuits have rate control applied to them and an aggregate rate control is applied to the total of a logical grouping of circuits. This is relatively efficient to implement in code.

In ATM the leaky bucket principle is called generic cell rate algorithm (GCRA). This is a continuous-state leaky bucket algorithm.

9.3.3 Credit-Based Flow Controls

The GFC protocol described in 9.3.2.2, "Generic Flow Control at the UNI" on page 9-23 for control of data flow into the network over the UNI is an example of a credit-based flow control. In this section we are discussing flow controls *within* the network itself rather than at the end-user interface (the UNI).

Credit-based flow control protocols are not new. Indeed, they were a critical part of many early communication networks including ARPANET (the US Advanced Projects Research Agency Network) that first became operational in 1968. Credit-based controls are used in HDLC line controls, X.25 (at both the link level and at the packet level), in many parts of IBM SNA, and in OSI.

The principle of credit-based flow control was actively considered by the ATM Forum as the basis for ATM flow control for ABR class of service (only).[5] While it was rejected by

---

[5] It is clearly inappropriate for CBR or VBR traffic.

the Forum in favor of rate-based controls, credit-based controls are used in a number of proprietary ATM implementations.[6]

The basic principle is very simple: Before a node can send data to another node it must receive a "credit" for the amount of data it is allowed to send. In the original ARPANET this was the length of the receive buffer that had been allocated to receive data from this node. After some data has been received, the receiver sends more credits to the sender to enable the sender to continue transmitting data.

There is a problem here that has to do with propagation delay. It takes time for data to go from sender to receiver and more time for a reply to be received. So, if the receiver waits until all credits available to a particular sender have been used up before sending more credits, then the sender must wait (at least twice the propagation delay) before it can commence sending again. This can be a significant waste of link time. So, protocols were developed to allow a receiver to keep sending more credit to an active transmitter allowing sufficient margin for propagation delays so that (provided there was no congestion) the sender could send continuously at full rate. This is illustrated in Figure 9-11.

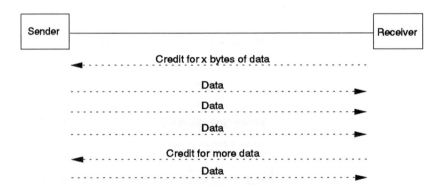

Figure   9-11. Credit-Based Flow Control

In principle, credit-based controls may be performed over any circuit. In ATM this could be a performed on:

- The physical link between switches
- On an individual VC or VP connection from switch to adjacent switch
- On an individual VC or VP connection end-to-end across the network

---

6   A good discussion of credit-based flow controls in the ATM context can be found in [17].

That is, credit-based control can be performed on any circuit between any two locations where the circuit is known.

There are many detailed implementations.

- In the HDLC family of link controls you have a "rotating window" system which works on the number of blocks of data sent rather than the number of bytes. For example, you might have a window size of 5. This means that the sender is able to send 5 blocks of data (of any length up to some maximum) before it must wait for permission to send more from the receiver. When the receiver receives a block of data it sends an updated "window" to increase the allowance at the sender. If the receiver doesn't send an update then the sender must wait after sending its "window" (allowance) until it receives an update before resuming the transmission of data.

- Other systems work on the number of bytes of data outstanding rather than the number of blocks.

Figure   9-12. *Stage-by-Stage Credit-Based Flow Control*

The proposal in ATM was to implement this from switch to adjacent switch on each VC or VP connection separately. This would certainly have solved the problem of congestion and of optimization of link capacity, but many people believed that it required far too much buffering and far too much logic (processing) within each switch. This, it was said, would increase the cost of the switch to an unacceptable level. Nevertheless, it is available in a number of proprietary switches.

9.3.4 Explicit Forward Congestion Indication (EFCI)

In the ATM header, there is a bit called the Explicit Forward Congestion Indication (EFCI) bit. It is intended that switches should set this bit to notify the receiver of congestion along the path. This is a part of existing ATM and a number of switches on the market already set this bit.

The problem is that its use relies on conforming end-user equipment and there are no widely used protocols that make use of it. The first concern with EFCI is that it tells the receiver (*not* the sender) that there is congestion. (The path in the other direction might be fine.) The receiver has to notify the sender to slow down. Another concern is that the network can't easily enforce a slowing down. The sender can just ignore it and the network can do nothing. This leads to the situation that exists in frame relay where good, conforming devices are penalized and non-conforming devices benefit. (The "bad boys" win!)

A workable protocol could be built for using EFCI but nothing exists today. In the next section it will be seen that EFCI is being incorporated into the wider mechanism of rate-based flow control by the ATM Forum.

Another suggestion is that when a switch sees congestion on a forward path that it should *generate* a cell in the backward direction and return that immediately to the sender. This would allow much faster response. The difficulty with this approach is the granularity of ATM switches - in many switches it is very hard to generate a cell in the reverse direction. This is because there is often no data path on which a cell like this might flow - the two halves of the connection are independent.

9.3.5 Rate-Based Flow Controls

The concept of rate-based flow control[7] is new in ATM and has not been used in traditional networking protocols. The concept is simple - *The network continuously tells each sender the rate at which it is allowed to transmit data into the network.* This allows the network to adjust the rate of data sent to it on each connection.

There are many kinds of traffic for which control of this type is not appropriate:

1. CBR traffic has a service contract and the network must fulfil it. You can't ask CBR traffic to slow down - that's why it's CBR.

2. VBR traffic does vary, but the variations are due to traffic characteristics at the source and again the network can't slow it down or speed it up. It could, but if it did the application would fail! VBR traffic needs a service contract just like CBR traffic.

So, there is a special service category for traffic that is able to use rate-based control. This is called ABR or Available Bit Rate service. When an ABR connection is set up, the connection request carries information about the ABR characteristics requested. These are:

- Peak cell rate (PCR)
- Minimum cell rate (MCR) - this will be "guaranteed" by the network
- Initial cell rate (ICR)
- Additive increase rate (AIR)
- Number of cells between RM cells (Nrm)
- Rate decrease factor

After call setup transmission begins with an RM cell, thereafter every Nrm'th cell is an RM cell (see Figure 9-13 on page 9-33). A good ballpark value for Nrm is 16; in this case, every 16th cell on the connection would be an RM cell. The ICR is the starting cell rate allowed to the sender.

---

[7] A good discussion of the ATM Forum rate-based flow control protocol and its history may be found in [2].

Each RM cell contains information about the current cell rate:

- Current cell rate (CCR)
- Minimum cell rate (MCR)
- Explicit rate (ER)
- Direction indicator (tells whether this RM cell is flowing away from or towards the sender)
- Congestion indicator (CI)
- Block Start (BS) bit

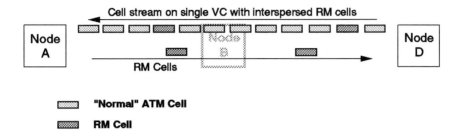

Figure 9-13. *Rate-Based Flow Control Procedure*

As the RM cell travels through the network, switches may update the ER field (that is, reduce the allowed rate but not increase it) and set the CI bit. Switches may also save some of the parameters in order to determine fair allocation between different connections.

When the RM cell reaches its destination it is turned around (the direction indicator is reversed and the RM cell returned to the sender). The destination can also reduce the ER field if it cannot handle the data and, if this is done, it will also set the CI bit.

There is an interesting feature here for compatibility with switches that do not know about RM cells but do set the EFCI bit. If an EFCI bit has been set in any data cell since the last RM cell was received, then the CI bit is set in the turning-around RM cell.

Switches are allowed to reduce the ER field in the RM cell as it returns to its origin through the network, but a switch should only modify the RM cell in one direction.

When the RM cell is received back at the original sender the sender must take action based on its contents. If CI=0 then it is allowed to increase its cell rate up to the returned value of ER (in increments of AIR). If CI=1 then it must decrease its rate either to ER or to CCR-decrease factor whichever is the least. Notice here that when the rate is decreased the decrease applied is a proportion of the current rate. That is, the decrease is exponential. When a rate is increased the increase is by linear increments.

There is a time-out provision so that if a returned RM cell does not arrive, the sending rate is automatically decreased by a defined factor.

For a sender that restarts transmission after a period of idleness there is a danger that it would be allowed to restart transmission at the full ER that applied some minutes or hours ago. When a source restarts it sends a new RM cell with the BS indication set and it must start at the ICR rate.

The cell rate adjustment is always bounded by the PCR and the MCR. The network will always allow a source to send at the MCR rate. The source (obeying all the rules) still may never increase its sending rate above the PCR.

There is a question here that is not yet resolved. How should the network police the rate of cell reception. There is a time difference between the entry switch and the end-user device and the switch may not be easy to synchronize with the end user. This question is in process of resolution.

As mentioned in the introduction to this chapter, many people have strong reservations about the suitability of rate-based techniques. These reservations hinge on a number of concerns:

1. The network propagation delay in a large WAN means that congestion is likely to become severe before anything can be done about it. This translates to a need to operate links at perhaps lower utilization and for larger queues in switches.

2. The processing required in intermediate switches is regarded by some as difficult and expensive.

3. The serious problem is what to do in end-user equipment adapters, specifically in servers. A LAN server may have a few hundred client workstations with active connections to it. The processing needed on the adapter card for the ABR function could be very great - great enough to require an additional microprocessor and additional storage. Perhaps as much as doubling the cost. But then server adapters are relatively few and there is no problem in the clients.

Time will tell.

Chapter 10. Network Management

The functions that must be performed by the management system in an ATM network include the following:

Configuration Management

> This is the operational control of the ATM switch. It includes functions such as:
>
> - Add and remove modules to/from the ATM switch.
>
> - Enable and disable ATM switch modules, ports, etc.
>
> - Detect and report changes in the switch configuration. For example, most ATM switches allow the user to "hot plug" adapter cards and many other components such as fans, power supplies, and the like. This function detects and reports changes made by hot plugging and may take actions (such as automatic activation) when changes are detected.

Fault Management

> This is the detection and diagnosis of network faults. It can (should) be largely automatic, but it must also be possible to initiate these tests through operator command. Fault management comprises the following functions:
>
> 1. Automatic detection of:
>
>   - Software and hardware errors
>
>   - Changes in the status of ATM modules within a switch
>
>   - Status changes of ATM links and trunks
>
> 2. Monitoring of critical parameters:
>
>   - Per port statistics (error counters, etc.)
>
>   - Per connection counters
>
>   - Per SVC counters
>
>   This should be done with user-definable thresholds and sampling rates.
>
> 3. Dynamic testing (on demand) of:
>
>   - Hardware modules
>
>   - ATM interfaces (ports)
>
>   - ATM connections, VCs, VPs, and links via the OA&M protocols

10-1

Statistics Collection

Many types of statistics are required for successful operation and control of an ATM network. Some of them are:

- Counters of cells transmitted and received per port
- Counters of cells received in error (per port)

    Most of the time it is not possible to keep a count of transmitted cell errors since they are not detected at the transmitter (you count these at the other end of the link).

- Counters of cells per connection (VC and/or VP)

    We need to know the number of cells transmitted and received and the number of cells discarded. In many situations it is just not possible to count discarded cells on a per connection basis, but it may be possible to keep counts of discarded cells in some situations.

- Counters per signaling channel

    This is the total number of incoming and outgoing calls, etc.

In addition to this, there are necessary billing statistics. In some networks (such as LAN networks) keeping billing statistics is just an unnecessary cost overhead. In wide area carrier networks billing statistics are a crucial part of the system.

In general, statistics kept for maintenance purposes are not adequate for billing purposes and two separate sets of statistics are kept.

Some statistical counters will usually have thresholds associated with them such that the management system is notified when a specified limit is reached.

Switched Virtual Connection Management

This function is primarily for billing but may also be used for maintenance. Calls are monitored and when a call completes statistics are sent to the billing system (via the management process). For each completed call the collected information will include:

- Calling and called numbers (addresses)
- Call start time and duration
- Call characteristics (QoS, peak cell rate requested)
- Total number of cells sent and received
- Cause and diagnostics attached to call clearing

There is also a control function to force the clearing of a call by operator command.

Permanent Virtual Connection Management

The two functions here are:

1. Monitoring

   • Identification and listing of all PVCs

   • Keeping billing statistics

   • Keeping a record of the characteristics of each PVC (such as QoS, peak cell rate, status)

2. Control

   • Add/restart/delete PVCs

   • Add/restart/delete parties to existing PVCs (point-to-multipoint case)

10.1 System Structure

The structure of an ATM management system is shown diagrammatically in Figure 10-1. Broadly, this is the same structure as is used for the management of most communication networks.

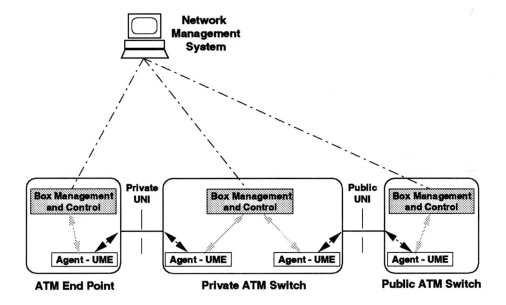

Figure 10-1. ATM Network Management System

There are three components:

Access Agents

> The access agents do the real work in any network management environment. Spread throughout the operational structure (hardware and software) of the system there are many processes that directly monitor and control individual elements of the system. "UNI Management Entities" (UMEs) are illustrated in the figure.

Box Management and Control

> This is the entity that controls and monitors everything that happens within an ATM "box". The function may be quite small (as in the case of a personal-computer ATM endpoint) or it may be very large (as in the case of a full-scale ATM wide-area switch).

> This function may be split up into different modules, or even separate computers, or it may be just a single software module. Most of its operation is done by communicating with access agents within its domain. In most ATM switches, there will be an operator console function (screen/keyboard) that communicates with the box management and control process.

> In its turn, the box management function can be an agent for a network-wide network management system.

Network Management System

> The network management system communicates with every box in the network and provides centralized operation and control for the network. Typically, each box will operate "stand alone" (without the management system) when required, but full network operational control is obtained through the management system. This often (usually) means a level of automated operation and control.

10.1.1.1 Status

At the present time, most of the ATM management system is not fully defined by ITU-T standards. In fact, the only part that is defined is a small part of the OA&M function. This is discussed in 10.3, "Operations Administration and Maintenance" on page 10-6. In the interim, the ATM Forum has addressed an important part of the management system and produced an interim "implementation agreement".

10.2 Interim Local Management Interface (ILMI)

The Interim Local Management Interface (ILMI) was defined by the ATM Forum to provide standardized management information and formats until the official ITU-T standard is produced. In terms of the functions shown in Figure 10-1 on page 10-3,

ILMI does *not* define standards for either network management or box management. Neither does it define how information is to be transferred between network management and box management.

ILMI defines the information to be collected by agents. In particular, an agent called the "UNI Management Entity (UME)" is defined. Further, the ILMI defines the protocol to be used in communicating this information with a *peer* UME. ILMI uses the Simple Network Management Protocol (SNMP)[1] for data transfer across the UNI and for the information formats used.

The ATM UNI management information is represented in a MIB (Management Information Base). This MIB contains six types of information:

Physical Layer (Common and PMD Specific)

> There is a different set of attributes applicable to each different physical interface type. Status information reflects the state of the physical link.

ATM Layer

> There is one ATM layer per physical interface. The information provided here is the common information that applies to all VPs and VCs on this interface.
>
> Configuration information includes:
>
> - The size of the VPI and VCI address fields (maximum number of bits in use)
> - Number of configured VPCs and VCCs
> - Maximum number of VPCs and VCCs allowed at this UNI
> - The UNI interface port type

ATM Layer Statistics

> This contains aggregate statistics for all VPs and VCs on this physical connection. The information includes totals of the numbers of cells transmitted and received and the number of cells dropped (due to header errors) on the receive side.
>
> In addition, there are optional statistics that can be used to identify performance problems, aid in problem diagnosis, and collect traffic engineering data.

---

[1] Of TCP/IP fame.

Virtual Path Connections

The information provided here includes:

- The traffic descriptors for both the send and receive side of the connection. These include the specified peak cell rate, the average cell rate, cell delay variation tolerance, etc.

- The operational status of the VPC.

- The transmit and receive QoS classes in use.

Note that traffic details (counts of cells transmitted and received) per VPC are not provided here.

Virtual Channel Connections

Provided information is much the same as for a VP connection:

- The traffic descriptors for both the send and receive side of the connection. These include the specified peak cell rate, the average cell rate, cell delay variation tolerance, etc.

- The operational status of the VCC.

- The transmit and receive QoS classes in use.

Note that traffic details per VCC are not provided.

Address Registration Information

This is to allow an ATM endpoint to register its address with the ATM switch.

The MIB is structured in such a way as to allow for extension over time to include new items without requiring any changes in the management protocol or framework. Of course, real ATM products will need additional information about aspects of the product not covered by standards. In this case, there is the ability to define extensions to the MIB to carry the additional information.

10.3 Operations Administration and Maintenance

The OA&M protocols specified as part of the ATM layer are designed to perform the following functions:

Performance Monitoring

A managed entity (such as a link or VP/VC) is monitored to ensure continuing correct operation. This may be done continuously or by periodic testing. Reports of the result are made available to the management system.

Defect and Failure Detection

This includes the detection and reporting of malfunctions. This may also be done by continuous monitoring or by periodic testing.

System Protection

This is the necessary accommodation of faults by the system. The process could include deactivating a failed component and activating a standby. It could mean rerouting traffic around a failed link.

Failure or Performance Information

This is reporting of failure or malfunction information to other management entities.

Fault Isolation

This function may be operator-initiated or automatic. It provides a set of mechanisms for investigating the causes of a fault when the fault report contains insufficient information.

In order to perform these functions, tests at five functional layers are defined:

F1   Section level

F2   Line level

F3   Path level

F4   Virtual path level

F5   Virtual channel level

The first three levels are performed by the link protocols and differ depending on the functions available in those protocols. Sonet/SDH has by far the most functionallity in this area, and the three layers of maintenance testing correspond exactly to Sonet/SDH functions. Lower function is available over PDH connections.

Of course, the level of maintenance testing that you need depends very much on the environment in which the system is operated. Sonet/SDH is a networking system in its own right and requires significantly more function than a point-to-point connection in the LAN environment, for example.

The two higher layers are ATM loopback tests. These tests operate on VPs and VCs, both as end-to-end tests and for individual segments of a connection. The objective of these functions is to monitor performance and report degradation. Performance degradation is a good indicator of the presence of a fault or of a fault situation developing. The same tests can be initiated on command and used for fault isolation.

The two flows (F4 and F5) are illustrated in Figure 10-2.

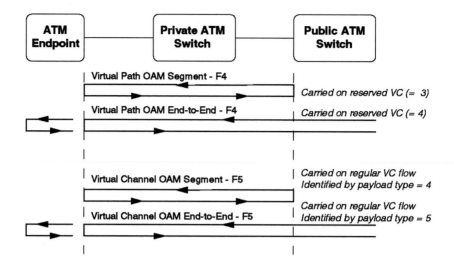

Figure 10-2. OA&M Flows

VP Tests

Cells performing the VP tests include the appropriate VPI number for the VP being tested. The VCI numbers used are special (VCI=3/4) and are reserved for this purpose.

VC Tests

We cannot use the reserved VC numbers for the VC tests since we need to send the testing cell along the VC we are testing. The cell header must contain the correct VPI/VCI for the connection under test.

OA&M cells in this case are distinguished by special values of the Payload Type (PT) field in the cell header (PT=4/5).

Chapter 11. LAN Emulation

LAN emulation is not a part of ATM itself. Nevertheless, it is a critical function which uses ATM and which will be needed immediately by most ATM users.[1] Throughout this book (and in most published material on ATM) constant reference has been made to the use of ATM as a LAN. Several proposals for LAN emulation over an ATM network have been discussed in the ATM Forum. This chapter seeks to analyze the problems inherent in creating virtual LAN structures and to discuss the solution being adopted by the ATM Forum.

11.1 ATM in the Local Environment

When speaking of LAN emulation over ATM, what has usually been meant is that workstations will be ATM endpoints and these will communicate with one another through a central ATM switch (or a network of switches) to which all workstations are connected. That is, ATM will be used to perform the local-area networking function.

Most people, however, think of a LAN as the traditional shared-media structure exemplified by Ethernet, token-ring, and FDDI. An ATM LAN, while it performs the same logical function as that performed by the traditional shared-medium system, is a very different structure.

To use ATM in the LAN environment we need:

- Appropriate link connection protocols (PMDs)

  These have been specified and are being implemented very quickly.

- Appropriate ATM services

  Since link capacity in the local environment is effectively infinite (and very low in cost) we can afford to use non-assured (best-effort) data transfer services. We do not need facilities like billing for data transmission (this is meaningless in a LAN environment).

- A "higher-level" networking system

  ATM covers only the most basic communication functions (you need much more than ATM to get a useful operational system). This is also true on a LAN and there are many to choose from (TCP/IP, IPX, APPN, etc.).

---

[1] Much of the material in this chapter was abstracted from papers presented by IBM to the ATM Forum by Mr Bill Ellington and Dr Wayne Pace IBM NS division, Raleigh, NC and Dr Linh Truong of IBM Research in Zurich, Switzerland.

In practice, ATM LANs are not going to exist in isolation. They will need to interface to existing LANs in various ways and if they are to be made available in any kind of reasonable time frame, then they will need to be able to reuse existing software. Even if ATM equipment was suddenly to become available at very low cost and everyone decided to move to it,[2] there would still be a need to provide a smooth transition from the shared-media LAN world to the ATM LAN.

Thus, there are two generic alternatives for building an ATM network within a local area:

"Native" ATM Network

This is the case where a LAN is conceived of as being simply a "network in a local area" rather than a traditional shared-media LAN system. ATM (with an appropriate higher-layer networking system) would be used in much the same way as traditional wide-area networking systems. You could not easily reuse existing LAN software in this environment, but you could make use of almost any of the existing wide-area networking systems (such as TCP/IP or SNA/APPN).

This approach is certainly the most efficient, but it becomes very difficult to use existing LAN application software or to interface to existing LANs.

ATM Switched Virtual (Emulated) LAN

The concept of an ATM switched virtual LAN is to construct the system such that the workstation application software "thinks" that it is a member of a real shared-media LAN.

This would enable the reuse of the maximum amount of existing LAN software and significantly lessen the cost of migration to ATM. The concept is illustrated in Figure 11-1 on page 11-3.

There are many ways to do this (discussed later in this chapter). The situation is helped by the fact that existing LAN software has usually been built to interface to many different types of LAN. (For example, most IBM LAN software will interface to token-ring, Ethernet, token-bus, PC-LAN, and FDDI, all without change to the application software.)

A sub-objective here is to allow multiple *unrelated* switched virtual LANs to be constructed over the same ATM network.

---

2 Both of these events are extremely unlikely.

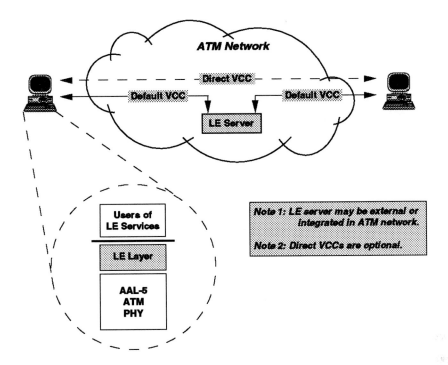

Figure 11-1. *LAN Emulation - ATM to ATM*

Regardless of which of the above alternatives we decide to use, there are two functions that must be accommodated.

ATM-Device to LAN Communication

Natively attached ATM devices must be able to communicate with devices attached to a LAN. This can be done through bridging, routing, or via an integrated networking architecture that supports many different physical types of attachment (such as SNA or TCP/IP).

One of the biggest motivations for using ATM is the desire to put high-bandwidth devices (such as servers and engineering workstations) onto ATM connections and to leave existing PCs unchanged, that is, connected to their existing LANs. This suggests the need for ATM (LAN emulation) devices to communicate with real LAN-attached devices in a transparent way. This is illustrated in Figure 11-2 on page 11-4. The best way to do this would be to bridge between the virtual LANs and the real (traditional) LAN.

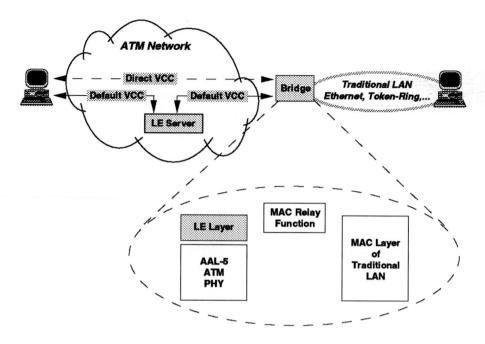

Figure 11-2. *LAN Emulation - ATM to LAN*

LAN Interconnection

Even without the need to interconnect LAN-attached devices to native ATM equipment we would still need to build LAN-to-LAN connections over ATM. Again, there are many ways to do this, such as simply using ATM virtual connections as links between traditional LAN bridges. This is illustrated in Figure 11-3.

Figure 11-3. *LAN Emulation - LAN to LAN*

11.1.1 Emulating LANs over ATM

The objective is to replace the existing LAN system with an ATM-based system with as little change to the workstation software as possible, consistent with gaining the extra speed and function that ATM brings.

There are many potential ways of achieving this (at different levels in the protocol stack), but the most attractive appears to be LAN emulation at the MAC level. This approach allows the widest possible coverage of existing applications and potentially also the cleanest and most trouble-free software interface.

11.1.1.1 Traditional LAN Architecture

The challenge in developing a virtual LAN architecture that can meet the above objectives is to accommodate the differences between the two environments:

- LANs are connectionless. Each frame sent contains the address of the destination LAN adapter. ATM is a connection-oriented system and requires that a connection be established between end stations before data can be transferred.

- Broadcast and multicast operations are easy and natural on a LAN and are extremely efficient, because a frame sent on the medium will be received by all other users (of course, with the latent problem of "broadcast storms" in a bridged environment).

- ATM addresses are different from LAN addresses in more than just format. An ATM address can (and will) be structured to help the system find the location of the destination end device. Default LAN addresses are device serial numbers "burnt in" to the LAN adapter card at the time of manufacture (although an optional ability exists for the user to specify a "locally administered" LAN address). Any LAN emulation system will need to make use of real LAN addresses for some functions and, therefore, a database must exist somewhere that allows mapping from LAN addresses to ATM addresses.

11.1.1.2 System Approaches

A number of potential system approaches are immediately apparent:

Broadcast Approach

If we could set up all the users of a virtual LAN into a broadcast structure such that anything sent by one workstation would be received by all of the others, then we have the functional problem solved. This would emulate a LAN and perform all of the functions easily.

It would also be so inefficient that it would negate the reason for having ATM at all. This effectively makes an ATM network into a shared-media LAN and destroys much of the advantages of ATM along with it.

There is another problem here: at the present time there is no standardized way to set up a multicast group in ATM such that everything sent by any station is broadcast to all other members of the group. What only is supported so far is an ability to set up multicast trees, in which only *one* node (the root) can multicast to all other members (the leaves). This means that you have to set up multiple multicast trees, one for every member of the group.

This is unworkable because of the very large numbers of VCCs needed (VCCs take table space in adapters and switches) and because *all* multicast trees of the group (emulated LAN) have to be modified the moment a member enters or leaves the group (a user's workstation is powered on or off).

There is another problem with this approach. Adding a member to a multicast tree can be initiated by the root or (in future) initiated by the new leaf. How then do all current members of the group (each being a root) get to know about the new member (if they have to add it to their respective multicast trees) or how does the new member get to know about all currently active members (if it has to initiate joining all existing multicast trees)?

Connectionless Server Approach

We could set up a point-to-point ATM connection (VCC) from each LAN workstation to a single "connectionless server". This is consistent with the way in which connectionless services are provided in ATM. The connectionless server could act in a number of ways.

1. It could just reflect everything sent to it in a non-intelligent way to all members of the emulated LAN. This is truly inefficient because all of the data is sent to all workstations.

2. It could reflect only the broadcasts to every station but send data frames addressed to individual stations only to their correct destinations.

   This solution is not as bad in terms of data traffic. All of the data passes through the ATM network twice (sending station to server followed by server to destination) but at least data is only sent to destination workstations and not to every workstation.

However, with either of these approaches the server now becomes part of the data flow through the system and its throughput becomes the main system throughput limitation. It must have sufficient capacity to handle the total data throughput of the system. In addition, the ATM connections to it also have to handle the total system throughput. Of course, since it is now a critical system component it must be protected from failures (by duplexing components, etc.).

Direct Virtual Channels Approach

Each workstation could have a multicast tree enabling it to send to each other user in the virtual LAN. It could also have a dedicated virtual channel connection to each other user in the virtual LAN. In this case, it would send broadcasts on its broadcast VCC and data on the appropriate connection to the destination end user.

This approach would work quite well for a small number of devices in the virtual LAN, but there are two major problems:

1. A prohibitive number of virtual channel connections is required. Large numbers of VCCs do not present any performance problem, but they take table space in adapters, etc. The number of VCCs required grows as the square of the number of workstations. In practical ATM systems, each adapter will have the ability to have somewhere between 1000 and 4000 active VCCs and VPCs. This is a very significant limitation in this situation.

   This solution also has the problem referred to above that you cannot have an any-to-every multicast structure in current ATM. You must have a separate multicast tree (one per end station).

2. Another problem is setting up such a structure. How does a new workstation joining the virtual LAN find out the ATM addresses needed, etc.?

3. This solution restricts the ability to move users around the network (changing ATM addresses as they move).

Fast Circuit-Switched Approach

In this method of operation, a workstation that wants to send some data would establish a direct switched connection with the destination workstation. The connection would be released (cleared) on some criteria such as the length of time that has expired since the last data was transferred or knowledge about the functions required by the higher-layer protocol (obtained from that layer).

This is actually not so silly - fast circuit switching has been operational in many data networks for at least 15 years. To make this work we have to overcome a few problems:

1. There is a time delay inherent in setting up the connection. The sending workstation must make a request to the network over the signaling VCC and the network must respond, after contacting the destination workstation. In a local ATM environment, this can be done in perhaps tens of milliseconds (say 50 ms).

   While a delay of this kind is fine if it happens once at the start of a large file transfer, it is not acceptable if it happens for each frame sent.

2. If workstations were to make a separate switched connection request for every block of data to be sent it would place a very great load on the switching control function within the ATM network. The operation of such

a system would be limited by the ability of the ATM network to set up (and clear) switched connections. This is not insurmountable; you could design a network with a very large capacity to set up and clear connections, but many "off-the-shelf" ATM networks will have quite limited ability to set up and clear connections.

3. The sending workstation has to have a way of finding out the destination workstation's ATM address (all it knows is the LAN address and there is no easy mapping). The only workable way is to have an address server which maintains a central directory and provides address translation support for all attached stations.

This is a promising approach for point-to-point data transfer, but this system will not handle broadcasts.

From the above discussion, it is apparent that there is no easy and immediately obvious solution. Looking at the problem in terms of the functions that must be performed can assist in understanding:

Data Transfer

Most data transfer over a LAN actually uses a *connection*. The network delivery mechanism is connectionless, but there is a connection built between the end stations in order to ensure the integrity of the data transfer (802.2, for example, does this). Most data transfers actually are sequences of many frames of data from one end station to another. There is some ad-hoc data transfer (small numbers of frames between arbitrary end stations) but this is actually quite rare.

This leads to the possibility that elements of the fast circuit-switched approach could be used. Using this approach data is sent on direct VCCs between end stations. The necessary (switched) VCCs are set up as required.

Ad-hoc data transfer of one or only a few frames could be handled by relaying through a server.

Broadcasts

There are many kinds of broadcasts in LAN systems and they are used for different purposes.

Given that we need to handle broadcasts through a server mechanism, perhaps some of the broadcasts (in fact most of them) could be filtered by the server and only sent to the correct destination. For example, a "where are you" broadcast frame could be pre-empted by the server (since the server knows where the destination actually is) and sent onward *only* to the correct destination.

You cannot always do this. For example, the server may not know all of the functional capabilities of each attached workstation. Broadcasts to functional addresses may need to be sent to all the members of the virtual LAN. Bridges need to see all the broadcasts for a number of reasons.

Addressing

The translation between LAN address and ATM address requires that some device must have a database that maps from one to the other. (Manual entry of the LAN and ATM addresses of all members of the virtual LAN into every workstation is not a workable possibility.) User end stations need access to this database in order to find out where other stations are.

11.2 LAN Emulation over ATM (ATM Forum)

The discussion in the previous section leads us to the design of the ATM Forum's LAN Emulation over ATM. The basic concept is that it allows the implementation of one or multiple virtual LANs over an ATM network to emulate either an IEEE 802.5 (token-ring) or Ethernet/IEEE 802.3 LAN. Of course, these virtual LANs are not restricted to the local environment but can be established across any ATM network. Different virtual LANs implemented over one ATM network are completely independent from each other and users connected to one virtual LAN *cannot* directly communicate with users connected to a different virtual LAN. A workstation may be connected, of course, to more than one virtual LAN. Such a workstation could then be a bridge or router to provide connectivity to the members of the virtual LANs to which it is connected.

Communication between different LAN emulation (LE) components can be performed using either switched or permanent VCCs or a mixture of both. When using permanent VCCs, of course, there is the burden for the system administrator to predefine all the necessary connections.

11.2.1 LAN Emulation Components

An emulated LAN is implemented in various components that include:

- LAN emulation clients (LECs), that is, user workstations, bridges, routers, etc.

- An LE server (LES)

- An LE configuration server (LECS)

- A broadcast and unknown server (BUS)

Users connect to the virtual LAN via LE clients, which request services through the *LAN Emulation User-to-Network Interface (LUNI)*. The three components (LES, LECS, and BUS) may be distributed over different physical boxes or may be grouped together in one physical box, but logically they are distinct functions. The LAN emulation services may be implemented in ATM intermediate systems (e.g. switches) as part of the ATM network, or in one or several ATM end devices (e.g. workstation, router, etc.).

As illustrated in Figure 11-4 on page 11-10, each LEC has to support a variety of VCCs across the LUNI for transport of control and data traffic.

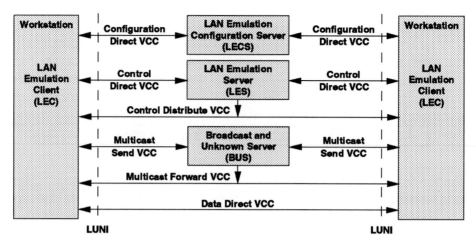

Figure 11-4. *LAN Emulation Components*

11.2.1.1 LAN Emulation Client (LEC)

Each workstation connecting to the virtual LAN has to implement the LE layer (also called LE entity), which performs data forwarding and control functions like address resolution, establishment of the various VCCs, etc. The LE-layer functions could be implemented completely in software, in hardware on a specialized LAN emulation ATM adapter, or in a combination of both. The layered structure of the LEC is shown in Figure 11-5 on page 11-11.

The LE layer provides the interface to existing higher-layer protocol support (such as IPX, IEEE 802.2 LLC, NetBIOS, etc.) and emulates the MAC-level interface of a real shared-media LAN (802.3/Ethernet or token-ring). This means that no changes are needed to existing LAN application software to use ATM services. The LE layer implements the LUNI interface when communicating with other entities in the emulated LAN.

The primary function of the LE layer is to transfer LAN frames (arriving from higher layers) to their destination either directly or through the BUS.

A separate instance (logical copy of the LE client) of the LE layer is needed in each workstation for each different LAN or type of LAN to be supported. For example, if both token-ring and Ethernet LAN types are to be emulated, then you need two LE layers. In fact, they will probably just be different threads within the same copy of the same code but they are logically separate LE layers. Separate LE layers would also be used if one workstation needed to be part of two different emulated token-ring LANs. Each separate LE layer needs a different MAC address but can share the same physical ATM connection (adapter).

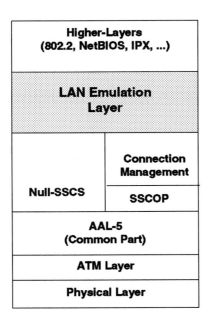

Figure 11-5. *LAN Emulation Client Functional Layers*

Figure 11-2 on page 11-4 illustrates the connection of an ATM station (LEC) with a station connected to a traditional LAN. The "ATM bridge" illustrated contains an LE layer similar in function to the LE layer in an ATM end station. The LE layer within the bridge makes the ATM virtual LAN appear as though it is a real LAN to the bridge. This allows existing LAN bridging methods (both source routing and transparent bridging) to be used without modification. But the LE layer needs to provide special support for transparent bridges.

Connecting two traditional LANs across an ATM network (as illustrated in Figure 11-3 on page 11-4) could be implemented with existing (non-ATM) remote LAN bridges with an ATM VCC used as a point-to-point link in between. However, this is not what is meant here. Bridges can be connected to each other through the ATM network to form a small (in this case) trivial emulated LAN in between. So, each real (shared-media) LAN is bridged to a backbone virtual LAN. Of course, this allows for multiple (more than 2) LANs to be connected to the same virtual LAN.

11.2.1.2 LAN Emulation Server (LES)

The basic function of the LES is to provide directory and address resolution services to the LECs of the emulated LAN. Each emulated LAN must have an LE server. An LE client may register the MAC address(es) it represents with the LE server. When an LE client wants to establish a direct connection with a destination LEC it gets the destination's MAC address from the higher-layer protocols and has to ask the LE server for the destination's ATM address. The LE server will either respond directly (if the destination client has registered that address) or forward the request to other clients to find the destination.

An emulated token-ring LAN cannot have members that are emulating an Ethernet LAN (and vice versa). Thus, an instance of an LE server is dedicated to a single type of LAN emulation. The problems of translation bridging between different LAN types are not ones that ATM can solve.

The LE server may be physically internal to the ATM network or provided in an external device, but logically it is always an external function which simply uses the services provided by ATM to do its job.

11.2.1.3 Broadcast and Unknown Server (BUS)

The BUS handles data that, on a real LAN, is sent to the broadcast MAC address (X′ FFFFFFFFFFFF′), all multicast traffic, and unicast data frames that are sent by a client before the destination ATM address has been resolved (by the LE server). The BUS then will forward the data frames either over a multicast send VCC (the return path) or over the multicast forward VCC to the destination(s). Of course, a client could send unicast frames without ever trying to establish a direct connection to the destination; this could be acceptable if it happens for a few frames, but would overload the BUS, for example, in the case of a file transfer.

The BUS works in a store-and-forward fashion, such that a frame's AAL-5 "cell train" has to be completely received by the BUS before the frame can be forwarded to its destination(s) (AAL-5 cells of different frames must not be intermixed). Also, all data frames sent through the BUS have to pass the ATM network twice, not very effective when sending large files. Nevertheless, the BUS is essential for the functioning of the virtual LAN; it is the BUS which presents the image of a shared-media LAN.

11.2.1.4 LE Configuration Server (LECS)

The LECS assigns the individual LE clients to the different virtual LANs that can exist on top of the ATM network. During initialization, an LE client may request the ATM address of an LE server, that is, to which virtual LAN it is connected. An LE client is not required to request this information from the LECS; an LE server's ATM address may be configured (system defined) in the LE client.

Using an LECS to assign clients to the different virtual LANs allows for central configuration and administration of multiple virtual LANs in an ATM network. The LECS could make its decision to assign an LE server, for example, based on a client's ATM or MAC address according to a defined policy, or simply based on a system-defined database.

11.2.2 LAN Emulation VC Connections

Data transfer in the LE system (consisting of control messages and encapsulated LAN frames) uses a number of different ATM VCCs as illustrated in Figure 11-4 on page 11-10.

11.2.2.1 Control Connections

Control VCCs connect an LE client to the LE configuration server and an LE server, but are never used for user data traffic. These connections may be permanent or switched and are established when an LE client connects to the virtual LAN.

Configuration Direct VCC

> A bi-directional configuration direct VCC may be established between an LE client and the LECS to obtain configuration information (e.g. the LE server's ATM address).

Control Direct VCC

> A bi-directional, point-to-point control direct VCC must be established (and kept active) between each LE client and the LE server to send control traffic (e.g. address resolution). The server use this VCC to send replies to the client.

Control Distribute VCC

> The LE server may optionally establish a unidirectional control distribute VCC to distribute control information (e.g. query for an unregistered MAC address) to all LE clients connected to the virtual LAN. This can be a point-to-point VCC to each LE client. If the ATM supports point-to-multipoint connections, then the LES might instead establish one point-to-multipoint VCC to all LECs (of course, this then has to be changed through signaling whenever a client enters or leaves the virtual LAN).

11.2.2.2 Data Connections

Data connections are direct VCCs from an LE client to other LE clients and to the BUS. They are used to carry user data traffic and never carry control traffic (except for a flush message for cleanup).

Data Direct VCC

For unicast data transfer between end systems, data direct VCCs are set up through ATM signaling as bi-directional, point-to-point connections once the LE client has received the destination's ATM address from the LE server.

Outgoing from an LE client, a VCC has to be established for every MAC address and SAP ID residing in the node to every destination MAC address and SAP ID. That means that if two nodes exchange NetBIOS and APPN traffic in parallel, then they will need two separate VCCs, one for NetBIOS and one for APPN.

As long as a data direct VCC has not been established (the protocol flows with the LE server may take some time) an LE client may send initial data frames through the BUS, but as soon as a data direct VCC is established it has to be used and no data must be sent through the BUS. (This needs careful control to ensure that when the direct VCC becomes available frames are not delivered out of sequence to the destination.) Data direct VCCs stay in place until one of the partner LECs decides to end the connection (because there is no more data) based on installation options defining relevant timeouts, etc.

Multicast Send VCC

During initialization, an LEC has to establish a bi-directional, point-to-point multicast send VCC to the broadcast and unknown server (the BUS's ATM address is provided by the LE server) and must keep this VCC established while being connected to the virtual LAN. This VCC is used by the LEC to send broadcast and multicast data frames and unicast frames until a data direct VCC is established. The BUS may use this VCC to send data (including multicast) to the LEC.

Multicast Forward VCC

When an LE client establishes its multicast send VCC to the BUS, the BUS learns about the new member of the virtual LAN. The BUS then will initiate signaling for the unidirectional multicast forward VCC to the LEC, which is used to forward data frames from the BUS. This VCC can be either point-to-point or point-to-multipoint (of course, a point-to-multipoint VCC is more effective for multicast operations).

Every LEC must be able to receive data frames from the BUS, either over the multicast send VCC or the multicast forward VCC, or even intermixed, but will not receive duplicates.

11.2.3 LE Service Operation

In operation, the LAN emulation service performs the following functions:

Initialization

> During initialization the LEC (workstation) obtains the LE server's ATM address and establishes the control VCCs with the LE server and the BUS. It also discovers its own ATM address; this is needed if it is to later set up direct VCCs.

Address Registration

> In this phase the LEC (workstation) registers its MAC address(es) with the LE server.

Address Resolution

> This is the method used by ATM end stations to set up direct VCCs with other end stations (LECs). This function includes mechanisms for learning the ATM address of a target station, mapping the MAC address to an ATM address, storing the mapping in a table, and managing the table.

> For the server this function provides the means for supporting the use of direct VCCs by end stations. This includes a mechanism for mapping the MAC address of an end-system to its ATM address, storing the information, and providing it to a requesting end station.

Data Transfer

> To transmit a frame the sending LE layer must:

> - Decide on which of its VCCs (to destination LEC or BUS) a frame is to be transmitted.

> - Encapsulate the frame (AAL-5 is used).

> It must also decide when to establish and release data direct VCCs. To do this it may need to access the LE server for address resolution purposes.

LAN Frame Receive

> The basic function here is to determine if a received frame is to be processed by this workstation. As on a real LAN, many frames are received which need to be filtered out and not passed to the workstation.

> After it is decided to pass the frame to the workstation, the frame must be decapsulated.

> It is important to note that there is no end-to-end error recovery provided by the LE system. This is just the same as a traditional shared-media LAN. The LE system will detect errors and discard error frames, but it does nothing to recover the error.

In a bridge, the LAN frame receive function is the same as that of an end station but without filtering.

11.2.3.1 Operation in Real Systems

In many practical LAN networks this system is going to work very well indeed. While LANs allow any-to-any data transport, the overwhelming majority of LAN users *never* make use of that function. Typical LAN users connect to a very few servers (such as communication servers, file servers, and printers). Many LANs exist for no purpose except to share printers.

In this situation, the LE architecture described above can be extremely effective. After a short time workstations will have established VCCs with all of the servers that they usually communicate with. Data transfer is then direct and very efficient. Timeouts can be set such that the switched VCCs stay there.

11.2.4 Summary

Provided the supporting network has the ATM facilities of switched VCC setup and multicast, a relatively efficient LAN emulation service can be built. Such a system would operate in the following way:

- Each user end station contains software that provides the appearance of a LAN to the existing LAN software in the workstation. This software together with the necessary ATM interfacing hardware is an ATM endpoint as far as the ATM network is concerned.

- There is a LAN emulation service somewhere in the network which provides address resolution, administration, broadcast forwarding (and filtering), and some regular data transfer facilities to the end stations.

- End stations (the LE layer software within the end stations) are connected through the ATM network to the LE service.

- Broadcasts are performed on behalf of end stations by the BUS, but a good level of filtering is available to improve efficiency.

- Data transfer takes place on direct VCCs between the end stations. These are set up by the end stations using supporting functions from the LE server.

This structure maintains full LAN function and can support most higher-layer LAN protocols. Reliance on the LE service for data transfer is minimized by using switched VCCs for the transport of most bulk data.

Appendix A. Standards

There are a number of bodies producing standards for ATM. They are summarized as follows:

ITU-T

> The International Telecommunication Union - Telecommunication (ITU-T) is the new name for the CCITT organization. This is a body set up under the auspices of the United Nations to make technical recommendations for country telecommunications carriers. Voting membership is restricted to organizations that provide telecommunications common carrier services in a particular country. IBM is not a member.

> Under its charter the ITU-T does not have the legal authority to make recommendations covering equipment (or networks) that are the property of end-user organizations. Its prerogative stops at the property boundary. Hence it is interested exclusively in providing standards (recommendations) for wide area networks provided by common carriers.

> Where telecommunications technical standards are concerned, the ITU-T is clearly the senior standards body. Most people accept that if multiple standards conflict, then the ITU-T recommendation takes precedence. ATM development was started by the ITU-T (then the CCITT).

ETSI

> The European Telecommunication Standards Institute is a body primarily concerned with choosing which of the ITU-T standards will be used in Europe (which options, etc.).

> ETSI has its own set of ATM standards, which generally follow the ITU-T.

ANSI

> The American National Standards Institute provides unique standards for the US. ANSI is involved in ATM for historical reasons. The US telephone network is very different from the rest of the world (due to accidents of history). Where ITU-T has specified the standards for outside the US, ANSI has specified them for the US.

> This does *not* mean that there will be a different ATM in the US.

> It will be necessary to run ATM over US PDH link connections, and ANSI is actively involved in specifying the necessary protocols to allow this.

A-1

ATM Forum

The ATM Forum is a non-profit consortium of companies and organizations interested in ATM development. Currently over 200 companies are involved, and these represent 95% or more of the telecommunications and data communications industries.

The ATM Forum has no authority of any kind to produce standards. Real standards are the domain of the International Organization for Standardization (ISO). The ATM Forum produces "implementation agreements" that member companies agree to follow when producing ATM equipment.

In fact, there is not much conflict. The ATM Forum is primarily interested in the use of ATM in the LAN environment. The ITU-T is interested in the wide area. The two bodies complement one another rather than conflict.

Another way of looking at it is to say that the ATM Forum is primarily interested in data communications and the ITU-T primarily interested in telecommunications. But there is lots of overlap here.

International Organization for Standardization (ISO)

ISO will be involved when the time comes to make ITU-T or ATM Forum recommendations into real standards. As yet its involvement is minor.

IEEE

The Institute of Electrical and Electronics Engineers is a professional body which produces standards in the LAN area. The IEEE-802.6 committee is responsible for the DQDB (SMDS) LAN architecture. It is their position that 802.6 *is* the ATM LAN.

Internet Activity Board (IAB)

Sponsored by the Internet Society (ISOC), the IAB is responsible for setting the standards related to the Internet. This means everything related to TCP/IP.

The IAB has produced a number of RFCs (RFC = Request for Comment, which really means "standard") for the operation of TCP/IP over ATM, for LAN interconnection over ATM, and for resolution of the addressing issues related to the use of ATM with the Internet. The IAB does not produce ATM standards, but is very interested in standards for using ATM.

A.1.1 Roadmap to ATM Standards

Table A-1 gives an overview of the major ATM standards[1] by the different standardization bodies. (The ATM Forum's "implementation agreements" are not included).

Table A-1. *ATM Standards*

	ITU-T	ITU-T related	ETSI	ETSI related
Signaling UNI	Q.2931			
Signaling NNI	Q.2761/4			
CBDS	I.364	F.812	dETS DE/NA-53203	ETS 300.217
Frame Relay		F.811	dETS BISDN/FRBS	prETS 300.FR
FR Interworking		I.555	dETS DE/NA-53204	
SSCS (FR)	I.365.1			
SAAL	I.SAAL		dETS SAAL	
AAL-5	I.363	I.362	dETS AAL-5	
AAL-3/4	I.363	I.362	ETS 300.300	ETS 300.299
AAL-1	I.363	I.362	prETS DE/NA-52617	
ATM layer	I.361	I.150	ETS 300.298	
ATM performance	I.35B			
BISDN UNI	I.432	G.957	ETS 300.301	
PHY architecture		G.803/4		dETR DE/TM-3010
PDH UNI		G.703	prETS DE/TM-3007	ETS 300.126
SDH UNI	G.708	G.707 G.957	ETS 300.228	ETS 300.147

Note:
dETR = draft European Telecommunication Report
dETS = draft European Telecommunication Standard
ETS = European Telecommunication Standard
ETSI = European Telecommunication Standards Institute
prETS = pre-European Telecommunication Standard
ITU-T = International Telecommunication Union - Telecommunication

The following are the full references for the key standards. Care should be exercised because some of them are still in draft stage. Standards are subject to revision. People who require accurate current information have no alternative but to obtain the most recent editions of the standards indicated.

1. Rec. G.652-1993 Characteristics of Single Mode Fiber

---

[1] This table of standards and the roadmap which follows is the work of Mr Marc Boisseau of IBM CER La Gaude.

2. Rec. G.702-1988 Digital Hierarchy Bit Rates
3. Rec. G.703-1991 Physical/Electrical Characteristics of Hierarchical Digital Interfaces
4. Rec. G.707-1993 Synchronous Digital Hierarchy Bit Rates
5. Rec. G.708-1993 Network Node Interface for the Synchronous Digital Hierarchy
6. Rec. G.709-1993 Synchronous Multiplexing Structure
7. Rec. G.804-1994 ATM Cell Mapping into Plesiochronous Digital Hierarchy (PDH)
8. Rec. G.832-1994 Transport of SDH Elements on PDH Networks: Frame and Multiplexing Structures
9. Rec. G.957-1993 Optical Interfaces Relating to SDH Equipments and Systems
10. Rec. I.311-1993 B-ISDN General Network Aspects
11. Rec. I.361-1993 B-ISDN ATM Layer Specification
12. Rec. I.362-1993 B-ISDN ATM Adaptation Layer (AAL) Functional Description
13. Rec. I.363-1993 B-ISDN ATM Adaptation Layer (AAL) Specification
14. Rec. I.364-1993 Support of Broadband Connectionless Data Service on B-ISDN
15. Rec. I.365.1-1994 Frame Relaying Service Specific Convergence Sublayer (FR-SSCS)
16. Rec. I.432-1993 B-ISDN User-Network Interface - Physical Layer Specification
17. Rec. I.610-1993 B-ISDN Operations and Maintenance Principles and Functions
18. ANSI T1.630-1993 Broadband ISDN -- ATM Adaptation Layer for Constant Bit Rate Services Functionality and Specification
19. ETSI prETS 300 353, B-ISDN ATM Adaptation Layer (AAL) Specification, Type 1, December 1993.

Note: The prefix Rec. implies a published ITU-T (formerly CCITT) Recommendation, according to the "Catalogue of ITU-T Recommendations, July 1993," or those that have been approved during 1993 under Resolution 1 procedures.

Figure A-1 on page A-5 shows a "roadmap" to the more significant ATM standards as they exist in March of 1994.

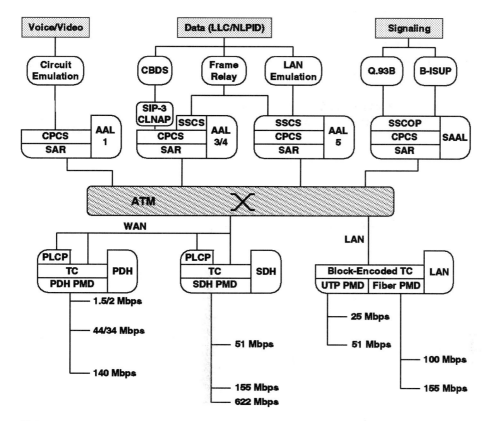

Notes:

- AAL-2 is not mentioned as it is being reworked by the standards body.
- 51 Mbps is only a Sonet speed.

Legend:

AAL	ATM Adaptaion Layer	**PMD**	Physical Medium Dependent
ATM	Asynchronous Transfer Mode	**NLPID**	Network Layer Protocol Identifier
B-ISUP	Braodband Integrated Service User Part	**SAAL**	Signaling AAL
CBDS	Connectionless Broadband Data Service	**SAR**	Segmentation and Reassembly
CLNAP	Connectionless Network Access Protocol	**SDH**	Synchronous Digital Hierarchy
CPCS	Common-Part Convergence Sublayer	**SIP-3**	SMDS Interface Protocol Layer-3
LAN	Local Area Network	**SMDS**	Switched Multimegabit Data Service
LLC	Logical Link Control	**SSCOP**	Service Specific Connection-Oriented
PDH	Plesiochronous Digital Hierarchy		Protocol
PLCP	Physical-Layer Convergence Protocol	**SSCS**	Service Specific Convergence Sublayer
		TC	Transmission Convergence

Figure A-1. Roadmap to the ATM Standards

A.1.2 Staged Development

The standards bodies are developing ATM in different stages. This is due to the immense size of the standardization task. The stages relate to what functions are available at what times. This has enabled the building of early products, whereas if people waited for the standards to be fully complete before product design was commenced, then ATM would not be available for some years.

The stages relate mainly to the development of signaling protocols. The ITU-T calls its stages "releases". The ATM Forum calls them "phases". The process is the same but Forum Phase 1 is not equivalent to ITU-T Release-1.

Release-1

> Release-1 is primarily aimed at supporting existing services, such as telephony and constant bit rate services through ATM.

Release-2

> The R-2 signaling protocol will support VBR services, point-to-multipoint connections, and the ability to add and drop connections during the lifetime of the call.

Release-3

> Expected to be available in 1996 or later, Release-3 function will support multimedia and distributive services, the negotiation of QoS parameters, and negotiation of other attributes during the progress of a call.

ATM Forum Phase-1 contains a subset of ITU-T Release-1 features and some features from ITU-T Release-2.

Appendix B. SDH and Sonet

Sonet (Synchronous Optical Network) is a US standard for the internal operation of tele-phone company optical networks. It is closely related to a system called SDH (Synchro-nous Digital Hierarchy) adopted by the CCITT as a recommendation for the internal operation of carrier (PTT) optical networks worldwide.

Sonet and SDH are of immense importance because of the vast cost savings that they promise for public communications networks.

Traditionally, public telephone company networks have been built by using a cascade of multiplexors at each end of a high-speed connection. In physical realization, this resulted in the configuration illustrated in Figure B-1.

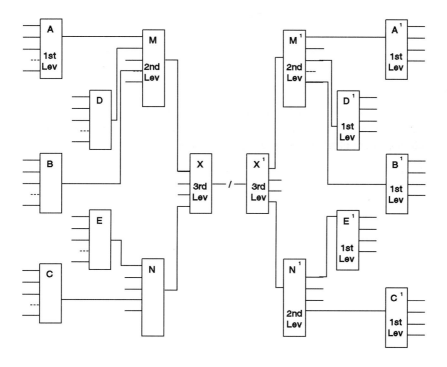

Figure   *B-1.* *The Multiplexor Mountain.* Each multiplexor illustrated exists as a sepa-rate physical device, although many multiplexors may be mounted together on a single rack.

B-1

In order to use a high-speed interexchange link, it was necessary to multiplex a very large number of slower-speed circuits onto it in stages. The faster the link, the more stages required.

There are a number of important points to remember here:

1. The internals of this structure are proprietary. Each pair of multiplexors in the system has to be manufactured by the same supplier. In the figure, the concept of multiplexor pairs is illustrated. A pair of multiplexors "see" a clear-channel connection between them, even though the connection might really go through several higher-layer multiplexors. (In the figure, multiplexors A and A′, B and B′ are multiplexor pairs.)

2. The multiplexing structure in the US is different from the structure used in Europe, and both are different from the structure used in Japan. This leads to compatibility problems when interconnecting systems between countries, and also means that equipment designed and built in one country often cannot be used in another.

3. There is an enormous cost benefit to be gained by integrating the multiplexing function with the internal functioning of the telephone exchange and hence removing the multiplexors entirely. Modern telephone exchanges are digital time-division multiplexors in themselves.

4. If access is needed to a single tributary circuit (or small group of circuits), then it is necessary to demultiplex the whole structure and then remultiplex it.

Sonet and SDH eliminate these problems. A single multiplexing scheme is specified that allows:

1. A standardized method of internal operation and management so that equipment from many different manufacturers may be used productively together.

2. Multiple speeds of operation such that, as higher and higher optical speeds are introduced, the system can expand gracefully to operate at the higher speeds.

3. Worldwide compatibility. A single optical multiplexing hierarchy applies throughout the world and accommodates the existing speeds used in both Europe and the US.

4. Many levels of multiplexing and demultiplexing to be accomplished in a single step. (You do not have to demultiplex the higher levels to gain access to the lower levels.)

5. Many different payloads (different-speed channels) to be carried through the system.

6. Access to low bandwidth (T-1, E-1 style) tributaries without the need to demultiplex the whole stream.

7. Considerably better efficiency than before. For example, the floating payload feature of Sonet eliminates the need for the customary 125-μsec buffers required at crosspoints in the existing ("plesiochronous") multiplexing schemes.

B.1.1 Sonet Structure

The basic structure in Sonet is a frame of 810 bytes, which is sent every 125 μsec. This allows a single byte within a frame to be part of a 64-Kbps digital voice channel. Since the minimum frame size is 810 bytes, then the minimum speed at which Sonet will operate is 51.84 megabits per second.

```
810 bytes × 8000 frames/sec × 8 (bits) = 51.84 Mbps
```

This basic frame is called the Synchronous Transport Signal level 1 (STS-1). It is conceptualized as containing 9 rows of 90 columns each as shown in Figure B-2.

- The first three columns of every row are used for administration and control of the multiplexing system. They are called "overhead" in the standard but are very necessary for the system's operation.

- The frame is transmitted row by row, from the top left of the frame to the bottom right.

- Of course it is necessary to remember that the representation of the structure as a two-dimensional frame is just a conceptual way of representing a repeating structure. In reality it is just a string of bits with a defined repeating pattern.

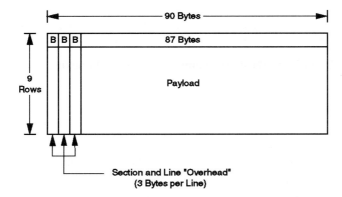

Figure B-2. Sonet STS-1 Frame Structure. The diagrammatic representation of the frame as a square is done for ease of understanding. The 810 bytes are transmitted row by row, starting from the top left of the diagram. One frame is transmitted every 125 microseconds.

The physical frame structure above is similar to every other TDM structure used in the telecommunications industry. The big difference is in how the "payload" is carried. The payload is a frame that "floats" within the physical frame structure. The payload envelope is illustrated in Figure B-3 on page B-4.

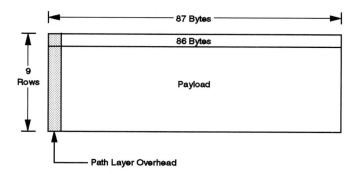

Figure B-3. Sonet Synchronous Payload Envelope

Notice that the payload envelope fits exactly within a single Sonet frame.

The payload envelope is allowed to start anywhere within the physical Sonet frame and in that case will span two consecutive physical frames. The start of the payload is pointed to by the H1 and H2 bytes within the line overhead sections.

Very small differences in the clock rates of the frame and the payload can be accommodated by temporarily incrementing or decrementing the pointer (an extra byte if needed is found by using one byte (H3) in the section header). Nevertheless, big differences in clock frequencies cannot be accommodated by this method.

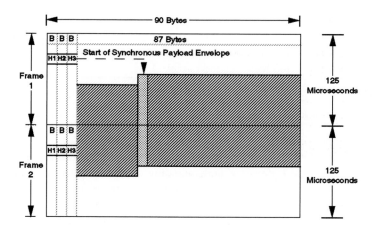

Figure B-4. Synchronous Payload Envelope Floating in STS-1 Frame. The SPE is pointed to by the H1 and H2 bytes.

Multiple STS-1 frames can be byte-multiplexed together to form higher-speed signals. When this is done they are called STS-2, STS-3, etc. where the numeral suffix indicates the number of STS-1 frames that are present (and therefore the line speed). For example, STS-3 is 3 times an STS-1 or 155.52 Mbps. This multiplexing uses the method illustrated in Figure B-5 on page B-5.

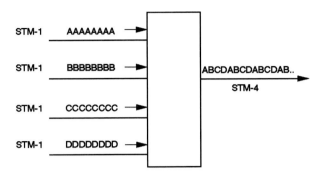

Figure **B-5.** *STM-1 to STM-4 Synchronous Multiplexing*

An alternative method is to phase-align the multiple STS frames and their payloads. This means that a larger payload envelope has been created. This is called "concatenation" and is indicated in the name of the signal. For example, when three STS-1s are concatenated such that the frames are phase-aligned and there is a single large payload envelope, it is called an STS-3c.

B.1.2 SDH

In the rest of the world, Sonet is not immediately useful because the "E-3" rate of 35 Mbps does not efficiently fit into the 50-Mbps Sonet signal. (The comparable US PDH signal, the T-3, is roughly 45 Mbps and fits nicely.)

The CCITT has defined a worldwide standard called the Synchronous Digital Hierarchy, which accommodates both Sonet and the European line speeds.

This was done by defining a basic frame that is exactly equivalent to (Sonet) STS-3c. This has a new name. It is Synchronous Transport Module level one or STM-1 and has a basic rate (minimum speed) of 155.52 Mbps. This is shown in Figure B-6 on page B-6.

Faster line speeds are obtained in the same way as in Sonet - by byte interleaving of multiple STM-1 frames. For this to take place (as in Sonet) the STM-1 frames must be 125-μsec frame aligned. Four STM-1 frames may be multiplexed to form an STM-4 at 622.08 Mbps. This (again like Sonet) may carry four separate payloads byte multiplexed together (see Figure B-5). Alternatively, the payloads may be concatenated (rather than interleaved), and the signal is then called STM-4c.

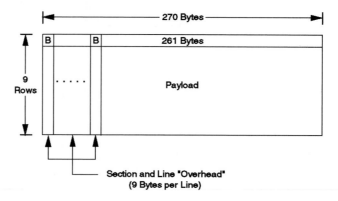

Figure *B-6.* *SDH Basic Frame Format*

B.1.3 Tributaries

Within each payload, slower-speed channels (called tributaries) may be carried. Tributaries normally occupy a number of consecutive columns within a payload.

A US T-1 payload (1.544 Mbps) occupies three columns; a European E-1 payload (2.048 Mbps) occupies four columns. Notice that there is some wasted bandwidth here. A T-1 really only requires 24 slots, and three columns gives it 27. An E-1 requires 32 slots and is given 36. This "wastage" is a very small price to pay for the enormous benefit to be achieved by being able to demultiplex a single tributary stream from within the multiplexed structure without having to demultiplex the whole stream.

The tributaries may be fixed within their virtual containers or they may float, similar to the way a virtual container floats within the physical frame. Pointers within the overhead are used to locate each virtual tributary stream.

B.1.4 Status

Sonet/SDH standards are now firm and equipment implementing them is beginning to become available. However, there are many desirable extensions that have not yet been standardized. For example, there is no standard for interfacing customer premises equipment to STS-3c (STM) available as yet. However, it is likely that this will happen in the future, since the FDDI standard contains an interface to STS-3c for use as wide area operation of FDDI rings.

Table B-1. Sonet Speed Hierarchy				
Signal Level	**Bit Rate**	**DS-0s**	**DS-1s**	**DS-3s**
STS-1 and OC-1	51.84 Mbps	672	28	1
STS-3 and OC-3 (STM-1)	155.52 Mbps	2,016	84	3
STS-9 and OC-9	466.56 Mbps	6,048	252	9
STS-12 and OC-12 (STM-4)	622.08 Mbps	8,064	336	12
STS-18 and OC-18	933.12 Mbps	12,096	504	18
STS-24 and OC-24	1244.16 Mbps	16,128	672	24
STS-36 and OC-36	1866.24 Mbps	24,192	1008	36
STS-48 and OC-48 (STM-16)	2488.32 Mbps	32,256	1344	48
STS-n and OC-n (STM-n/3)	$n \times 51.84$ Mbps	$n \times 672$	$n \times 28$	n

B.1.5 Conclusion

Successful specification of a system which integrates and accommodates all of the different line speeds and characteristics of US and European multiplexing hierarchies was a formidable challenge. Sonet/SDH is a complex system but it is also a very significant achievement. It is expected that equipment using SDH will become the dominant form of network multiplexing equipment within a very short time.

B.2 The Bandwidth Fragmentation Problem

Existing telecommunication backbone systems are almost exclusively based on TDM structures. The system is cost effective and efficient in an environment where bandwidth allocation is done in a small number of fixed amounts.

In the future, high-speed backbone wide area networks owned by the PTTs will need to become a lot more flexible. It is predicted that there will be significant demand for arbitrary amounts of bandwidth and for "variable bandwidth" such as is needed for a video signal. Many planners in the PTTs believe that TDM technology is not sufficiently flexible to satisfy this requirement. This is partly because of the perceived "waste" in using fixed rate services for variable traffic (such as interactive image, variable-rate voice or variable-rate encoded video) and partly because arbitrary variable amounts of bandwidth are very difficult to allocate in a TDM system. This latter problem is called "bandwidth fragmentation".

The problem of bandwidth fragmentation on a TDM link is exactly the same problem as storage fragmentation in main storage buffer pools within a computer system.

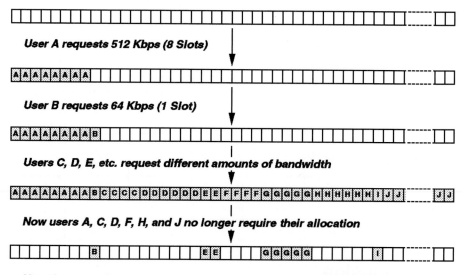

Figure B-7. Bandwidth Fragmentation

For the example in Figure B-7, assume that we have a 4 Mbps link which consists of 64, 64-Kbps slots. The example is a trivial one but it illustrates the point. In computer memory variable-length buffer pools (before virtual storage fixed the problem), it was found that after operation for a long period of time perhaps only 20% of the memory would be in use and the other 80% would be broken up into fragments that were too small to use. This is a significant waste of resource. In addition, the control mechanisms needed to operate a scheme such as this would be complex and more expensive than alternative schemes based on cell multiplexing.

A mechanism like the computer's virtual storage could be used to concatenate multiple 64 Kbps channels into wider logical channels, but that requires significant hardware and will only work when communication on the link is peer-to-peer. In the new Sonet/SDH system it is possible for multiple devices to access the same link and extract groups of channels (tributaries) without the need to demultiplex the whole channel. A virtual channel allocation system would take away this ability.

This problem is the primary reason that Broadband ISDN uses a cell-based switching system.

B.2.1 Synchronous Transfer Mode (STM)

Synchronous Transfer Mode was a proposed TDM system for implementing Broadband ISDN. It was worked on for some time by standards committees. It uses the same principles as SDH (and can be thought of as an extension of SDH). STM was abandoned in favor of the Asynchronous Transfer Mode (ATM) cell-switching approach. One of the reasons for this was the difficulty of managing bandwidth allocation (bandwidth fragmentation).

B.3 Plesiochronous Digital Hierarchy

PDH is the digital networking hierarchy that was used before the advent of Sonet/SDH. The link speeds are included here for reference.

Table B-2. *PDH Speed Hierarchy - USA*

Level	Speed in Mbps	Number of Channels
DS-0	64 Kbps	1
T-1, DS-1	1.544	24
T-2, DS-2	6.312	96
T-3, DS-3	44.736	672
T-4, DS-4	274.176	4032

Table B-3. *PDH Speed Hierarchy - Europe*

Level	Speed in Mbps	Number of Channels
E-1	2.048	30
E-2	8.448	120
E-3	34.368	480
E-4	139.264	1920
E-5	564.992	7680

Appendix C. Synchronization

It seems ironic that one of the most important issues in the design of *Asynchronous Transfer Mode* networks is *synchronization* of the network. The fact is that if we want to handle *any* traffic type that is inherently timing dependent, then we have to provide end-to-end network clock synchronization. This is not quite the same as the kind of synchronization that is used within a telephone network or within a TDM carrier structure. The parts of an ATM network that need to be synchronized are the input and output interfaces. Data transfer within the ATM network itself is asynchronous.

Traffic types that require this level of synchronization are:

1. Any constant-bit-rate (CBR) service

2. Voice (whether compressed or not)

3. Video (whether compressed or not)

4. Multimedia

ATM networks that do not have these types of traffic (such as data networks) do not need to be synchronized. The requirement for synchronization at the adaptation layer was discussed in 3.4, "AAL-1" on page 3-8.

C.1.1 Need for Synchronization

The need for synchronization can be illustrated by referring to Figure C-1.

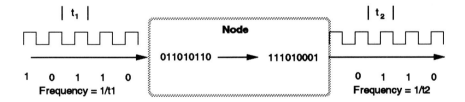

Figure   C-1. *Synchronization*

A continuous, unbroken stream of bits passes through a communications node. The bit stream arrives at the node at a particular rate (speed). When the bit stream is sent out from the node the transmitted stream also has a particular rate associated with it. If the receive clock rate and the transmit clock rate are *identical*, then you only need perhaps 3 bits of buffering within the node and you can pass the bit stream through without any problems. If, however, the receive and transmit clocks are operating at *different* rates, then we have a problem.

C-1

- If the bits are received faster than they are transmitted, then some will be lost. This situation is called overrun.

- If the bits are transmitted faster than they are received, then at some point a bit will be needed for transmission and there will not be one available (so a randomly determined bit will be added to the stream). This situation is called underrun.

Generically, overruns and underruns are often referred to as "clock slips". In traditional packet networks (and *within* an ATM network) this does not matter at all. Data transfer of packets or cells is asynchronous.

But when input and output bit streams are continuous (go on forever) this can cause a problem. You can, of course, allow for a certain amount of buffering within the node, but if the streams are unbroken, at some time you are going to run out of buffers. The problem is exactly the same even if a packet or cell network takes the place of the node shown in the figure.

The real problem is that we cannot manufacture timing sources that provide really *exact* timing. Crystal-controlled oscillators are used in most communications equipment and they are generally accurate to about 1 part in a million. This sounds fine until you have to receive and retransmit a few hundred million bits (which at modern link speeds can be significantly less than one second). Atomic clocks are extremely accurate but are too costly to have one at every communications interface within a network.

C.1.2 Timing Source

Looking back at Figure C-1, if the node could control both the rate at which it receives data and the rate at which it sends data, then there would be little problem. In some situations you have just this. There are many ways of having a receiving node control the timing.

It is common to assume that the transmitter end of every communication link actually controls the timing. Thus, the clock in the two directions would be going at slightly different rates. In fact, this does happen sometimes, but it is quite unusual (at least on electrical connections).

Most electrical links have a primary end and a secondary end. The secondary is required to recover the clock it receives and use that to control and stabilize its own transmit oscillator. So if node B is the primary end of a particular link and node A is transmitting to B the link rate will be controlled by node B's clock. (One reason for this is that echo cancellation on copper connections is significantly easier if both directions of a link are synchronized.)

But there is also the situation where the node cannot control either its own transmit or receive timing. In this case there is no solution. If the transmit and receive data streams are different in speed, then at some point data will either be lost or corrupted.

It is clear that if an unbroken, synchronous data stream is to be carried through a multi-node network, then we have to do something to ensure that all the clocks run at the same speed.

C.1.3 Clock Tolerance

If the network is to be planned to have no clock slips, then we must consider the difference in rates between clocks at the edges of the network. If these are identical and the appropriate startup transmit delay and buffer size are set up to support the delay jitter within the network, then no clock slips will occur.

Telephone network engineers try to maintain a very tight clock reference to minimize any loss within the network. This means that any link connecting private network equipment to the public data network will have a very accurate clock reference inherent in its data stream.

The standards for clocks within a carrier network are as follows:

- Stratum-1 $= +/- 1 \times 10^{-11}$
- Stratum-2 $= +/- 1.6 \times 10^{-8}$
- Stratum-3 $= +/- 4.6 \times 10^{-6}$
- Stratum-4 $= +/- 32 \times 10^{-6}$

C.1.4 Node and Network Synchronization

In telephone networks, extreme care is taken to synchronize the entire network to the same clock. Extremely accurate atomic clocks (called "Stratum-1" clocks) are situated at critical points within the network and timing is propagated throughout the network along with the data.

- Within each node (telephone exchange, for example) a single clock source is carried to each link (I/O) interface.
- Within a network of nodes a network clock is used to control each node clock.

In practice, a network clock is subject to some distortion as it is propagated through the network. The technique most commonly used is for the node clock to be synchronized with the network clock, but the node clock is the one actually used for interface timing. That way, if the network clock is lost for any reason the node clock will continue and the network will continue to function for some time until the node clock has drifted too far from the correct frequency.

The problem is not just one for the network itself but extends right down to the end-user devices. If a TV camera is generating a stream of bits at a given rate and the network is transporting them at a different rate, then we have the same problem. **Timing-sensitive end-user devices should be synchronized to the same clock as the network itself.**

This is a significant design issue for the I/O device itself. Personal computer buses are asynchronous and so do not have a way of distributing a clock internally between adapters. This is one of the reasons that the newer personal videoconferencing PC applications do most of their processing work outboard of the PC on an adapter card - the real data flow does not go anywhere near the PC bus or main memory.

In an ATM network, cell streams are not particularly timing sensitive. Provided links are of sufficient capacity there is no requirement in ATM to synchronize links *between* ATM switches. (Other factors such as the use of SDH protocols for interswitch connection may require them to be synchronized, however.) In ATM, we only need to synchronize the data streams on external interfaces where the devices are bit rate sensitive.

C.1.5 Clock Propagation within the Network

Figure C-2 shows timing distribution taking place throughout a hypothetical network.

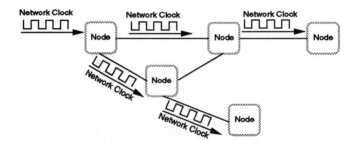

Figure   C-2. Clock Propagation

- An external clock source is used to synchronize the node clock in the first node.

- This node clock then controls data transmission on the node's external links.

- Connected nodes *may* derive a timing reference along with the data from any link connected to the first node. The link used for this is normally carefully chosen.

- These connected nodes then synchronize their clocks to the derived timing reference.

- This process takes place stage-by-stage throughout the network until all the nodes are synchronized to the same network clock. (In practice, the network clock will vary a little bit due to skew, etc. but the average rate will now be extremely stable throughout the network.)

One issue is precisely how is the network clock to be derived from an incoming link. It is possible to take any line and divide its line clock until a common network clock rate is reached. This is not the common method, however.

Telecommunications equipment is universally synchronized to a 125-μsec clock signal. The use of framing on link protocols attests to that. The frame rate is usually one frame every 125 μsec. This gives a network clock rate of 8 kHz. Node timing in ATM will usually be derived from the frame rate on one or other attached links. In ATM, in some of the link protocols that do not have 125-μsec frames a special 125-μsec strobe signal is introduced instead.

C.1.6 Clock Propagation within a Node

Depending on available timing sources a node could select either:

- An external carrier line
- An external line connecting to another node belonging to the same end-user network
- A specially attached clock reference line
- An internally generated clock

Within the node there must be a mechanism to distribute the clock to the I/O adapters. This will usually consist of one or more clock distribution lines connected to each adapter across the backplane.

- In a typical switch, each link adapter will be controlled by its own local oscillator, but that oscillator will be regulated (its rate will be determined) by the node clock. If the node clock fails for any reason, then the local oscillator will be able to continue operation at much the same rate for some time before it drifts too far away from its desired rate.
- The node clock will be controlled by a selected external clock reference source.
- The clock rate used as reference will usually be 8 kHz (125 μsec between pulses). This is not necessary - a very much higher rate may be used and divided when it reaches the adapter.
- End-user equipment that processes timing-dependent data streams also needs to receive and to use the network clock.

Abbreviations

AAL	ATM adaptation layer
ABR	available bit rate
ADPCM	adaptive differential pulse code modulation
ADSL	asymmetric digital subscriber line
AM	amplitude modulation
ANSI	American National Standards Institute
APPN	Advanced Peer-to-Peer Networking
ASCII	American (National) Standard Code for Information Interchange
ATM	asynchronous transfer mode
Bps	bytes per second
bps	bits per second
BRI	basic rate interface
B-ICI	B_ISDN inter-carrier interface
B-ISDN	Broadband ISDN
BUS	broadcast and unknown server
CAD	computer-aided design
CBR	constant bit rate
CCITT	Comite Consultatif International Telegraphique et Telephonique (International Telegraph and Telephone Consultative Committee) now ITU-T
CDMA	code division multiple access
CLP	cell loss priority
CMOS	complementary metal oxide semiconductor
CPCS	common part convergence sublayer
CPN	customer premises network (node)
CRC	cyclic redundancy check
CS	convergence sublayer
CSMA/CD	carrier sense multiple access with collision detection
dB	decibel
DE	discard eligibility
DLCI	data link connection identifier
DQDB	distributed queue dual bus
DS	digital signal
DTL	designated transit list
DXI	data exchange interface
ECC	error correction code
ETSI	European Telecommunication Standards Institute
FCS	frame check sequence
FDDI	fiber distributed data interface
Gbps	gigabits per second
GFC	generic flow control
HDLC	high-level data link control
HDSL	high-bit-rate digital subscriber line
HDTV	high-definition television
HEC	header error check
IDU	interface data unit
IEEE	Institute of Electrical and Electronics Engineers
IISP	interim inter-switch signaling protocol
ILMI	interim local management interface
I/O	input/output
IP	internet protocol
ISDN	integrated services digital network
ISO	International Organization for Standardization
ITU-T	International Telecommunication Union - Telecommunication
KB	kilobyte
Kbps	kilobits per second
LAN	local area network
LAPB	link access procedure balanced
LAPD	link access procedure for the D_channel (ISDN)
LASER	light amplification by the stimulated emission of radiation
LE	LAN emulation
LEC	LAN emulation client
LECS	LAN emulation configuration server
LES	LAN emulation server

X-1

LGN	logical group node	**SDU**	service data unit
LLC	logical link control	**SMDS**	switched multi-megabit data service
LPDU	logical link control protocol data unit	**SNA**	Systems Network Architecture
LUNI	LAN emulation user-to-network interface	**Sonet**	synchronous optical network
		SOH	section overhead
MAC	medium access control	**SPE**	synchronous payload envelope (Sonet/SDH)
MAN	metropolitan area network		
MB	megabytes	**SRTS**	synchronous residual time stamp
Mbps	megabits per second		
MIB	management information block	**SSCF**	service specific coordination function
NBBS	Networking BroadBand Architecture		
		SSCOP	service-specific connection-oriented protocol
NNI	network node interface		
NRZI	non-return to zero inverted	**SSCS**	service-specific convergence sublayer
OA&M	operations, administration, and maintenance		
		STM	synchronous transfer mode
OC-n	optical carrier level n	**STM**	synchronous transport module
OSI	open systems interconnection	**STP**	shielded twisted pair
PBX	private branch exchange	**STS**	synchronous transport signal
PC	personal computer	**TA**	terminal adapter
PCM	pulse code modulation	**TC**	transmission convergence
PDH	plesiochronous digital hierarchy	**TCP/IP**	transmission control protocol/internet protocol
PDU	protocol data unit		
PG	peer group	**TDM**	time division multiplexing
PGI	peer group identifier	**TE**	terminal equipment
PGL	peer group leader	**TTP**	telephone twisted pair (Wiring)
PLCP	physical layer convergence protocol	**UBR**	unspecified bit rate
		UNI	user-to-network interface
PMD	physical medium dependent	**UTP**	unshielded twisted pair
PNNI	private network-to-network (node-to-node) interface	**VAD**	voice activity detector
		VBR	variable bit rate
POH	path overhead	**VC**	virtual circuit (X.25)
PT	payload type		virtual connection (Frame Relay)
PTSP	PNNI topology state packet		
PTT	post, telegraph, and telephone (company)		virtual channel (ATM)
		VCC	virtual channel connection
QoS	quality of service	**VCI**	virtual channel identifier
RAM	random access memory	**VP**	virtual path
SAAL	signaling ATM adaptation layer	**VPC**	virtual path connection
SAP	service access point	**VPCI**	virtual path connection identifier
SAR	segmentation and reassembly	**VPI**	virtual path identifier
SDH	synchronous digital hierarchy	**VT**	virtual tributary
SDLC	synchronous data link control	**WAN**	wide area network
SDT	structured data transfer		

Glossary

A

anisochronous. Literally, "not equal". Used in the communications engineering context to mean bit streams of unequal rates (this causes a problem in time division multiplexing systems).

asynchronous. Any two events that are not tied together exactly in time are said to be asynchronous.

asynchronous transfer mode (ATM). A transfer mode in which the information is organized into cells. It is asynchronous in the sense that the recurrence of cells containing information from an individual user is not necessarily periodic.

ATM peer-to-peer connection. A virtual channel connection (VCC) or a virtual path connection (VPC).

ATM user-to-user connection. An association established at the ATM layer to support communication between two or more ATM service users (that is, between two or more next higher layer entities or between two or more ATM entities). The communication over an ATM layer connection may be either bidirectional or unidirectional. The same virtual channel identifier (VCI) is used for both directions of a connection at an interface.

ATM layer link. A section of an ATM layer connection between two active ATM layer entities (ATM entities).

ATM link. A virtual path link (VPL) or a virtual channel link (VCL).

ATM traffic descriptor. A generic list of traffic parameters that can be used to capture the intrinsic traffic characteristics of a requested ATM connection.

B

broadcast. A value of the service attribute "communication configuration", which denotes unidirectional distribution to all users.

C

cell. ATM layer protocol data unit.

cell header. ATM layer protocol control information.

connection admission control (CAC). The set of actions taken by the network at the call setup phase (or during call re-negotiation phase) in order to establish whether a virtual channel/virtual path connection can be accepted or rejected (or a request for re-allocation can be accommodated). Routing is part of connection admission control actions.

congestion control. The set of actions taken to relieve congestion by limiting its spread and duration.

connectionless service. A service which allows the transfer of information between service users without the need for end-to-end call establishment procedures.

constant bit rate service. A type of tele-communication service characterized by a service bit rate specified by a constant value.

X-3

F

framed interface.   An interface where the serial bit stream is segmented into periodic physical frames. Each frame is divided by a fixed partition into an overhead and an information payload portion.

G

general broadcast signaling virtual channel.   A virtual channel independent of service profiles and used for broadcast signaling.

H

heterochronous.   If two bit streams have nominally different bit rates they are said to be heterochronous.

I

isochronous.   Literally "in the same time". An isochronous bit stream is one that goes at a constant rate. The term isochronous is often used colloquially to mean "digitally encoded voice". The term is not often used in the world of data communications but is a common term in the voice communications and engineering context.

J

jitter.   Undesirable variations in the arrival time of a transmitted digital signal.

M

mesochronous.   The Greek prefix "meso" means "middle". If two isochronous bit streams have no precisely controlled relationship, but have exactly the same bit rate, they are called mesochronous.

If two bit streams start at some point of origin as synchronous streams and arrive at some destination by different routes or networking schemes they will be mesochronous at the point of arrival.

meta-signaling.   The procedure for establishing, checking and releasing signaling virtual channels.

multipoint-to-point connection.   A multipoint-to-point connection consists of a simple tree topology considered as a root node connected to many leaves. A multipoint-to-point connection has zero bandwidth from the root node to the leaf nodes and a non-zero return bandwidth from the leaf nodes to the root node.

multipoint-to-multipoint connection.   A multipoint-to-multipoint is a collection of ATM VC or VP links and their associated endpoint nodes. Any information sent on the connection by a node is received by all of the other nodes. A receiving endpoint node cannot distinguish which other endpoint sent the information unless some higher layer information is present for the purpose.

N

network node interface.   The interface between two ATM switches.

network parameter control.   The set of actions taken by the network to monitor and control traffic at the Inter-Network Node Interface to protect network resources from malicious as well as unintentional misbehavior by detecting violations of negotiated parameters and taking appropriate actions.

O

OA&M. Operations, Administration and Maintenance

OA&M cell. A cell that contains ATM LM information. It does not form part of the upper layer information transfer.

P

packet. In data communication, a sequence of binary digits, including data and control signals, that is transmitted and switched as a composite whole. Synonymous with *data frame*.

In ATM, "An information block identified by a label at layer 3 of the OSI reference model."

packet transfer mode (PTM). A transfer mode in which the transmission and switching functions are achieved by packet oriented techniques, so as to dynamically share network transmission and switching resources between a multiplicity of connections.

physical connection. The ability of two connectors to mate and make electrical contact. In a network, devices that are physically connected can communicate only if they share the same protocol. See also *logical connection*.

physical layer. In the Open Systems Interconnection reference model, the layer that provides the mechanical, electrical, functional, and procedural means to establish, maintain, and release physical connections over the transmission medium.

plesiochronous. Literally "nearly the same". If two bit streams have nominally the same bit rate, but are controlled by different clocks, they will have bit rates that are nearly the same but not quite.

point-to-multipoint connection. A point-to-multipoint connection is a collection of associated ATM VC or VP links and associated endpoint nodes, with the following properties:

1. One ATM link, called the root link, serves as the root in a simple tree topology. When the root node sends information, all of the remaining nodes on the connection, called leaf nodes, receive copies of the information.

2. Each of the leaf nodes on the connection can send information directly to the root node. The root node cannot distinguish which leaf node is sending the information without additional (higher layer) information.

3. Leaf nodes cannot communicate directly with each other.

ATM Forum Phase 1 signaling does not support traffic (except OA&M cells) sent from a leaf to the root.

port. (1) An access point for data entry or exit. (2) A connector on a device to which cables for other devices such as display stations and printers are attached. Synonymous with *socket*.

protocol. (1) A set of semantic and syntactic rules that determines the behavior of functional units in achieving communication. (2) In SNA, the meanings of and the sequencing rules for requests and responses used for managing the network, transferring data, and synchronizing the states of network components. (3) A specification for the format and relative timing of information exchanged between communicating parties.

protocol control information. Information exchanges between corresponding entities, using a lower layer connection to coordinate their joint operation.

protocol data unit (PDU). A unit of data specified in a layer protocol and consisting of protocol control information and layer user data.

S

segment. A single ATM link or group of interconnected ATM links of an ATM connection.

selective broadcast signaling virtual channel. A virtual channel allocated to a service profile and used for broadcast signaling.

signaling virtual channel. A virtual channel for transporting signaling information.

sublayer. A logical sub-division of a layer.

switched connection. A connection established by signaling.

synchronous. Literally "locked together". When two bit streams are said to be synchronous it is meant that they are controlled by the same clock and are in the same phase.

T

telephone twisted pair. One or more twisted pairs of copper wire in the unshielded voice-grade cable commonly used to connect a telephone to its wall jack. Also referred to as "unshielded twisted pair"

U

unassigned cell. A cell identified by a standardized virtual path identifier (VPI) and virtual channel identifier (VCI) value, which has been generated and does not carry information from an application using the ATM layer service.

unshielded twisted pair (UTP). See *telephone twisted pair*.

usage parameter control. The set of actions taken by the network to monitor and control traffic at the User Network Interface, to protect network resources from malicious as well as unintentional misbehavior by detecting violations of negotiated parameters and taking appropriate actions.

V

virtual channel (VC). A concept used to describe unidirectional transport of ATM cells associated by a common unique identifier value.

virtual channel connection. A concatenation of virtual channel links that extends between two points where the adaptation layer is accessed.

virtual channel link. A means of unidirectional transport of ATM cells between a point where a virtual channel identifier value is assigned and the point where that value is translated or removed.

virtual path. A concept used to describe the unidirectional transport of ATM cells belonging to virtual channels that are associated by a common identifier value.

virtual path connection. A concatenation of virtual path links that extends between the point where the virtual channel identifier values are assigned and the point where those values are translated or removed.

virtual path link. The group of virtual channel links, identified by a common value of the virtual path identifier, between the point where the VPI value is assigned and the point where the VPI value is translated or removed.

virtual path switch. A network element that connects VPLs. It translates VPI (not VCI) values and is directed by control plane functions. It relays the cells of the VP.

virtual path terminator. A system that
unbundles the VCs of a VP for independent
processing of each VC.

Bibliography

[1] Hamid Ahmadi and W.E. Denzel.
A Survey of Modern High-Performance Switching Techniques.
IEEE J. Selected Areas in Communication, September 1989.

[2] Flavio Bonomi and Kerry W. Fendick.
The Rate-Based Flow Control Framework for the ABR ATM Service.
IEEE Network, March/April 1995.

[3] Jean-Yves Le Boudec.
The Asynchronous Transfer Mode: A Tutorial.
Computer Networks and ISDN Systems, 1992.

[4] Jean-Yves Le Boudec, Erich Port and Hong Linh Truong.
Flight of the FALCON.
IEEE Communications Magazine, February 1993.

[5] George E. Daddis and H.C. Torng.
A Taxonomy of Broadband Integrated Switching Architectures.
IEEE Communications Magazine, May 1989.

[6] Jan P. Vorstermans and Andre P. De Vleeschouwer.
Layered ATM Systems and Architectural Concepts....
IEEE JSAC Vol. 6, No 9, December 1988.

[7] John J. Degan, Gottfried W.R. Luderer and Avinash K. Vaidya.
Fast Packet Technology For Future Switches.
AT&T Technical Journal, March/April 1989.

[8] W.E. Denzel, A.P.J Engbersen and G. Karlsson.
A Highly Modular Packet Switch for GB/S Rates.
XIV International Switching Symposium, October 1992.

[9] Harry J.P. Dutton and Peter Lenhard.
Prentice Hall.
High-Speed Networking Technology - An Introductory Survey.
1995.

[10] A.E. Eckberg.
B-ISDN/ATM Traffic and Congestion Control.
IEEE Network, September 1992.

[11] ATM Forum.
ATM User-Network Interface Specification - Version 3.1.
Prentice Hall, 1995.

[12] H.J.Fowler and W.E.Leland.
LAN Traffic Characteristics with Implications for ATM Congestion Management.
IEEE JSAC Vol. 9, No 7, September 1991.

[13] IBM, number SC31-6826.
ISDN Data Link Control - Architecture Reference.
1991.

[14] IBM, number SC31-6827.
ISDN Circuit-Switched Signaling Control - Architecture Reference.
1991.

[15] Ilias Iliadis.
Perf. of a Packet Switch with
Shared Buffer and Input Queueing.
*Teletraffic and Datatraffic in a
Period of Change*, Elsvier Science
Publishers B.V. (North-Holland),
1992.

[16] Ilias Iliadis and W.E. Denzel.
Performance of Packet Switches
with Input and Output Queueing.
Proc. of ICC/Supercomm'90,
Atlanta, GA., 1990.

[17] H.T. Kung and Robert Morris.
Credit-Based Flow Control for
ATM Networks.
IEEE Network, March/April 1995.

[18] Will E. Leland, Walter Willinger,
Murad S. Taqqu and Daniel V.
Wilson.
On the Self-Similar Nature of
Ethernet Traffic.
IEEE Network, September 1993.

[19] Steven E. Minzer.
Broadband ISDN and Asynchro-
nous Transfer Mode (ATM).
IEEE Communications Magazine,
September 1989.

[20] Peter Newman.
ATM Technology for Corporate
Networks.
IEEE Communications Magazine,
April 1992.

[21] K.K. Ramakrishnan and Peter Newman.
Integration of Rate and Credit
Schemes for ATM Flow Control.
IEEE Network, March/April 1995.

[22] James D. Russell.
Multimedia Networking Perform-
ance Requirements.
*The Sixth Triangle Conference on
Computer Communications*, April
1993.

[23] Ken-Ichi Sato, Satoru Ohta and Ikuo
Tokizawa.
Broad-Band ATM Network Archi-
tecture Based on Virtual Paths.
*IEEE Transactions on Communi-
cations*, August 1990.

[24] Youichi Sato and Ken-Ichi Sato.
Virtual Path and Link Capacity
Design for ATM Networks.
*IEEE Journal on Selected Areas in
Communications*, January 1991.

[25] Kotikalapudi Sriram, R. Scott
McKinney and Mostafa Hasheim
Sherif.
Voice Packetization and Com-
pression in Broadband ATM Net-
works.
*IEEE J. on Selected Areas in Com-
munications*, April 1991.

[26] Fouad A. Tobagi.
Fast Packet Switch Architectures for
B-ISDN Networks.
Proceedings of the IEEE, January
1990.

[27] ITU-TS Study Group 18.
I.113, I.121, I.150, and I.211.
Draft Recommendations, December
1993.

[28] ITU-TS Study Group 18.
I.211, I.327, I.311, I.361, I.413,
I.432 and I.610.
Draft Recommendations, December
1993.

Index

Numerics

A

B